UNGUARDED
GATES

UNGUARDED GATES

A History of
America's Immigration Crisis

Otis L. Graham Jr.

ROWMAN & LITTLEFIELD PUBLISHERS, INC.
Lanham • Boulder • New York • Toronto • Oxford

ROWMAN & LITTLEFIELD PUBLISHERS, INC.

Published in the United States of America
by Rowman & Littlefield Publishers, Inc.
A wholly owned subsidiary of The Rowman & Littlefield Publishing Group, Inc.
4501 Forbes Boulevard, Suite 200, Lanham, Maryland 20706
www.rowmanlittlefield.com

PO Box 317
Oxford
OX2 9RU, UK

British Library Cataloguing in Publication Information Available

Library of Congress Cataloging-in-Publication Data

Graham, Otis L.
  Unguarded gates : a history of America's immigration crisis / Otis L.
Graham Jr.
    p. cm.
Includes bibliographical references and index.
  1. United States—Emigration and immigration—History—Congresses. 2.
United States—Emigration and immigration—Government
policy—Congresses. 3. Immigrants—United States—History—Congresses.
I. Title.
  JV6450.G73 2003
  325.73—dc21
                              2003010197
  ISBN-13: 978-0-7425-2228-2 (cloth : alk. paper)
  ISBN-10: 0-7425-2228-8 (cloth : alk. paper)
  ISBN-13: 978-0-7425-2229-9 (pbk. : alk. paper)
  ISBN-10: 0-7425-2229-6 (pbk. : alk. paper)

Printed in the United States of America

♾™ The paper used in this publication meets the minimum requirements of
American National Standard for Information Sciences—Permanence of Paper
for Printed Library Materials, ANSI/NISO Z39.48-1992.

To the memory and life of
Hugh Davis Graham

CONTENTS

ACKNOWLEDGMENTS

Many people have helped me in the long task of writing this book, and I can mention only a small number. Robert Maynard Hutchins came first chronologically, as he encouraged me to begin the study of immigration issues at the Center for the Study of Democratic Institutions in Montecito, California, in 1977. Leon Bouvier and David E. Simcox, especially, have patiently educated me over the years in matters demographic, and each has been generous with textual criticism of the current work. The late Richard Estrada was never too busy to share with me his intimate knowledge of contemporary immigration, always enriched by a profound grasp of the history of both the United States and Mexico. I owe a special debt to former governor Dick Lamm of Colorado for his steady encouragement, and his bracing conviction that our obligations to our children require far-reaching changes in our underlying assumptions and in public policy. Vernon Briggs combines economics and history in a masterful way, and has been generous in giving me his critical attention to several drafts. Jessica Vaughan and Peter Nunez gave me the benefit of their experience working on immigration issues within the State Department and Department of Justice, respectively. I am especially grateful for suggestions from historians John Higham, James T. Patterson, Betty Koed, and Barbara Lindemann and from that astute student of the law and politics of ethnicity, George LaNoue.

I benefited greatly from a chance to present my ideas on immigration reform in the Ronald Reagan years in conferences at Oxford University (thanks to Gareth Davies) and Cambridge University (thanks to Tony Badger). These two talented historians of the United States provided me with useful critical hearings.

Research assistants Ryan Anderson, Jason Eudy, and Matt Jaeger supported my work with meticulous library research and many a penetrating question.

I am also grateful to Sherman Hayes, librarian, and his staff at the Randall Library at the University of North Carolina, Wilmington, where I completed this work with the benefit of a year as a Fellow of Randall Library. I wish to thank Rowman and Littlefield's editors Steve Wrinn and Mary Carpenter for their wise counsel.

My wife, Delores, sustained my spirits and improved every page with her keen editorial skills. She is the wind beneath my wings.

My brother, the late Hugh Davis Graham, loaned his unmatched historical judgment and knowledge to this as to all my projects and improved every draft with his keen sense of style. He is missed beyond the power of words to express.

It is safe to say that none of the above have agreed along the way with everything I have written, and any errors that remain have somehow escaped their remedial efforts and are my responsibility alone.

OLG Jr.
Chapel Hill, N.C.

INTRODUCTION

The American future is shaped by many complex forces. One of the most powerful—immigration—is, on balance, now taking America where it doesn't want to go—toward porous borders and uncontrolled entry, endless population growth, imported-worker competition with American labor, social fragmentation.

To understand how we have moved onto a road to a more troubled future we need to turn to our history.

This is so because our predicament finds us as a nation confused and misguided by our historical memories and myths, which tell us a flawed and misleading story, that immigration has always taken us where we *wanted* to go.

This is confusing because it is part of the truth, but only a part. Immigration of Europeans, Latin Americans, Asians, and others, as well as the forced immigration of many Africans, on balance and over the course of our colonial and national experience did advance economic development and nation-building, which was where we wanted to go. As a people we feel justifiably proud of this achievement (on the whole) and have long recognized that the Americans engaged in this nation-building were immensely aided by newcomers bringing renewed energy and their own cultural contributions.

On balance. The rest of the truth is that immigration's potential has a negative component, whose costs sometimes appear to exceed benefits. Immigration to the New World brought enormous injury to indigenous populations and the natural environment. In the nineteenth century immigration reached a scale and composition that brought or exacerbated substantial problems among Americans already here and seemed to many of them to actually threaten the unique national project of democratic nation-building. An extended period of such problematic immigration began in the decades before the Civil War, as a Great Wave of European immigration brought an unprecedented large number from Germany and Ireland. The flow of immigrants resumed after the war with source regions shifting to eastern and southern Europe. This era of mass immigration, substantial in numbers and also very different in cultural inheritances, generated in American political life a demand for control over this source of immense social change.

This book begins with the story of the process of moving from essentially an open-border policy and small-scale immigration to a new era in which the national government undertook to moderate and manage migrating human populations so that immigration would mesh with and promote our national purposes, rather than conflict with them. It then tells the modern story of how immigration, shaped by immigration policy, changed from bringing mostly positive to mostly negative contributions.

Regulation of immigration came slowly, because Americans always have been ambivalent about immigration. Between the 1880s and the 1920s a policy decision was finally reached. A system of national regulation of immigration was put in place, based on the national origins of the population of 1920 and aimed at greatly reduced numbers. With the help of external events such as world wars and economic depression worldwide, this system of regulation sharply lowered the incoming numbers and allowed the country to absorb and thus on the whole benefit by the large inflows of the First Great Wave.

Then in the 1960s a Second Great Wave began to surge across national borders, generated by global population growth, lowered transportation costs, and a widespread awareness of the wealth gap between developed and underdeveloped nations. Immigration policymakers, not recognizing this era of expanding immigration pressures, took a step toward expanding legal admissions. A reform of American immigration law and policy in 1965 was intended to bring important ethical improvements in the form of opening equal access to all nationalities, while having little practical effect. But the reforms of 1965 brought other, surprising effects of vast importance—a threefold expansion of legal immigrants, augmented by burgeoning numbers of illegal immigrants, and a radical shift in the source countries of American immigration. We are still sorting out the far-reaching impacts of this half-century (to date) experiment in porous borders between America and a world undergoing an unprecedented expansion of human population.

Today, after four decades of Second Great Wave immigration, legal and illegal, the American government's performance in the task of managing immigration is at the top of any list of government failures. This was true well before the deadly September 11, 2001, acts of terrorism by foreigners commandeering American airliners after residing and training in the United States under various mixtures of legal and illegal entry and extended illegal residency. Americans for decades have sensed that we are now in a phase of our national life in which immigration is on balance taking America where it doesn't want to go. All public-opinion polls since large-scale immigration resumed in the 1960s have reported pluralities (in the 1960s) and thereafter majorities (in all ethnic groups) in favor of reducing immigration. These polls are one form of expression of a sustained and tenacious vote of no confidence in the government's gate tending.

And with good reason. The numbers of legal immigrants has hovered around one million for two decades, augmented by illegal immigration, always estimated by official bodies as lower than subsequently found. An internal population of nine to ten million illegal immigrants is acknowledged by the early years of the twenty-first century. On the legal side, these new Americans are selected by a system placing primary emphasis on kinship, which means family ties to recent immigrants, rather than on national needs.

The costs of this new mass immigration collect across the ledger. They include labor market competition with native workers, rising social service costs, nurturing of illegal trade in drugs and indentured labor, the immigration contribution (70 percent at the end of the century, and rising) to population growth with all the costs that come attached to it in this era of global ecocrisis, an intensifying intersection of mounting human numbers with an era of erratic global warming and other stresses of a global ecosphere mauled by more than six billion people in the process of expanding to or beyond ten billion. Other costs are more speculative, such as the concerns that the radical shift in immigrants' countries of origin from Europe to Latin America (especially Mexico), Asia, and the Middle East may overwhelm the nation's capacity for assimilation. A century later, the national question is being asked again—is our fundamental national cohesion and coherence being lost?

Against this are weighed immigration's benefits—cheap labor for harvest agriculture and urban menial tasks, relatively cheap skilled labor in certain industries, a more culturally diversified cuisine and society, and scattered stories of urban revitalization.

Assessing this complex picture of immigration impacts in the mid-1990s, a national commission led by former congresswoman Barbara Jordan confirmed that immigration patterns were not aligned with the national interest and urged reforms. The numbers coming in legally should be reduced by almost half, and selected with more emphasis on the needs of the American economy. Illegal entry should be firmly combated. By this time that part of the nation's public policy elite knowledgeable about immigration had reversed an earlier complacency and begun to frequently express the alarm long felt by the public. The Brookings Institution in 2000 gathered a panel of historians and political scientists to reflect on the federal government's greatest achievements and failures since World War II, and it ranked controlling immigration as second among the top five failures. In a 2001 review of the literature on immigration's impacts, one of the nation's most respected social scientists, Harvard's Christopher Jencks, confirmed this overall negative assessment of the costs imposed by the four-decade run of mass immigration. Alarmed at the environmental and demographic affects from a likely doubling of the U.S. population to 500 million by 2050, a doubling attributable almost entirely to immigration, Jencks joined many other end-of-century writers in questioning whether such a "vast social experiment" had been authorized by the American people or was in their best interest. The nation's policy-studies elite had finally caught up with the American public, which had been expressing the same convictions to pollsters since the early 1970s. On the one occasion when voters were allowed a direct vote on the immigration status quo—at least, on the illegal part of it—Californians by a wide margin in 1992 endorsed Proposition 187, which withheld social services from illegal immigrants. A broadly negative perception of the American immigration policy regime faced no serious intellectual challenge at the end of the century. Apologists for the mass immigration status quo were few and fell back on historical analogy, arguing that similar waves of mass immigration of a century earlier had also been met by objections but the nation had nonetheless prospered.

Yet U.S. policymakers ignored this critical appraisal of the immigration regime, and in the first year of the twenty-first century drifted toward further dismantling of controls. President George W. Bush in 2001 proposed a virtual open border with Mexico, and, incredibly, congressional policymakers seemed receptive.

This presents us with an enormous puzzle. The vast social experiment in the form of mass immigration rushes on, entering its fifth decade. It is a product of policymaking in the world's foremost democracy, yet it has from the first been unpopular with the public and viewed with increasing skepticism by policy analysts. The costs of America's porous borders were piled to even more stunning heights on the morning of September 11, 2001. That day's terrorist attacks harshly illuminated a defect that had not formerly been high on the list of flaws in immigration policy, that our porous borders and governmental abandonment of virtually all interior immigration controls allowed terrorists to glide easily in and out of the country, illegally and legally, for periods of their choosing, as they contemptuously trained and prepared for mass murder in this affable and wide-open society.

Perhaps the events of that day and the threat of more foreign-based terrorism will force a reconsideration of U.S. immigration policy, even one that goes beyond new antiterrorist filters to address the core flaws that the Jordan commission has already identified, and result in a turn toward lower numbers and selection criteria that advance national needs rather than kinship relations. But the sustaining forces that lie behind a national policy of virtually open borders are formidable, and two years after September 11 brought little real movement toward substantial reform of immigration policy, beyond the bureaucratic repositioning of the Immigration and Naturalization Service. If substantial immigration policy reform toward lower numbers and stricter enforcement eventually comes from the heightened concern over terrorism, then the "vast social experiment" in mass immigration to the United States will have lasted four decades. If not, the expansionist policy will extend into the future, taking America where the public, if not the elites, does not want to go.

Either way, the puzzle remains: How could this have happened? How could the United States for almost half a century have been steering into a future of intensifying environmental constraints with a population-expanding immigration policy that does not have public support?

For understanding our situation we must follow history into the present, revisiting and rethinking the story of modern America's remarkable, turbulent, and unfinished encounter with that most emotional, difficult, and nation-changing of all public policy subjects—immigration.

It should be noted that in thinking about a title for this book, one of my editors—Mary Carpenter or Laura Roberts—suggested *Unguarded Gates*. I agreed that this phrase signaled the book's central theme as well as any other two words—and then recalled that a Gilded Age writer, Bostonian Thomas Bailey Aldrich, author of many books and poems and once editor of *The Atlantic Monthly*, had earlier used that title for a poem he published in 1895. His "Unguarded Gates" was to have a longevity that none of his other poems achieved, for it lyrically expressed not only a love of America but also the worry of many contemporary Americans over the volume and cultural characteristics of the "new immigration" that began in the 1880s. Historians of American immigration have been fond of quoting some of Aldrich's language ("Wide open and unguarded stand our gates, and through them presses a wild, motley throng . . ."), calling attention not to his love of country but to his evident xenophobia. Should we abandon the title, as sullied by Aldrich's characterization of the immigrants he saw debarking in Boston harbor? But that would amount to a virtual agreement to permanently identify the concern he expressed ("O Liberty, white goddess, is it well to leave thy gates unguarded?") with Aldrich's own apparent ethnic prejudices. One purpose of this book is to restore to the idea of immigration limitation, so often stigmatized and diminished as synonymous with xenophobia, its multiple historical meanings and its potential for advancing the public good. Aldrich had his own conception of the hazards of unguarded gates, I have mine, and there are others. They should contend across the spectrum of opinion. As a matter of good judgment as well as law, you cannot copyright a title, nor singularly own the expression of an idea.

I

IMMIGRATION ISSUES FROM THE FOUNDERS TO THE CREATION OF A SYSTEM OF LIMITATION

NATION OF THE NATIVE BORN
UNREADY FOR THE GREAT WAVE

It is not clear who invented the phrase "America is a nation of immigrants," but this now-hackneyed thought is not true for any of our national history and applies only in the British colonies for the first few decades in the first half of the seventeenth century. Thereafter, most Americans (by which we mean North Americans in the territory now the United States) were native-born, and that has remained true for the rest of our history to this date. America is a nation of the native-born. But it is certainly true, as historian Victor Greene observed, that "the immigration stamp is upon us," in that we are all descendants of immigrants, even if quite distantly.

Whatever else this implies, our history tells us that immigration in the American story has always, from first to last and at every point, been controversial among the people who live here—associated always with both costs and benefits. This reality has been lost in the current romanticized historical view that immigration is always a Good Thing, both for host society and immigrants. This was not the view of the first human residents of the Americas, the indigenous peoples in this hemisphere when European explorers and immigrants began to arrive. For native populations, European immigration meant death by disease, warfare, and social disorganization, a virtual genocide in which their populations fell 90 percent by 1600. In North America, an Amerindian population estimated at 2 to 20 million (a range lately narrowed among most anthropologists to 4 to 7 million, though there are fierce disagreements) had dropped to perhaps 250,000 when the twentieth century

opened. This is the primal American experience with immigration—
grotesquely negative, unique, and (we fervently hope) unrepeatable. Yet it
should anchor our understanding that immigration is morally complicated,
immensely powerful in charting human destiny, and always a shifting mixture
of goods and bads. That is why nations create immigration policies, hoping to
minimize the latter and maximize the former.

When these death-bringing European immigrants became Americans by
birth, their own response to further immigration was ambivalent. Industrious immigrants were indispensable in expanding colonial populations, and
they were welcomed in the abstract and usually on arrival. But the quality
of immigrants from the Old World was a constant issue of concern. "Slums
and alleys were raked for labor to stock the plantations," wrote historian
Marion Bennett; dependent kinfolk were sometimes dumped on ships
headed for America, and the British government was notorious for shipping
felons to the southern colonies especially. Colonial assemblies enacted restrictions against paupers "likely to become a public charge" and criminal
immigrants as early as 1639, and restrictions on the admission of those
"lame, impotent, or infirm" followed.

Independence placed such decisions firmly in American hands. The
Founders welcomed immigration in principle, while having serious
reservations about its capacity for harm to the fledgling nation. George
Washington wrote to a group of Irish immigrants that "the bosom of
America is open to receive not only the opulent and respectable stranger,
but the oppressed and persecuted of all nations." On another occasion he
spoke of his hopes that "the poor, the needy and oppressed of the Earth"
would "resort to the fertile plains of our western country," where of
course he was a landowner. But he often was of a different mind. "I have
no intention to invite immigrants, even if there are no restrictive acts
against it. I am opposed to it altogether," he wrote to a friend in England.
To John Adams he wrote: "My opinion with respect to immigration is,
that except of useful mechanics and some particular description of men
and professions, there is no use of encouragement."

Jefferson in his *Notes on the State of Virginia* raised fundamental questions
about populating the country by immigration. Natural population increase
would provide Virginia with four and a half million (which he thought a maximum population for the state, and possibly too large a number) in eighty-two
years, so there seemed no need to accelerate that growth by "the importation
of foreigners." And there would be "inconveniences to be thrown into the
scale" if immigration were the path chosen. "It is for the happiness of those
united in society to harmonize as much as possible" in matters of civil gov-

ernment, but immigrants could be expected to come henceforth mostly from countries of absolute monarchy, bringing habits and outlooks rendering our polity "a heterogeneous, incoherent, distracted mass." A few "useful artificers" might "teach us something we do not know," but the drafter of the Declaration of Independence specifically discouraged building the future nation out of immigration. Hamilton, this time, agreed with his political rival: "The opinion advanced in [Thomas Jefferson's] *Notes On Virginia* is undoubtedly correct. . . . The influx of foreigners must . . . tend to produce a heterogeneous compound; to change and corrupt the national spirit . . . to introduce foreign propensities."

These sentiments were widely shared, from Jefferson to Hamilton across the political spectrum, and do not reflect a divided mind but rather a principled ambivalence. The generation of the Founders expected immigrants to help populate the vast country and welcomed those who shared the American work ethic and would adopt our national values and customs. They had continuing concerns about the habits, particularly the language, political principles, and morals, of those stepping off the boats and repeatedly made it clear that some people would be unwelcome. How to guarantee the immigration of only what James Madison called "foreigners of merit and republican principles" but not "the common class of vagrants, paupers and other outcasts of Europe" according to Congressman James Jackson of Georgia. Policymakers expressed such worries without devising an effective filter against bad immigration—since immigration levels were quite low. The young republic was essentially open to immigrants joining the earlier settlers.

The Europeans (and, involuntarily, Africans) continued to leave their homelands and come, though annual arrivals in the first three decades of the republic were estimated at less than ten thousand a year (no records were kept until 1820), well below 1 percent of the resident population in any given year. The United States was growing primarily by the natural increase of its population, as Jefferson preferred. These early decades were a lull before a larger demographic convulsion that would eventually force Americans to rethink their empty-continent optimism. Europe had entered an astonishing century-and-a-half surge of population growth generating a mass movement of peoples of which the settling of the British colonies was only the first ripple. During the nineteenth century and into the twentieth, Europeans, in the words of historian Alfred Crosby, "swarmed and swarmed again," driven by population pressures, starvation, and civil and religious unrest. A "Caucasian tsunami" of some fifty to sixty million immigrants came to colonize the rich soils and temperate zones of what Crosby calls the "Neo-Europes" of North America, Argentina, Australia, and New Zealand.

A heavy pulse of Germans began to reach the United States in the 1830s, of Irish beginning in the 1840s, boosting the annual average immigration to 120,000 a year between 1820 and 1860, an average that masked the erratic surges out of Europe that brought nearly 3 million in the 1850s alone. This was the first stage of the Great Wave. The Civil War and subsequent economic depression of the 1870s brought a lull. Then, in the 1880s, the Europeans "swarmed again" as industrialization and farm mechanization moved south and east on a disruptive journey through European regions with rapidly growing populations and chronic unemployment. Over the next fifty years nearly 30 million Europeans migrated to the United States. They were the New Immigrants from new places—Italians from the southern regions of their peninsula, the multiple ethnic subsets of the Russian Empire, Poles, Serbs, Croats, Bulgarians and Hungarians from the Austro-Hungarian Empire, Armenians, Greeks, and Portuguese. Two million of the world's 7.5 million Jews relocated to America out of central and Eastern Europe in these years. To the other American coast, to California, came Chinese and Japanese.

This was the Great Wave, the most massive of all human migrations to date, provoking a protracted, soul-searching national debate that culminated in the 1920s in a decision to take control of the nation's demographic destiny and end the era of uncontrolled immigration to the United States.

GREAT WAVE AND THE AMERICAN FUTURE

The Great Wave washing out of Europe was generated by unprecedented population growth during the two-century demographic transition from high to low birth and death rates. The transition was disastrously slow. Death rates came down first and fastest, the decline in birth rates lagging by decades. A stupendous surge of population growth was the result. This vast migration of millions of humans from their homelands was driven by the pull of industrial–urban expansion and the push of rural poverty and unemployment, political and civil wars, and especially in the case of the Eastern European Jews, religious persecution or the well-founded fear of it.

Remembering that Jefferson's America absorbed less than ten thousand immigrants a year, the size of the Caucasian tsunami when it hit in the 1880s was beyond historical experience. Some twenty-seven million immigrants arrived in the United States between 1880 and 1930, when the wave was curbed by restrictive policies and the worldwide depression. In the years after 1900, arrivals averaged close to or above one million a year.

There was much return immigration to Europe, but still the permanent demographic impact was enormous. The foreign-born population in the early years of the twentieth century is estimated at 13 to 15 percent of the total. Since the South was home to only 2 percent of the foreign born, the rest of the country, especially the seaboards, had populations that were approximately 20 percent foreign born. Economic historian Richard Easterlin estimated that at its peak, in the decade 1900–1910, immigration constituted roughly 40 percent of U.S. population growth and much more than that if their descendants are added.

The societies producing this surge of humanity toward America and the other neo-Europes were not in the western tier of European nations but the eastern and southern peripheries. Whatever their many shortcomings in practice, the western European societies peopling America in the seventeenth to nineteenth centuries had been early and advanced incubators of constitutional democracy, religious pluralism (within a Christian framework), and unprecedented progress in science, technology, and economic development. By contrast, Great Wave arrivals were from nations or regions within the Russian and Austro-Hungarian empires that by Western standards were profoundly backward. These mostly peasant peoples had "lived much closer to serfdom," in historian John Higham's words, than earlier arrivals. To heighten the sense of a cultural gap between Americans and newcomers, much of the Great Wave was not Protestant but Roman or Orthodox Catholic, or not Christian at all but Jewish—or, on the West Coast, practitioners of oriental religions entirely foreign to Americans.

AMERICAN DESTINATION: A TROUBLED SOCIETY

This tide of new people from different homelands than had historically provisioned America also arrived at an inauspicious time for absorbing more people from anywhere, let alone from alien traditions. The powerful energies of urbanizing industrialism within the United States were dislocating America's rural populations. Mechanization on the farm and the lure of industrial jobs siphoned millions into expanding cities unable to cope with crowding and pollution or to maintain basic social services. The United States had entered that phase of economic development that economist Walt Rostow called "take-off" into industrialization. In the long run and at the bottom line, this meant rising living standards that doubled American per capita income between the 1860s and World War I. The bad news was that these early decades of industrialization were plagued with disorder. First was a savage business cycle, in which economic growth was interrupted between the Civil War and the beginning of the twentieth century by three grinding depressions, one arriving in the middle of each decade. Immigrants setting out for the United States in these years were acting on their belief that America was and would continue to be the greatest wealth-producing economic machine in the world. In the short run, however, workers and businesses in America were in depression circumstances during almost half the years from the Civil War to the new century, with high unemployment even in good years. Labor unrest and massive strikes plagued basic industries. The rise of agrarian radicalism, the growth of labor organization, and the stirrings of a socialist movement clouded the future. These economic strains merged with a set of political and social worries—political corruption, urban congestion and vice, child labor, alcohol and tobacco abuse, and degradation of natural environments. A broad progressive reform movement began to build, and in the first two decades of the twentieth century a main theme of American history would be the multifaceted interventions taken to address these problems through research, public education, formation of activist social institutions, and a resort to governmental power.

Into this America came the streams of Great Wave immigrants, igniting a sustained controversy that became inextricably a part of the broader social reform impulse. Great Wave immigration was seen by progressive-era reformers as another uncontrolled force threatening political democracy, the aspirations of labor, social order in the cities, and American identity itself.

2

IMMIGRATION REFORM: BEGINNINGS OF NATIONAL POLICY

In 1876 the Supreme Court ruled that individual states could not regulate immigration. What regulation there had been was ineffectual inspection at seaports for obvious physical or mental disease, which meant mainly the port of New York. New York City charity officials who helped settle the especially needy, alarmed at the prospect of losing the fees they collected from shipowners, urged the federal government to take over immigration control and exclude immigrants unable to support themselves. Congress was not eager to shoulder these responsibilities, but under pressure from seacoast states it enacted the Immigration Law of 1882, naming the secretary of the treasury as responsible executive (the law did not tell him what his objectives should be, beyond collecting a new head tax). The law barred "criminals, lunatics, idiots, and those likely to become a public charge" (language going far back into Colonial days). This was hardly a firm federal grip on immigration. Inspection at the docks was still left to the states, and the law was not intended or expected to restrict immigration. Those few who were to be excluded had always been, on paper, excluded. There were no criteria for selecting from the many applicants those whom America would permit to enter. When history textbooks date the beginnings of federal immigration policy as 1882, they have something else in mind.

The long road to immigration reform did begin that year, but in an unlikely place—on the West Coast, with the question of the Chinese. Mine owners and railroad builders in the region, desperate for cheap and docile labor ready for backbreaking tasks, began importing Chinese "coolie" (the term was an English version of a Hindu phrase for unskilled laborers transported from the Orient) labor about 1850, along with a few female Chinese for prostitution. The initial reception from California citizens to the almost entirely male labor force, described by one citizen as "sober, industrious, and inoffensive," tended to be genial. The reception turned hostile at the end of the 1860s, when the gold rush had waned and the Union Pacific Railroad was completed (1869), but oriental immigration continued. Chinese numbers by the 1870s reached 10 percent of the state's population and one-quarter of its labor force, a low-wage labor pool beginning to compete with American labor. The specter of continuing and unlimited flows of Chinese peasant labor threatened more than a downward pressure on wages. "Transported and largely controlled by certain Chinese societies," John Higham wrote, "they awakened fears of a new kind of slavery in a nation already convulsed by the struggle over African slavery."

Beyond posing an economic threat to American workers, the Chinese were almost universally thought entirely unassimilable for permanent settlement. They fled, or were sent into virtual slavery, from a once-respected ancient civilization that by the mid-nineteenth century had fallen into the chaos of civil war and banditry of the Taiping Rebellion (1851–1864) with its ripples of disorder stretching through the rest of the century. The American image of China, once favorable, veered toward the view that this disintegrating and stagnant empire, and therefore its citizens, had little to teach the civilized world in the arts of government or civil society. In America the Chinese kept strictly to themselves in their residential enclaves and to the American eye retained peculiar customs and questionable health standards, operating private courts of justice through their secret societies, or tongs, which were also said to control gambling and opium rings. The fact that Chinese migrating to Hawaii met with far less cultural resistance and showed less ethnic isolation suggests that their unassimilability on the West Coast was at least partially a result of white society's increasingly negative perception of them. In any event, resistance to their growing numbers mounted and occasionally became vicious. There were taxes on and boycotts of Chinese laundries and other businesses, community expulsions, even riots. Organized opposition to Chinese immigrants came from a coalition of workers, small farmers, and shop owners, energized by the harsh depression of the mid-1870s. Denis Kearney of the California Workingmen's Party, composed substantially of immigrants, mostly Irish, provided passionate, even angry leadership behind the slogan "The Chinese must go!" Employers also came in for harsh criticism for using the Chinese as pawns.

Anti-Chinese sentiment erupted also on the East Coast when significant numbers of Chinese laborers arrived and some were used as strikebreakers in Massachusetts and New Jersey. Black newspapers often joined the condemnation of the "disease-breeding, miserly, clannish, and heathen Chinese," in the words of the *Washington Colored American*.

In response to a remarkable intensity of complaint on the West Coast, which was increasingly expressed nationwide (the platforms of both political parties endorsed restriction of Chinese immigration in 1876 and 1880), Congress moved rapidly toward a historic reversal of the tradition of laissez-faire in immigration matters. A Chinese exclusion law in 1879 was vetoed because it violated the Burlingame Treaty of 1868. The treaty was renegotiated, and Congress by wide margins passed the Chinese Exclusion Act of 1882, suspending the admission of Chinese laborers for ten years. (Chinese "other than laborers"—teachers, students, merchants, government officials—could and did legally travel to the United States; in any event, Chinese immigrants were declared ineligible for citizenship, though their American-born children were citizens.) It was the first sharp curtailment of immigration to America and was extended with minor adjustments for sixty years, until 1943 when Chinese exclusion—which had never been total—was eased.

A new tradition of restricting U.S. immigration through federal policy had begun. Unfortunately, it was a fumbling start on the necessary task of gaining national control over the country's demographic destiny and labor markets. West Coast Americans' understandable concerns over an unlimited flow of cheap oriental labor had sometimes veered into panic or anger, leading on occasion to acts of violence against very peaceful invaders, with much racist language harsh to the modern ear. In the public debate, the arguments for continuing the laissez-faire policy on national immigration were remarkably puny—a combination of sentimental invocations of "hospitality to all suppressed nationalities" along with the argument, candidly stated by the Reverend Henry Ward Beecher, that without the Chinese, we Americans would have "no race that will be willing to do what we call menial work."

Against this, restrictionists built a compelling argument that swung huge majorities behind immigration reform. "We do not object to the Chinese because of their race or their language or their religion," editorialized a labor union journal, whose readers surely agreed only in part, "but we do object to an organized effort to introduce cheap laborers into the Republic." Even those initially hesitant to break with the nation's open door tradition concluded that, in addition to the labor problem,

Americans and Chinese were simply too different to permit large and sustained oriental immigration with the resultant social conflict. "If they are brought rapidly, in large numbers, into any Western country, there will be unpleasant friction," said University of Michigan President James Angell, who had led negotiations to rewrite the Burlingame Treaty. In the crisis, democratic government had a responsibility to respond to over-whelming majority opinion. "The public peace is disturbed," said re-spected Republican Senator George Edmunds of Vermont, "and if you can save it by giving time for reason to restore itself and passion to cool, is it not wise? . . . Then let us protect the Chinamen by having them hold up a little while. . . . While all mankind are of one kin . . . one destiny," the Chinese were very different in culture and religion, and "no repub-lic can succeed that has not a homogeneous population." Edmunds was one of many, observes historian Andrew Gyory, who "did not condemn the Chinese or call them inferior; he simply stressed their differentness."

Thus a beginning had been made in the emotionally difficult transition from traditional laissez faire toward immigration limits. In retrospect, and even to moderates at the time, some of the terms of the debate needlessly offended another nationality and stigmatized those of Chinese origin re-maining in America. A drastic reduction in Chinese immigration could have been amply justified in terms of labor-market impacts and problems of as-similation of oriental immigration on a vast scale, without slurs on foreign-ers, and without denying citizenship to those already here. Some in the 1880s justified the curb on the Chinese in just this way, but the restriction-ist impulse activated many who did not hesitate to generate support through appeals to other popular emotions.

The main lesson of this first stage of immigration reform was lost on many contemporaries as well as most historians. Massive immigration of a surplus and thus low-wage population vastly different culturally from Americans generated severe social conflicts across the entire range of so-ciety (with the exception of large employers, always eager for cheap la-bor without concern for social repercussions). Those conflicts arose from real as well as perceived economic, social, and cultural threats to living and labor standards achieved and cherished by the native population. People will react to these forces, as they should in a self-governing re-public. The formula for turning those responses hostile and lengthy is unresponsive government. The Chinese Exclusion Act, with its mislead-ing, inept title and other flaws apparent to people living a century later (and to some at the time), prevented what had been building as a mas-sive and sustained immigration of Chinese laborers to Jinshan—"the

Golden Mountain." The U.S. government's first step to control one of the forces tearing at the social fabric allowed the level of social conflict between Caucasians and Chinese (and other Asians) on the West Coast to slowly (too slowly for anyone's preference) drain away to be replaced by the occidental–oriental accommodation and amity that prevailed on the West Coast in the latter half of the twentieth century.

The progressive reform impulse now moved on to a confrontation with the rest of the uncontrolled Great Wave, as reformers erratically searched for a national immigration policy to replace the laissez-faire stance so inappropriate to the modern era.

3

GREAT WAVE AND THE SEARCH FOR NATIONAL POLICY

As we have seen, 1882 produced the first federal restriction of immigration, dealing with the Chinese, and the first general federal immigration law, extending a colonial and state tradition of excluding those found on inspection to be convicts, lunatics, idiots, and paupers. There quickly followed in 1885 a ban on immigrants brought in under the contract labor system in which employers or agents advanced sums to those without the means to finance the voyage. But these were tiny steps, weakly enforced. Reformers pondered other grounds for exclusion, broad enough to cut the numbers in a way that barring paupers and lunatics would not. More positively, what were the criteria for choosing those most valuable to the country, providing a basis for excluding all others? And how to give the weak, minimalist government in Washington not just the legal mandate but the bureaucratic capacity to regulate immigration, now that the 1876 Supreme Court ruling placed that responsibility clearly with the national government?

These questions and others arose in the 1880s. Public pressure for acceptable answers began a forty-year reform buildup. The appeal for immigration control came from many quarters, "from society," in the words of one scholar, Keith Fitzgerald, who analyzed the lists of witnesses participating in key congressional hearings related to immigration from 1875 to 1891. The Knights of Labor were the principal sponsors of the 1885 Contract Labor Act. By the time a House special committee to investigate the immigration problem began its work in 1888, however, hearings elicited calls for restriction from the new American Federation of Labor (AFL), labor leaders, journalists, public officials, some chambers of commerce, and governmental and private charities overwhelmed by the numbers of the indigent and ill. The social support for restriction was broad and diverse. Had black Americans been invited to testify before governmental bodies in these years, their representatives would certainly have added their appeals for stemming the tide of foreign labor, as Tuskegee Institute's Booker T. Washington had done in his Atlanta Exposition address in 1895.

Against a background of severe economic depressions in the mid-1880s and again in the mid-1890s, along with labor unrest, strikes, and spectacular episodes of violence such as the 1886 Haymarket bomb explosion at a foreign-led anarchist political rally that killed seven policemen, the political machinery began to respond. The Immigration Law of 1891 established the post of Commissioner of Immigration in the Treasury Department (a curious place to lodge immigration regulation). By 1893 both houses of Congress for the first time had standing committees on immigration. The national government was taking the first halting steps toward equipping itself to make immigration policy.

Even so, it was lagging quite far behind public opinion. Newspapers and magazines reflected a swelling discussion, and in 1884, 1888, 1892, and 1896 the platforms of both major political parties recognized large-scale immigration as a problem, though occasionally with an ambivalent salute to past immigrants. Acknowledging the need for some sort of filter or selection process, part of the Democratic platform in 1892 was to "heartily approve all legitimate efforts to prevent the U.S. from being used as the dumping ground for the known criminals and professional paupers of Europe" but "denounce any and all attempts to restrict the immigration of the industrious and worthy." Both major parties and the National Peoples' Party (Populists) were especially adamant about immigration reform in the depression year 1896, though how the government would limit immigration was unclear. Organized labor began a lengthy debate on the issue beginning in the mid-1890s and gradually shifted ground toward restriction. The head of the AFL Samuel Gompers wrote, "I have always felt that restricting opportunities for others is a grave responsibility. . . . America is the product of the daring, the genius, the idealism of those who left homes and kindred to settle in the new land." But those sentiments steadily lost ground in the face of the numbers and character of the New Immigration and its apparent impacts. The new "immigrants crowded into any available employment," Gompers later said, "into unskilled callings and worked at starvation wages. They undermined standards and labor organizations."

In the 1880s 5.2 million came, in the 1890s 3.7 million. In the first decade of the new century 8.8 million came, a "long-term upward trend in immigration between 1880 and 1914 which was apparent to contemporaries and influenced public opinion," in the words of labor historian A. T. Lane. One-fifth of the workforce in the country was foreign-born as the century closed, and the foreign stock (foreign-born and their children) comprised 34 percent of the total white population in 1880, rising to 40 percent by 1910.

NEW IMMIGRATION AND THE URBAN CRISIS

The American industrial city at the end of the nineteenth century was a vortex pulling in labor from wherever it was in surplus—the farms of New England and the Midwest, but also the crowded rural villages of Poland, Russia, and Italy's Mezzogiorno. From 1880 to 1910 the American urban population tripled. Chicago grew by an average 50,000 a year through the 1890s. New York counted 984 people per acre in the city's Sanitary District A, or 300,000 people in a six-block area, a greater density than Bombay. Over one hundred American cities, most in the East and Midwest, doubled in size in the 1880s, a growth rate that swamped social services. Economic dynamism drove the growth, but the price was high: "crowded tenement districts, chronic health problems, billowing smoke, polluted waterways, traffic congestion, unbearable noise, and mounds of putrefying garbage," in historian Martin Melosi's words. While most of America's population growth derived from the high fertility rate of the native population, the problems of the cities were greatly intensified and shaped by the long, relentless tide of the Great Wave out of Europe.

They were mostly unskilled peasants, with the major exception of the Jews, classified by port officials as nearly 70 percent skilled workers. They clustered in ethnic neighborhoods and gave the turn-of-the-century industrial city a memorable flavor of foreignness—an urban mosaic of non-English tongues and signage, exotic cuisine, dress, and holidays. Incredible density and unsanitary conditions became associated with the New Immigrant—1,231 Italians living in 120 rooms in New York, chickens and goats fed and slaughtered in halls or alleyways, a single tenement where journalist Jacob Riis (in his *How The Other Half Lives*) found Jewish parents raising fifty-eight babies and thirty-eight children over five years of age. The nation's urban population was 41 percent foreign born by 1920, and since the South had never become a popular destination for immigrants, in most major northeastern cities the proportion was closer to two-thirds.

The Great Wave had brought more than crowding. Chicago social worker Edith Abbott compiled a book of documents on *Historical Aspects of the Immigration Problem,* and the section "Pauperism and Crime and Other Domestic Immigration Problems" reported a range of problems from insanity, pauperism, criminality, and disease. None of these were new to America, all were copiously homegrown. But how much was imported, and was there a remedy? Cholera, called the "disease of the poor" because the bacterium enters the intestine through human fecal contamination of the water supply, escaped the Indian subcontinent around 1820, spread into Asia and Europe to take root from Russia to Sweden, then crossed the Atlantic, carried by sailors, rats, or immigrants—medical authorities were not sure—to ignite epidemics in 1832, 1845, and 1866. An outbreak of the disease in Russia in 1892 came when immigration to the United States was at an all-time high and after an outbreak of typhus fever was contained by a ruthless quarantine of arriving Jews. "The 'cholera scare' . . . of 1893, which had its origin among the steerage passengers of the great Atlantic liners," wrote a respected journalist in *The Atlantic Monthly* in 1895, "brought the results of unlimited and uncontrolled immigration vividly before the American people."

MAKING THE CASE FOR RESTRICTIONIST REFORM: THE ECONOMIC IMPACT

Epidemics of infectious disease were intermittent, relatively rare, and by no means always brought on by arriving foreigners. The major immediate, daily impact of mass immigration was economic, chiefly felt in the labor market. By the 1890s the relentless augmentation of the labor force by foreign workers had shifted the attitudes of the American worker from solidarity to resentment. An early and forceful complaint at the New Immigration's scale and impacts came from the fast-growing AFL. At their annual convention in 1896, a depression year, President Samuel Gompers expressed disappointment at the results of earlier efforts "to close the floodgates for hordes of laborers . . . brought to this country like slaves under contract," and led his federation of unions toward a restrictionist position whose details were as yet unclear. Labor newspapers and meetings reflected mixed feelings, such was the hold of the ethic of worker solidarity, but increasingly the rank and file pushed labor leaders to face the reality that a mass infusion of foreign labor put downward pressure on wages and served employers' need for strikebreakers. A factory workforce divided by language and nationality found class solidarity difficult, and management welcomed and even hired to create this disempowering diversity. Without restrictive legislation, the existing nonpolicy on immigration would produce, according to a 1905 editorial in a labor magazine, "more rackrent for slum landlords . . . more rake-offs for contractors, *padroni*, and foreign agents of transportation [companies], more voting cattle for our political stockyards . . . more non-unionists for manufacturing combines, more outlay for every charitable and penal institution in the country, and incalculably more misery for America's wage earners."

Labor leaders were surely thinking mostly of white labor, being white themselves. But historians of black labor in urban places and industrial occupations find (in the words of historian David Hellwig) that "more than whites [they] suffered from competition by the largely unskilled migrants," as "struggles for jobs and housing bred deep-seated hostilities," especially among the Irish, staunch political allies of the Democratic Party. "Blacks in Steelton [Pa.] were pushed down and out . . . rather than upward by immigrants who followed them," writes John Bodnar. "The influx of Croats, Serbs, Slovenes, Bulgarians, and Italians into Steelton, especially after 1900, had a devastating impact upon the town's Black working force." Black leaders, too, expressed complaints about the economic impact of the Great Wave on black workers and their futures, both north and south, though they were given precious little space in the forums of public discussion. In 1853, Frederick Douglass said: "Every hour sees the black man [in the North] elbowed out of employment by some newly arrived immigrant whose hunger and whose color are thought to give him a better title to the place." Booker T. Washington, speaking to an audience of mostly white business and industrial leaders at the Atlanta Exposition in 1895, agreed: "To those of the white race who look to the incoming of those of foreign birth and strange tongue and habit for the prosperity of the South, were I permitted I would repeat what I say to my own race, 'Cast down your bucket where you are.' Cast it down among the eight millions of Negroes whose habits you know . . . among these people who have, without strikes and labour wars, tilled your fields, cleared your forests, built your railroads and cities." A trickle of northward migrating Southern blacks had begun, but Washington knew that the ready availability of cheap foreign labor at the gates of Northeastern industries left no incentive among employers to welcome or recruit black labor. The Great Wave was not only happening, it was preventing something else from happening in the nation's labor markets—a labor shortage that would have opened opportunities for American blacks, requiring only a short migration up the eastern seaboard.

MAKING THE CASE FOR RESTRICTIONIST REFORM:
THE CIVIC IMPACT

The turn-of-the-century conversion of the rank and file and leadership of the labor movement to a restrictionist stance (some of whom, like Samuel Gompers, were immigrants themselves) was mainly driven by economic harm, as they experienced it. Harvard economist Claudia Golden has documented "substantial and rising negative effects of immigration on both laborer and artisan wages from the late 1890s to the early 1920s" and tied the political strength of restrictionist sentiment to those impacts. But shared across class lines was another concern rising from the heart of nineteenth century American political culture. It arose from a cluster of ideas historians now identify as republicanism, a channel of thought and conviction running at full strength in the Founders' generation and persisting through the nineteenth and into the twentieth centuries. The core of republicanism was the unshakable conviction among Americans that they occupied a unique place in history. They had sensed themselves as a people after a century and a half as colonial subjects of the Crown, demanded and won independence, established over a vast expanse of territory the only modern republic, one dedicated to freedom and (therefore) self-government. This was a rare, precious human experiment. Could Americans preserve, even expand it? The answer depended on the constant cultivation and strengthening of civic virtue, best seen in active citizenship seeking the common good before any special interest. Republicanism began with the belief that a magnificent start had been made (an easy assumption to make among white males, because for them it was true). More, the republic's fortunate citizens must always be vigilant against decay and backsliding, realists about human nature and the possibility of losing the republican experiment through the erosion of civic virtue.

Self-rule thus demanded the active political participation of every voter, and the white male electorate from the middle to end of the nineteenth century achieved astonishing levels of voter turnout. But participation meant more: keen attention to issues as debated in meetings and in an intensely partisan press, showing up for parades, conventions, meetings, a nonstop and usually emotional engagement in the unending political struggle. If citizens slipped back from active involvement in public affairs, republicanism affirmed and history confirmed, corruption was always poised to capture the apparatus of government.

The political heritage and habits of the New Immigrants gave multiple causes for alarm. They migrated from the decaying autocratic empires of Russia or that "political tower of Babel," Austria-Hungary (in historian

George Stephenson's phrase), their civic experience one of unrelieved subjugation. With such a background, it was no surprise that journalistic accounts and daily observations of life in the industrial cities in the East and
Midwest piled up stories of a pliant and uninformed, non-English speaking
and substantially illiterate immigrant public manipulated into voter fraud or
bloc voting when voting at all. Political corruption has a long history in
America. Yet the exploding industrial cities of the late nineteenth century
were by all reports in a class by themselves, and the Great Wave from Europe seemed a source of mounting misgovernment. The New Immigrants'
central instinct about government seemed to be to distrust and avoid it.
"They do not (unlike Americans)," Stephenson noted, "conceive of government as part of themselves." If "to be American was to be free," as stated in
Keith Fitzgerald's summary of the testimony before congressional committees in the 1890s, "to exercise that freedom politically, to be literate in the
free art of republicanism," then "entire races were unfamiliar with [these
qualities] . . . and probably mentally incapable of learning them."

CULTURAL-RACIAL DIFFERENCE: A GUIDE TO THE DEBATE

"Entire races . . . mentally incapable of learning them." Here was another
aspect of the concern about Great Wave immigration, and one that must be
understood historically.

When Germans began to enter the United States in large numbers, to the
mostly Protestant, white population they sounded and acted *different,* and
the Irish even more so. Pre–Civil War objections to this surge of immigration
focused mainly on cultural differences that would impede assimilability and,
if migration were uninterrupted, make Roman Catholicism ascendant. There
was no resolution of this issue through the political system, which at that time
was paralyzed by the slavery debate. The mass migration of Germans and
Irish eased for reasons internal to those nations. The Civil War distracted attention from these immigration questions, and with time an answer slowly
emerged in favor of confidence in assimilation even during periods of massive immigration. Germans and Irish, now Americans, fought bravely in the
Union army, erasing memories of some of the Boston Irish who had so little
loyalty to their new nation that they volunteered and fought with Mexico
against the United States in 1848. Over a long period of time American
Catholics proved more American than Catholic, defying the energetic efforts
of the clerical hierarchy to hold them to older, European ways. It helped in
the absorption of this mass of foreigners that the flow of Germans and Irish

abated. Round one in the debate over Great Wave immigration went (on points) to those confident of America's absorptive capacities. The election of Irish-Catholic John F. Kennedy as president of the United States in 1960 seemed a strong confirmation of that verdict. On the question of whether to worry about the absorption of massive immigration of foreigners, experience by the Civil War seemed to show the optimists ahead, when they also had luck in their corner. Non-English-speaking (though still western European) nationalities could be assimilated, if the numbers were not too large.

When the Great Wave resumed in and after the 1880s, the immigrants were even more obviously and fundamentally different. Their numbers, poverty, low average educational levels, and their tendency to cluster in industrializing cities compounded problems already festering in the United States. These generated a vast and rising volume of complaints that were, as we have seen, first economic and then civic: job competition; downward pressure on wages and standards; ethnic and linguistic fragmentation in the workforce preventing class solidarity; augmentation of crowding, crime, pauperism, and disease; and the establishment of separate, foreign-language neighborhoods, schools, and churches. Added to all this was the worry, discussed earlier, over a cluster of civic maladies made worse as peoples from despotic societies settled as politically passive masses in an active, participatory Anglo Saxon–based polity keenly attuned to the preservation of republican self-government.

These were differences that greatly concerned citizens of the new, experimental republic, and might be said to have opened, in the 1880s, round two of the debate among Americans who saw in mass immigration a multitude of current social costs as well as a long-term peril to the very nature of the republic and the identity of the American people, and those who were optimistic that uncontrolled immigration would again work out for the best as it had in the past.

Round two, to anyone recalling round one before the Civil War, would appear to be a new contest in a very different setting, even if the basic issue was familiar. Germans and Irish, coming as families, were one thing. Millions of displaced peasants from southern and eastern Europe, mostly male birds of passage with no apparent intent to take root in America, seemed quite another.

In the long debate over their assimilability, two very different levels of analysis were entwined, and in historical reconstruction, blurred. Were the new newcomers culturally so backward that not even the American environment could make them promising citizens in any reasonable length of time? Or were they beyond correction because they were "racially inferior"? Americans a century ago used such concepts and language of both racial and cultural hierarchy robustly and unapologetically, and with a confusing lack of precision.

Contemporary historians and their readers are offended by the racial judgments laced through the debates of that earlier time. Racism itself, as an ideology or set of beliefs, is of course embedded in American history and will be found in any historical account of this nation, whether of literature, politics, religion, or sport. We would expect racism, whatever we mean by that travel-weary term, to make some mark within the story of immigration reform, as it does in every aspect of American life before, during, and after the progressive era.

Of course, what Americans meant or understood by the term "race" has a history, which means that it has changed. The new element at the end of the nineteenth century was scientific racism, a historically temporary enhancement of the power of racialist ideas long present in American history. Scientific Racism refers to the new channels of intellectual energy opened to the idea of a racial hierarchy among humans by the immense influence of biology and developing from Charles Darwin's *Origin of Species* (1859). Darwin wrote almost nothing about humans in that book (turning to human evolution in his *Descent of Man*, 1871), but social scientists in Britain, Germany, and especially the United States, were enormously influenced by the idea that biology had tipped the scales in the old nature–nurture, or inheritance–environment, debate decisively toward nature and inheritance. After four centuries of discovery, exploration, and subjugation of non-European societies invariably unable to resist the accumulated prowess of the West, Darwinian biology converted many intellectuals to the idea that racial hierarchy was scientifically established. Many of America's most respected natural scientists, and also the rising elite of social scientists gaining influence within policy debates in the United States, developed in the decades around the start of this century a sense that science had confirmed a racial schema from Nordic supremacy down along a descending hierarchy of other races. In such schema, Africans usually occupied the bottom rung. Often the categories were ludicrously unscientific. Red, yellow, black, and white would do for some, Nordic and Alpine and Mediterranean for others. Not until the 1920s would social scientists begin to change their minds about this hierarchy of inherited traits (and indeed the very existence of discrete races).

Inevitably, the issue of the New Immigration, given its timing, would to some degree bear the imprint here and there of the "findings" of scientific racism. The Reverend Josiah Strong, whose reputation as a writer was made

by the success of *Our Country* (1885), wrote in 1893 that "there is now being injected into the veins of the nation a large amount of inferior blood
every day of every year." Francis A. Walker, variously Yale professor, president of the Massachusetts Institute of Technology (MIT), and chief of the
Bureau of Statistics, provided a quotation that few historians have passed up,
when he referred to the New Immigrants generally as "peasantry, degraded
below our utmost conceptions. . . . They are beaten men from beaten races."
Political science professor Thomas Woodrow Wilson, later two-term president of the United States, wrote in *A History of the American People*,

> Throughout the century men of the sturdy stocks of the north of Europe had
> made up the main strain of foreign blood which was every year added to the
> vital force of the country, or else men of the Latin-Gallic stocks of France and
> northern Italy; but now there came men of the lowest class from the south of
> Italy and men of the meaner sort out of Hungary and Poland, men out of the
> ranks where there was neither skill nor energy nor any initiative of quick in-
> telligence.

New York writer Madison Grant gave racial difference the dimensions of
a global conflict in *The Passing of the Great Race* (1916).

> The long-suppressed, conquered servile classes [are] rising against the master
> race. . . . The danger is from within and not from without. Neither the black
> nor the brown nor the yellow nor the red will conquer the white in battle. But
> if the valuable elements in the Nordic Race mix with inferior strains or die out
> through race suicide, then the citadel of civilization will fall for mere lack of
> defenders.

A generation later, Adolph Hitler would befoul and wound the world
with language of that sort. This has created a temptation to find Hitler bed-
fellows wherever in earlier times and other countries we find the language
of racial hierarchy and threat. This guilty association guarantees a misun-
derstanding of the American discourse of the early years of this century,
when racial and racist thinking, spurred by the prestige of Darwinian biology, was reaching a sort of peak. Racialist terminology and assumptions
were so widespread as to be virtually universal among whites (and many
nonwhites). In the relatively brief heyday of scientific racism, many of
America's best-educated, progressive elites were led to race-based assess-
ments of many contemporary social issues including immigration, guided
by the best science of their day.

But the language of race did not mean they were always or usually talking about race in its biological sense, if it has a biological meaning. Contemporaries often employed a very different, nonbiological logic for explaining human difference. There was widespread acknowledgment that the incoming migrants from eastern and central Europe brought many negative social characteristics often attributable to their race, but that generation of Americans used the word "race" carelessly. By it they usually—at least, in immigration discourse—meant nationality. They spoke of the Polish or the Italian "race," or even subgroups within nations, as when northern Italians were sharply distinguished from Italians from the southern Mezzogiorno. What was being identified by such usage was not inherited biological traits but deep historical and cultural deposits. Theodore Roosevelt, for example, spoke often and passionately about the "American race," but he knew very well that it was an interbred and mysterious amalgam—that is, a nation, a people.

Where appropriate, translating "race" into "nationality" or "culture" within the debate over the New Immigration assists the modern mind in actually engaging in the discussion. Those seeing in the New Immigrants from Europe (Asian immigration, a small part of the migratory surge at the end of the nineteenth century, was overwhelmingly seen in racial as well as cultural terms) a lower level of human capital than the first European settlers usually saw the strangeness and backwardness not as permanent, or racial, incapacities but as a history-based cultural gap. The issue posed by these central and eastern European migrants, in the view of many Americans, was whether their manifest social backwardness could in a reasonably short time and with no great cost be remedied in the American environment. Thus in the vocabulary of Americans "race" did not always mean they were talking about race. As the context requires, we should substitute "culture." And the pervasive language of cultural difference joined with judgments about inferiority and generally low civic and educational standards, while sounding to the modern ear harsh and unsympathetic, did not always imply contempt or hostility. Writer Peter Roberts, in his 1912 book *The New Immigration*, told his readers: "Foreigners do not bathe often," their women "are Drudges" with high fecundity, and "the evils Foreigners bring" include crime, filth, and voter fraud. Yet he more than balanced these generalizations by praising aspects of the incoming cultures making eastern seaboard cities so vivid, affirming that "I believe in the immigrant" and "when agencies of amelioration are brought to bear upon these patches of backward Europe in America, they yield to treatment and appear clothed anew."

4

LABELING OF REFORMERS

So gathered the troubles of late nineteenth century America: crowded, ill-governed, and vice-filled cities; menacing corporate monopolies; political corruption; labor–capital wars; rapid and wasteful depletion of the nation's forest and mineral reserves—and the Great Wave, reaching a million or more a year. These and other maladies aroused the muckraking journalists and other bell ringers who helped launch the progressive era, a national crusade to change the future rather than merely accept it. The pattern of reform ran through discovery and exposure of social maladies through journalism or other channels of communication, then organization for civic or political action, often to assign government a larger role in societal regulation. By the 1890s one could see national organizations forming for such action—the General Federation of Women's Clubs in 1890, the Sierra Club in 1892, the Anti-Saloon League in 1895, the Chicago forerunner of the Anti-Cigarette League in 1899, and the National Consumers League that same year, just to note a few.

Immigration reform followed a similar path. Before the 1890s, the impulse for restriction had been scattered geographically, expressed by various labor leaders and unions, local and national patriotic societies, and individual authors. National organizations devoted solely to this issue were the next stage. Some historians see immigration reform carried forward briefly by a fast-growing but short-lived national organization, the American Protective Association, a secret order that spread out of a base in Iowa in the late 1880s and held its first national convention in 1890. The APA deserves little space in the story. Its focus was on Americans: on the campaigns for separate schools by Catholic Americans, instigated by church leadership; on the Irish domination of local politics in selected cities; on Papal plots to control America, as described in lurid pamphlets. The organization collapsed in 1900 without making any contribution to understanding or solving the immigration problem.

The Immigration Restriction League (IRL), founded in Boston in 1894, was another matter. It arose out of the Good Government movement in northeastern cities that contributed in a major way to the entire progressive campaign and mobilized the academic talent of New England's top universities and intellectuals, among them the president of MIT Francis A. Walker, historian John Fiske, and Senator Henry Cabot Lodge, with much of the work done by three Harvard-educated founders—Prescott Hall, Robert Ward, and Charles Warren. The IRL sent letters to governors of states asking if immigrants were desired and, if so, which races—meaning nationalities—were preferred. Twenty-six governors responded, eight saying no more immigrants were wanted, the rest happy to have Scandinavians, Germans, and other Old Immigration groups. The league would be active in immigration reform politics for more than two decades, its representatives often traveling from their New England base to Washington to influence the ongoing debate.

LABELING OF REFORMERS

Most of the IRL's members shared Senator Lodge's disdain for the APA and its anti-Catholic, nativist cast. What did he and others mean by that clearly negative term? The *Random House College Dictionary* defines "nativism" as "the policy of protecting the interests of native inhabitants against those of immigrants," and *The Dictionary of American History* as "the policy of favoring native inhabitants of a country as against immigrants." This does not take us very far. Most normal people would tend to feel closer affiliation with fellow countrymen than with foreigners. If the definition allows that these interests can sometimes conflict, then it is an odd citizen who is not a nativist on those occasions, and the word is a synonym for patriot, defender of community. But when we encounter the word in the late nineteenth century it was taking on only a negative connotation, such as it strongly carries today. Nativism now equates to xenophobia, an irrational dislike of foreigners and discrimination against them to the (unfair) benefit of natives. This provides a label for those who take a dim view of foreigners entering their communities but have no decent reasons for doing so. But what of those situations when aspects of some particular immigration pattern imposes costs on the people who were there before? We entirely lack a working term for citizens defending their community interest when immigrants, wittingly or unwittingly, put them at risk. Oddly, the term nativism has come to run in only one direction, toward xenophobia, never toward patriotism or community defense. Clearly, the definition of nativism has been shaped by history (especially as interpreted by historians), not by its logical possibilities.

The word derives from a particular era in American history, the 1830s to the mid-1850s, when the first large waves of immigration came to the eastern seaboard, mostly from Ireland and Germany. Eastern cities were swamped by incoming migrants from the rural hinterland and overseas, and life was hard for all. But the immigrants seemed to intensify all existing problems and bring new ones. Economic historian Robert Fogel writes that the flood of immigrants arriving in America from 1841 to 1851, more than had come in the previous two centuries, put severe downward pressure on the wages and job opportunities of American workers, who "suffered one of the most severe and protracted economic and social catastrophes of American history." In New York, the city's population grew tenfold from 1800 to 1850. By 1850 half its residents were foreign-born and their proportion was growing twice as fast as the native born. New York's Irish were 30 percent of the population but accounted for 50 percent of arrests and 70 percent of indigent relief cases, while being heavily hit by infectious diseases.

Into this setting of gritty urban realities came also religious differences. American Protestants became deeply alarmed by the large numbers of Irish and German Catholic immigrants and their manipulation—it was feared—by the Pope and the church hierarchy to fundamentally change, and dominate, American society. Protestant agitation was widespread, the language of suspicion was vivid, and there was a violent edge. The chief concern was that Catholics, paternalistically mobilized and instructed by their church leadership in the Vatican and in America, were becoming a force undermining republican principles and institutions. This fear "eventually proved mistaken, but it was not wildly implausible at the time," in the words of historian Stephan Thernstrom. Catholic historians are sometimes more direct: "Reasonable Protestants, who were neither bigots nor paranoiacs, had ample grounds for concluding that the Roman Catholic Church was not a friend of democracy," wrote Charles Morris. The Roman Catholic Church was a deeply conservative, authoritarian institution, and under Pope Pius IX (1846–1878), Thernstrom reminds us, "was a major supporter of reactionary European monarchs and a staunch foe of republican revolutionaries like Louis Kossuth who were heroes in America." The Pope's own government—ruling twenty Papal States—was one of the most corrupt and surely the most authoritarian in Europe.

Protestants, convinced that republican principles arose out of Protestant thought and struggles in Europe, became increasingly worried that immigrant-augmented Catholic communities under their well-organized clerical leadership would threaten American political institutions and public schools. The Catholic hierarchy cooperated in the race toward more conflict. In a chapter titled "The Catholic Church Blunders, 1850–1854," historian Ray Allen Billington recounts how the American Catholic hierarchy, formerly cautious, conciliatory, and low profile given the small numbers of their flock in Protestant America, became emboldened by the waves of Catholic immigration from Germany and Ireland that surged through the 1830s into the 1850s. "Powerful and overbearing in Europe," where it often had close governmental ties and large majorities, the hierarchy watched the "flood of immigration from papal countries" and suddenly, ill advisedly "sought to be domineering in America." The church was growing rapidly. Why not dominate the American religious scene? For the first time, Catholic editors, writers, and clerics, at their head the fiery Archbishop John Hughes of New York, began to attack Protestantism and affirmed a duty to convert all such pagans. Conflict was precipitated by Catholic demands for a share of public-school funds to support their own schools and laws prohibiting the reading of Protestant Bibles in state-operated schools. A meeting of the American Catholic hierarchy in Baltimore in 1852 to plan separate Catholic public schools, hospitals, and newspapers was widely reported and, in places, rumor embellished. "Protestant reaction was immediate and violent," but mostly it was political. The American Party was born, the U.S. party system destabilized.

That American Catholics would in time prove highly independent of the political views of the Roman Catholic hierarchy was of course not known as the Irish and German Catholics surged into the United States in the middle and latter part of the nineteenth century. They did tend to cluster, and especially in the case of the Irish, voted as a bloc for ethnic comrades, legally or illegally. Urban political machines in the Northeast made sure that "hundreds who landed in the morning . . . frequently voted by nightfall," wrote Carl Wittke in We Who Built America. In New York, one historian wrote, Protestant fears of Irish political influence were "genuine fears rooted in real social experience." Constituting one-third of the city's voters by the mid-1950s, the Irish regularly carried nine to fourteen wards in elections and the native voters only two. This translated into Irish control of jobs and other patronage. Here and elsewhere, Catholics both as voters and elected officials opposed tax-supported public education, which Protestants saw as the key institution in building national solidarity. They were also known to be opposed to important Protestant civic crusades—including temperance and abolition of slavery. "Prostitution, violent crime, pauperism, drinking, gambling, and immoral amusements seemed on the rise and more open than ever before," a historian summed up the natives' view of New York in the 1850s. "How could bedrock republican virtues survive?"

These can be called religious tensions but not in the sense that mere religious affiliation was the only ground for hostility. Social values and institutions about which people felt deeply were challenged by newcomers from sharply different cultures. Large-scale immigration thrust these conflicting values together and social conflict was a natural result. There was some spontaneous violence, especially in the 1830s, a good deal of anti-Catholic (as well as anti-Protestant) pamphleteering of immoderate and angry tone, and then political organization. In the 1830s came the formation of the Native American Party and the growth of secret orders such as the Order of the Star Spangled Banner. Then in the 1850s the American Party, its members soon called "Know-Nothings" for their habit of refusing comment on their plans to journalists and others. Their program included strong anti-slavery sentiment and political reforms such as child labor laws and ending imprisonment for debt, but historians have tended to ignore or forget these, concentrating on what was surely the Know-Nothings's core belief, that one of the nation's greatest problems was Catholic political activity, made more potent every year by German and Irish immigration. They proposed little in the way of immigration restriction, never even mentioning immigration curbs in the party's 1856 platform. Instead they focused on keeping Catholic immigrants already in the country from gaining political power. Lengthening naturalization requirements was their chief policy goal and voting only for naturalized immigrants and citizens was another goal. Thus they wound up advocating a sort of provisional status for Catholic immigrants here and neglected the supply side of the problem they saw by failing to demand that the national government gain control of immigration. Your movement is bigoted nativism, they were told, apparently the first use of that new, clearly negative word in American politics. Not so, came the reply: "Our movement is plain Americanism."

Nativism had thus entered the American vocabulary and with an unsavory image. It had been applied to the Know-Nothings, whose chief concern was Catholics in the country, not the newly large-scale immigration, in which they showed little corrective interest. The term was not attached to the larger restrictionist effort. Senator Lodge and his IRL colleagues were immigration reformers aiming at a system for controlling the flow of foreigners. He himself had used the term nativist as it was then generally understood, meaning those in the American Party before the Civil War and the APL members at the end of the century who primarily focused on monitoring American–Catholic political activity. The Know-Nothings are best understood as immigrant reformers rather than immigration reformers. They were concerned about and hostile to (some of) the immigrants around them, failing to focus on the real source of the problems, which was unregulated immigration.

The history of Catholics in America has had the effect of belying the fears of the nativists of the 1850s. If in ensuing decades masses of Catholic voters had sapped the strength of the public school system and shifted American voting patterns sharply to the right, hostility to their arrival in mass numbers and to their separatist ways would not be called nativism with a negative ring, but either their term, "Plain Americanism," or simply patriotism. But by the twentieth century the political activities of the Catholic hierarchy in the context of the pre–Civil War urban crisis was forgotten, and American Catholics settled into the political mainstream. Looking back with the benefit of hindsight as well as forgetfulness of real social conflicts of long ago, the Native American Party's worries appeared, if not groundless, at least greatly exaggerated. Forgotten were the seriousness of the ethnocultural conflicts, the sudden and community-transforming scale of the pre–Civil War immigration, and the fact that Irish and to some extent German immigration ebbed before the Civil War. The central problem had subsided, if not at the level of community abrasiveness, at least as a national threat.

Therefore Know-Nothingism was remembered as mere xenophobia, a groundless and irrational dislike of the Other, mobilizing itself in secret societies preparatory to political action directed against the political influence of recent-immigrant Americans—or, nativism. This reduction is not a fair characterization of the American Party's overall ideology, which included some desirable political reforms and a staunch antislavery stand. But we are interested here in the emergence of powerful terminology associated with immigration politics. The term "nativist" arose in the mid-nineteenth century because we needed it, for characterizing the Know-Nothing approach to large-scale immigration, which focused on the enemy within rather than designing an immigration-control system and was quick to go beyond real problems to imagined ones—with the taint of occasional mob violence.

What was the future of the term? An immigration restrictionist like Henry Cabot Lodge applied the term nativist to the short-lived APL in the 1890s, and might well have pasted it on the Ku Klux Klan of the 1920s. Nativism defined in this way has always been marginal to immigration reform, but a nasty margin with the power to taint the restrictionist enterprise. It was a useful term for quite a while. Early historians of the immigration-reform debate that eventually led to the 1882 and 1906 curbs on Asian and the 1921–1929 curbs on European immigration—writers such as Roy Garis, Marion T. Bennett, Edward P. Hutchinson, and George M. Stephenson—made sparing use of the term "nativism." To them, those actively seeking restrictions on immigration were simply reformers, most in the mainstream, like Lodge, Theodore Roosevelt, and Samuel Gompers. No one labeled these men nativists in their day. They were moved by real social problems such as wage and job competition, high costs of poor relief, disease, neighborhood crowding, and deteriorating civic standards. They also were concerned about important matters on which the evidence was and remains complicated—such as the impression that the New Immigrants were not assimilating to national norms, eroding national cohesion, and bringing conflicting loyalties to the discussion of American foreign affairs.

That is quite a spectrum of worries spurred by the massive new demographic and cultural force in American life, the incoming millions of New Immigrants. It should be no surprise that massive immigration, and a wide-ranging discussion of its impacts, generated a growing body of restrictionist reform ideas. In places it also flushed out the marks of nativism as history had fifty years earlier revealed it—the dislike of Roman Catholicism, exaggeration of negative evidence, racist or at least ethnic derogation such as anti-Semitism, rumors of conspiracy, and secret political organization to monitor the immigrants among us rather than go to the root and establish some control over the flow. This was, in the nineteenth century and for a short distance into the twentieth century, immigration reform's irrational, unhelpful fringe, always brought on by large-scale immigration and subsiding when the numbers came down. After the 1940s, nativism has played no further role in American life.

Our view of immigration restriction, and the role of nativism within it, has been powerfully shaped by historian John Higham's *Strangers in the Land: Patterns of American Nativism: 1860–1925* (1954), one of the brilliant and enduring volumes in American historiography of the past half century. Higham traced what he saw as a nativist tradition through three outbursts of especially intense and well-organized anti-alien political activity—the 1790s, the Know-Nothing era before the Civil War, and the period of his main focus, the four decades prior to immigration restriction in the 1920s. Higham seemed to cast the entire forty-year history of the New Immigration debate as in part a story of nativism—which he defined as "intense opposition to an internal minority on the ground of its foreign connection."

Were immigration reform and nativism, then, the same thing? As we have seen, Henry Cabot Lodge emphatically thought not. He was a reformer in a restrictionist direction but a critic of those he saw as nativists. But the distinction has been collapsed by historians writing after Higham and journalists following their lead. The cause of reforming immigration policy so as to restrict it has been treated, in the years after *Strangers in the Land*, as an outbreak of nativism, essentially bigotry and fear of foreigners. Cross-referenced under "nativism" in the index to Leonard Dinnerstein and David Reimers' textbook *Ethnic Americans* (1988), for example, one finds "see also Bigotry, Discrimination, Prejudice." Nativism, one way of reacting to mass immigration in the decades before the Civil War, came to be spread as a label over all subsequent criticisms of unlimited entry of foreigners into the United States, to the present day.

This is profoundly unhistorical. And the first dissenter from this was Higham. Shortly after the publication of *Strangers in the Land* he published an article (1958) confessing "that nativism now looks less adequate as a vehicle for studying the struggles of nationalities in America than my earlier report of it. . . . The nativist theme, as defined and developed to date, is imaginatively exhausted." As a concept it directs our attention too much to "subjective, irrational motives" and neglects and even screens out "the objective realities of ethnic relations" and "the structure of society." By this he surely meant the institutional rivalries of established Protestant and immigrant-fed Catholic churches, as well as immigrant impacts on wages, living standards, communities, and political systems. It was, Higham reflected, a "bad habit" to label "as nativist any kind of unfriendliness toward immigrants," leading to a neglect of "the less spectacular but more steadily sustained contentions embedded in the fabric of our social organizations. . . . Status rivalries have not arisen from irrational myths but rather from objective conditions," he went on, which "have not usually reached the point of hatred and hysteria." In the second edition of *Strangers in the Land* (1963), he stated that if he were writing the book again he would "take more account of aspects of the immigration restriction movement that cannot be sufficiently explained in terms of nativism."

Higham's continuing second thoughts on the role of nativism in the story of ethnic relations and immigration policymaking in America have not been sufficiently heeded or discussed. One part of the story of the Great Wave's impacts on America, nativism, is an inadequate framework for understanding immigration reform politics. It is entirely misleading after the 1940s when nativism had eroded and "was all but finished" and had moved to the far fringes of American life, in the account of historian David Bennett who followed nativism to its mid-century disappearance, as Higham had not. The larger framework in which to set mass immigration in any era consists of the real socioeconomic strains and thus policy issues that these invariably generate. "Xenophobia did not matter" in generating the restrictionist pressures of the latter part of the nineteenth and early twentieth centuries, concluded Harvard economic historians Timothy Hatton and Jeffrey Williamson in their exhaustive 1998 study of immigration's impacts. Of course, xenophobia played a role, but labor market competition and the resultant widening of inequality "rather than ethnic or national origins really lay at the heart of the immigration debate."

The term "nativism" should thus be returned to its historical roots from its current dismissive and pejorative application to many in modern America who seek lower immigration numbers. It applies to organized efforts in the 1850s, 1890s, and 1920s, beginning in secret fraternal societies and eventually moving into politics, to identify one or more foreign groups (however defined) within America as dire threats to the American republic, and to propose for them limitations on their naturalization—probationary or permanently inferior status. We need a word for this exaggerated antiforeignerism where it has historically cropped up or if it reemerges. A litmus test is the tendency to devote energies to the unjustified (by objective conditions) attacks on immigrants within reach rather than to efforts within political channels to change national policy governing disruptive immigrant inundations. The short-lived APA of the 1890s was an example of nativism, as were the turn-of-the-century alien land laws and school-segregation policies for Orientals in California, as was the fitful attention given to immigrants by the Ku Klux Klan of the 1920s. These were on the margins of immigration reform at the front end of this century, troublesome fellow travelers in a larger mainstream that sought policy solutions to real problems.

5

IN SEARCH OF NATIONAL
IMMIGRATION POLICY

What was to be done? The high unemployment and social tensions of the 1890s had gathered a powerful coalition for immigration restriction—organized labor, intellectuals and social reformers, and most Republicans, with the southern wing of the Democratic Party beginning to swing toward limitations. Large-business interests remained mostly neutral, against a background of a huge labor surplus through the long depression of that decade. The Democratic Party could be counted on to resist restriction because of its voting base in Northeastern cities and its historic opposition to federal activism. Also favoring the status quo was tradition—a history of openness to immigrants and a record of successful assimilation of diverse European peoples.

On balance, restrictionist sentiment became politically ascendant in the 1890s. The largest problem was the lack of clear ideas, based on experience, as to what to do to bring under national control something that had never been controlled by public policy—mass migration. The New York State Federation of Labor in 1896 recommended suspension of all immigration for five years, until the demand for labor caught up with the supply, certainly not a viable idea for the long term. The idea of a literacy test came forward—reading portions of the Constitution in any language, and, in some versions, writing those passages also—and it seemed well designed to curb the New Immigration with its high illiteracy rates. Senator Lodge sponsored such a test, estimating that it would bar some 25 percent of the immigration from southern and eastern Europe. It passed Congress in 1896, but was vetoed by President Grover Cleveland as he left office in 1897. The House voted to override, but the Senate took no action. A similar measure easily passed the Senate in 1898, but failed by three votes in the House. If two votes had switched in the House, President McKinley almost certainly would have signed the first general restriction legislation, as the Republican Party platform endorsed a literacy test in 1896. The rest of McKinley's term was taken up with Spain, Cuba, war, and empire.

As the new century arrived, the Fifty-seventh Congress received 5,082 petitions in favor of restriction of immigration, some from every state. After Leon Czolgosz, son of recent Polish immigrants and a convert to European anarchist ideas, assassinated McKinley in 1901, President Theodore Roosevelt in his annual message of December 1, 1901, found "our present immigration laws . . . unsatisfactory. . . . There should be a comprehensive law enacted" to achieve three goals: exclusion of anarchists, an educational test of "some intelligent capacity to appreciate American institutions," and exclusion of those "who are below a certain standard of economic fitness" which would "stop the influx of cheap labor." Roosevelt had lined up at the head of the immigration reformers, but his ideas were half baked, part of an ongoing conversation among those who were attempting to be the architects of something very new—an immigration policy that limited the numbers and selected those who would enter rather than let America be built as it had formerly been, by the choices of foreigners. It would require three more decades of thought, fact finding, emotional debates, and legislative maneuvers—all in a context of a relentless human movement across the Atlantic—to devise a system that would finally control the Great Wave and allow this emotional issue to subside and move to the margins of the national agenda.

GATHERING FACTS AND KNOWLEDGE: THE ROLE OF SOCIAL INVESTIGATION

A hallmark of progressive thinking was the conviction that facts must decide important public questions, and gathering them was the precondition for sound action. A string of official investigations added information and opinion on the immigration problem. An immigration investigating commission reported to the secretary of the treasury in 1895, and the U.S. Industrial Commission (formed to shed light on the fierce conflicts between labor and capital) published in 1901 a 957-page report on the whole immigration question. This led to the 1903 transfer of the Immigration Bureau from the Department of the Treasury to the Department of Commerce and Labor, and eventually to the Department of Labor when it attained separate status in 1913.

When it came to Asian immigration, there seemed no need for further fact finding. In Teddy Roosevelt's second term, Americans on the West Coast began to respond to the rapid increase in Japanese (and to a lesser extent Korean, Filipino, and Asian Indian) immigration with denunciations by politicians, newspaper stories on the Japanese influx, and scattered anti-Oriental riots in 1906–1907. The Japanese were "a competent race," reported a study of broadly based American attitudes toward Japan, but their overpopulated island nation was colonizing along the west coast of the Americas, sending high-fertility settlers who were nonassimilable into Western culture and "present impossible economic competition to the Caucasian race."

The Japanese government protested sharply. President Roosevelt had considerable respect for the Japanese, but recognized the West Coast's determination to contain the Japanese migratory stream. His main concern was to minimize difficulties in the U.S.-Japan relationship, and he arranged a so-called gentleman's agreement with Japan in 1908. Japan agreed to end the emigration of its laborers to the United States. (Australia, New Zealand, Canada, and South Africa all put in place arrangements to exclude Japanese immigrants during this era, while the Japanese were preventing immigration to their islands of Koreans and Chinese.) Japanese immigration continued, but at a declining level (83,000 in 1911–1920, 33,000 in 1921–1930, 2,000 in 1931–1940), mostly in the form of brides. Curtailment of an immigration wave that had threatened to sprawl upward deflated the social tension on the West Coast. Here was a lesson that should have been learned several times, but was often forgotten: to reduce social conflict over immigration, lower the numbers.

TIME TO STUDY THE PROBLEM

There is a British ditty with a Gilbert and Sullivan lilt that runs:

> If you're pestered by critics and hounded by faction
> To take some precipitate, positive action
> The proper procedure, to take my advice, is
> Appoint a commission and stave off the crisis.
> — © Punch, Ltd.

This was the route taken in the Roosevelt presidency. Senator Lodge again in 1906 maneuvered though the Senate legislation carrying a literacy test, touted by one senatorial supporter as a way to "separate the ignorant, vicious and the lazy from the intelligent and industrious." This sounded like a major curb on immigration numbers to friend and foe and attracted a large majority in the House. But Republican Speaker Joseph Cannon stubbornly deadlocked the legislation, which included authorization for the president's negotiations with Japan. Roosevelt convinced Lodge to drop the literacy test from what became the Immigration Act of 1907 (which made a few additions to excluded classes, such as persons with physical and mental defects, further expanding the definition of "likely to become a public charge"). In return, Roosevelt appointed a commission to study immigration and come up with a plan for "a definite solution of this immigration business," as Cannon put it.

The Dillingham Commission (named after its chairman, Senator William P. Dillingham, R-Vt.) labored for three years and produced a forty-two-volume report that was neither a plan nor "a definite solution," but had "enormous influence on the future course of immigration policy," in the assessment of historian Lawrence Fuchs. Mountains of data were gathered on the economic and social characteristics and impacts of the New Immigrants, out of which commission staff and members constructed a picture confirmed by later research—that the new immigrants from southern and eastern Europe tended to be less skilled, less literate (35 percent were illiterate in any language), and chiefly male birds of passage whose attachment to America was questionable. The commission affirmed that "further general legislation concerning the admission of aliens should be based primarily upon economic or business considerations," though it acknowledged that restriction was "demanded by economic, moral and social considerations." It found an "oversupply of unskilled labor in the industries of the country as a whole, a condition which demands legislation restricting the further admission of such unskilled labor." In making immigration decisions, preference should be shown to those who "by reason of their personal qualities or habits" would be assimilated and "desirable citizens." How to select? The commission listed seven methods and favored a literacy test and a ban on unskilled workers entering without families while suggesting another method for consideration—"the limitation of the number of each race [meaning nationality] arriving each year to a certain percentage of the average of that race arriving during a given period of years," a murky statement tying immigration to the demographic aspects of the American past. This latter idea would prove formidably difficult to turn into policy, but it exerted a strong appeal, and the laws of the 1920s would be built around it.

6

REFORM COMES: NEW SYSTEM
FOR CHOOSING AND LIMITING
AMERICA'S IMMIGRANTS

The presidency of William Howard Taft disappointed progressives across the reform agenda, including those wanting some system of selecting and limiting immigration. Legislation embodying many of the Dillingham Commission's recommendations, chiefly the literacy test, passed in 1913 but was vetoed by Taft as he left office. He argued that he had "an abiding faith" that the American environment, particularly the school, would prove "an instrument for self-elevation," which "has always contributed to the strength of our people, and will continue to do so." The truth was that in the closely contested 1912 election all three candidates had pandered to the immigrant vote, and Taft and Woodrow Wilson had virtually promised ethnic politicians that they would reject the literacy test or any other plan to limit immigration. The Senate overrode Taft's veto, but the House vote fell five short. This was the sixteenth recorded congressional vote on the literacy test since 1896. The measure was steadfastly and for two decades the central policy idea of congressional restrictionists. It passed the House on five occasions and the Senate on four, its support so strong that three presidential vetoes were overridden in one house or another on the tortured way to passage in 1917. In that year, Congress overrode a second veto by Woodrow Wilson, who privately admitted that his veto came because of a campaign promise to Democrat-voting ethnic groups.

Screening potential immigrants by a literacy test (reading several sentences of the Constitution in any language chosen by the potential immigrant; his or her family members were exempt) had been blocked for twenty years by presidential vetoes, and now it was law. This principle of selection meant choosing future Americans for their promise as individuals rather than by any group affiliation. This was the selection strategy that restrictionism had taken for two decades (with regard to Europeans; Asians had been handled differently since they were thought unassimilable in large numbers, and in the 1917 law an Asian Barred Zone was established from which immigration of laborers, but not all applicants, was blocked), assuming it would yield the desired curb on numbers. But the literacy-test experiment came in a wartime context of the Atlantic sealed by a naval blockade and subject to deadly submarine warfare and could not be immediately tested. The Great Wave had finally been interrupted—but only temporarily.

REFORM'S PARALLEL TRACK: INTERVENING TO ASSIST ASSIMILATION

In the context of concern over "hyphenate" loyalties and wartime unity, both the government and citizens took a redoubled interest in an aspect of the larger immigration reform movement we have not yet addressed— Americanization, an organized effort to assist and accelerate the process of immigrant assimilation to American norms. This impulse long preceded the war. An Americanization movement could be discerned by the 1890s, a form of social intervention that should be seen as a component of the larger progressive era. It was never a single enterprise but flowered in many forms under many sponsors. Immigrant groups already established in America took the lead—most prominently German Jews, well-established and concerned about the unassimilable impression made by arriving Russian Jews. They established programs to aid new arrivals to learn English, understand American laws, and disperse out of eastern ghettos. New York's Educational Alliance, a Jewish social work organization, began Americanization programs in 1889, and the Finnish American women in Calumet, Michigan, organized an Americanization Club to learn American songs, history, civics, and English, all to "eliminate the hyphen" and become Americans.

This immigrant-generated enterprise was soon adopted by mainstream citizen groups—including settlement houses, churches, the YMCA, patriotic societies, employers and business leaders, unions, the General Federation of Women's Clubs—concerned to move recent immigrants as quickly as possible away from inherited and toward American customs. The first historian of the movement, Edward Hartmann, found two faces—a generous and welcoming visage and an anxiety-driven, coercive one. John Higham called these "Liberal" as against "100%" Americanization, respectively. The first, born in settlement houses and among immigrant groups, preached the doctrine of "immigrant gifts," conveyed a sense of welcome, and combined an acceptance of foreign cultural inheritances with assistance to accelerate the transition to the American language, customs, and habits that were the gateways to economic and social success. The second face of Americanization typically launched programs to school the immigrants in the importance of abandoning their old-world ways at once and offered classes in English, citizenship, and hygiene and promoted celebrations of American national holidays and heroes.

When war came, the issue of national unity naturally came to overshadow all else, and it was a matter of widespread anxiety that the population of the United States was substantially composed of people from Germany and regions of the Austro-Hungarian Empire. "Hyphenate" American voices had made the debate over American neutrality policy divisive, and many feared wartime disloyalty, especially in those of German and Irish origin, anarchists, socialists, or pacifists. Patriotic societies and governments at all levels turned toward programs of the "100% American" style, and soon state and local governments were going beyond mandatory civics and English classes to laws declaring English the sole language of instruction (fifteen states by 1919) or requiring that schoolteachers be citizens. "The conformist tendency," one historian wrote, "became paramount and the permissive, humanitarian side almost vanished." (Even in war, however, the "liberal" version did not completely disappear. "Don't Preach. Don't Patronize" were the two rules laid down by the Americanization Committee of the National American Woman Suffrage Association in 1917). This wartime injection of anxiety, impatience, and Anglo-conformity not only made Americanization efforts less effective, as immigrants resisted forced marches leading away from the habits of the mother country toward an unsettling new cultural pattern. It also gave Americanization a bad name ("Americanization is an ugly word," wrote an Italian American intellectual in 1919) that only one style of it deserved. The history of Americanization tells us two stories, and the encouraging one is that both private-sector and government efforts to aid immigrants in the assimilation and naturalization process have been and can be positive complements for the natural processes—participation in the economy, influences of school, media, and community life—promoting assimilation.

During the long progressive era it was discovered that a nation experiencing substantial immigration requires both an immigration policy combining limitation with selection, as well as what might be called an immigrant-assimilation policy. The first decides who shall and shall not enter as prospective citizens, and it is the senior partner. The second has to do with facilitating the naturalization and assimilation of those admitted. One thing is clear: in the absence of an immigration-restriction policy during the Great Wave, immigrant-assimilation policy swam against strong currents. When war and subsequent restrictive legislation gave America a half century of respite from mass immigration, assimilation accelerated rapidly, turning first- and second-generation Italians, Poles, and Hungarians and Jews of all nationalities into the patriotic Americans who voted for the social reforms of the New Deal and stormed the beaches of Normandy and the islands of the Pacific. Historians have recently begun to reconsider a fashionable scorn for the coercive and exclusionary impulses behind the Americanization and restriction movements. The attractive achievements of the nation-building decades through the middle of the twentieth century—liberal political reforms, the patriotic energies of World War II, an ebbing anti-Semitism, the inclusionary spirit of the Civil Rights movement—are hard to imagine without their nationalist predecessors.

REFORM COMES

Restrictionist energies had been surging through the American political system for decades, and had to show for it only the 1917 law that enacted the literacy test and tightened antiradical provisions. Historians have not been much interested in the literacy test strategy for controlling immigration because it had almost no trial, but it deserves closer attention. The Dillingham Commission estimated that in the form initially conceived in 1897, the literacy test would have reduced the number of eligible New Immigrants by 37 percent, cutting the flow from southern and eastern Europe by a third while increasing the level of education. If subsequent numbers were still too high, some sort of annual ceiling might have been imposed. But confidence in the literacy test eroded quickly at the end of the war. European literacy rates were improving, so that reading (the writing requirement had been dropped) a thirty- to forty-word passage (in any language) was no rigorous test, and the law allowed illiterate relatives to enter with those who passed. In 1920–1921 eight hundred thousand immigrants entered American ports, only fifteen hundred of them rejected by the literacy test. Immigration to the United States remained lightly regulated, and a rationale for selection remained elusive.

> There is no room in this country for hyphenated Americanism. When I refer
> to hyphenated Americans, I do not refer to naturalized Americans. Some of
> the very best Americans I have ever known were naturalized Americans.
> Americans born abroad. But a hyphenated American is not an American at
> all. This is just as true of the man who puts "native" before the hyphen as of
> the man who puts German or Irish or English or French before the hyphen.
> Americanism is a matter of spirit and of the soul. Our allegiance must be
> purely to the United States. We must unsparingly condemn any man who
> holds any other allegiance. But if he is heartily and singly loyal to this repub-
> lic, then no matter where he was born, he is just as good an American as any-
> one else.
>
> —Theodore Roosevelt, "Americanism," address to the
> Knights of Columbus, New York City, 1915
>
> Source: Philip Davis, ed., Immigration and Americanization (Boston: Ginn
> and Co., 1920), 648–51.

The outbreak of war in Europe brought a temporary lull, but immigrant
flows surged once again after the war. Wartime emotions vastly strengthened and somewhat altered the immigration reform impulse in the United
States. Both Roosevelt and Wilson warned of "hyphenated Americans" with
dual or multiple loyalties in wartime, a reminder that immigration vastly
complicated presidents' tasks in establishing a national foreign policy. Concerned that the war effort could be sabotaged by the spread of radical doc-
trines and political activities undermining the U.S. government or our capitalist economy, Congress in 1918 authorized the president to control the
entry of persons whose presence was deemed contrary to public safety and
to deport anarchists and other radical aliens. Deportation for radical beliefs
was further expedited by a 1920 law, at the peak of the Red Scare sparked
by the success of the Bolshevik Revolution in Russia, terrorist bombings in
the United States traced to anarchist groups, widespread labor unrest and
strikes in major industries, and a general anxiety about global unsettlement
in the wake of a war of unprecedented scope and destructiveness.

These war measures did not supply the systematic control of immigration
debated for so long. But the war itself, in damaging European economic systems, generated immense out-migration pressures and forced American policymakers to act. While the hostilities had for a time checked the flow of European immigration, half a million immigrants came in 1920, over fifty
thousand monthly toward the end of that year. The immigration commissioner

at the port of New York, relying as much on instinct as evidence, reported that "more than ten million are now waiting in various parts of war-stricken Europe to swarm to the United States as soon as they can obtain transportation." A commissioner of the Hebrew Sheltering and Aid Society of America published a statement declaring that "if there were in existence a ship that could hold 3 million human beings, the 3 million Jews of Poland would board it to escape to America." "A deluge of immigration was impending such as the country had never known," limited only by the carrying capacity of ocean liners, wrote sociologist Henry Pratt Fairchild. These predictions had a tinge of panic, but by February 1921, Ellis Island was so jammed that boats were redirected to Boston.

The congressional response was energetic, the mood one of urgency. Many bills were introduced in the Sixty-fifth Congress (1917–1919), and the House committee on immigration reported out a bill incorporating the AFL appeal for a prohibition on all immigration for four years. This was a good indication of widespread sentiment as well as a sign that an overall policy for managing immigration had not yet come forward. In the next Congress the House overwhelmingly (296 to 42) passed a bill suspending immigration for two years, but the Senate, feeling more pressure from employers, produced a bill based on a longer-term strategy. Annual immigration would be restricted to 3 percent of the foreign-born population in the United States in 1910, with nationalities given quotas. This passed both houses by huge margins (62 to 2 in the Senate, 295 to 41 in the House), but President Wilson killed it with a pocket veto in his last days in office, sending no veto message and leaving not so much as a memo on his thoughts.

The occasion was symbolic. The argument for continuing the open door nonpolicy was intellectually exhausted. The moment for creativity and new ideas belonged to the reformers, who had the momentum but as yet no coherent plan.

The presidential election of 1920 returned the Republicans, and Warren G. Harding of Ohio, to the White House. The GOP platform contained the strongest endorsement of immigration restriction in the party's history. The time for immigration reform had finally arrived, though it would take the entire decade to work out the details. The basic decision came easily. "There is a limit to our power of assimilation," declared the House committee on immigration in 1921, a year in which an economic recession pushed unemployment to five million. The committee reported out a "temporary measure" to "check the stream" until a long-term policy could be devised, and it passed the House without a recorded vote, and the Senate by 78 to 1. The Quota Law of 1921 limited the number of any nationality en-

tering the United States to 3 percent of foreign-born persons of that nationality who resided in the country in 1910. This puzzling rationale,
hatched by the Dillingham Commission, was predicted to produce totals of
200,000 for northern and western Europe and 155,000 for southern and
eastern, cutting immigration to approximately 360,000 "quota" immigrants.
The measure was temporary, but extended in 1922 for two more years, as
Congress wrangled over its long-term intentions. When the law expired,
warned the House immigration committee, "the largest migration of peoples in the history of the world may be expected to begin on July 1, 1924."
The law was not sufficiently restrictionist for African American leader A.
Philip Randolph, who wrote that instead of reducing immigration to some
percentage of the foreign born, "we favor reducing it to nothing . . . shutting out the Germans . . . Italians . . . Hindus . . . Chinese . . . and even the
Negroes from the West Indies. This country is suffering from immigration
indigestion . . . excessive immigration is against the masses of all races and
nationalities in the country."

The totals did decline under the interim measure of 1921, but irregularly.
The 800,000 immigrants admitted in 1921 were followed by 310,000 in
1922, then 523,000 in 1923, and 707,000 in 1924, much of the increase
coming from Mexico, Canada, and other nonquota countries. But the numbers were large and the non-English-speaking migrants from southern and
eastern Europe still predominated, which was not the result Congress had
intended. Sentiment quickly shifted toward tinkering with the formula—3
percent could be made 2 percent, and the base year shifted from 1910 to
1890, before the Great Wave had reached full tide. A majority favored this
change, though some commentators, especially ethnic leaders claiming to
speak for New Immigrant groups, complained that the change to the census of 1890 was wholly arbitrary and amounted to discrimination in favor of
"Nordics" and against those from their homelands.

What did the reformers want, as they finally closed in on their moment
of success? They came in many varieties across changing times, but students of history turn to what is a principal source of evidence on this, the
formal remarks of congressional politicians on the floor of both houses.
Here we find a mixed bag of argument and counterargument. Out of this
and other evidence historians fashion their interpretation of what happened
in the way of immigration policy reform in the 1920s, and why.

Here we need a reminder that historians' views of the American experi-
ence have been dramatically altered in the twentieth century by the Civil
Rights movement. Since at least the 1950s, when the white majority in the
United States began to awaken to the racial injustices of past and present,

historians have been developing a keen ear for racial or ethnic bigotry in all of American history, not just in the slaveholding South. This was a liberating and energizing turn in historical studies, permitting a new season of progress in the understanding of American history. Racist thought and expression was found virtually everywhere historians looked, including in the immigration reform debates of the 1920s. For example, leading restrictionist Congressman Albert Johnson publicized a State Department report that the United States was about to be swamped by "abnormally twisted" and "unassimilable" Jews, "filthy, un-American, and often dangerous in their habits." A Congressman from Maine justified his desire to protect the nation's "homogeneity" by advocating "one race, one country, one destiny." One could easily multiply such prejudiced sentiments expressed by some of those who voted to restrict immigration, suggesting that racial theorists like Madison Grant and Lothrop Stoddard were the tutors of Washington policymakers.

But a more careful reading of the congressional argumentation in committee hearings and on the floor reveals that many of the advocates of restrictionist reform, especially the leadership, were keenly aware that charges of ethnic discrimination even in 1920s America threatened political damage to both parties (outside the South), and seemed to sting those who were charged with abandonment of American ideals. And such charges were vigorously made by politicians from New York and other Northeastern cities where the New Immigrants were in heavy numbers. The proposed national origins legislation was "the worst kind of discrimination against a large class of individuals and absolutely opposed to our American ideas of equality and justice," said Richard Aldrich of Rhode Island.

This could not go unanswered. For the restrictionist reform impulse had to win a political victory in the America of the 1920s, which, despite the decade's reputation for unchecked bigotry, was actually a society that mixed bigotry with a strong dose of what we call American Ideals—essential human equality, fairness to all, social tolerance. Politicians in the 1920s (as before) knew this. Because it was so, many of the reformers from the rank and file and virtually all of the leadership (Johnson was an exception, and then only some of the time) were at pains not only to avoid invidious ethnoracial language but also to vigorously deny that their preference for an immigration stream composed mostly of the older nationalities represented discrimination in the derogatory sense. Several members of the House committee moving the legislation forward complained that all these charges of "discrimination" and the talk of "Nordic superiority" was injected by the opponents of restriction. "The committee has not dwelt on the desirability of a "Nordic" or any other particular type of immigrant," read the committee report. "We should not and do not condemn these as undesirable, when we mean near nonassimilable or slow of assimilation. The undesirable are the criminal, the insane, the paupers." Congressman Albert Johnson complained that the "Nordic superiority" language was coming entirely from the opposition: "This committee undertook not to discuss the Nordic proposition or racial matters." Congressional leadership urging a system of selection that would result in fewer immigrants from the new source countries and more from the old preferred another line of argument. All nations conceded to each other the right to decide who could make a home within their boundaries. Who could object to a policy that replicated the nation rather than weakened it with new elements who were unassimilable? Was unassimilable a racial slur? "Let me emphasize here," said Rep. William Vaile of Colorado,

> that the restrictionists of Congress do not claim that the "Nordic" race, or even the Anglo-Saxon race, is the best race in the world. Let us concede, in all fairness that the Czech is a more sturdy laborer, with a very low percentage of crime and insanity, that the Jew is the best businessman in the world, and that the Italian has a spiritual grasp and an artistic sense which have greatly enriched the world . . . [and] which the Nordic rarely attains. Nordics need not be vain about their own qualifications. It well behooves them to be humble. What we do claim is that the northern European, and particularly the Anglo-Saxons made this country . . . yes, the others helped. . . . They came to this country because it was already made as an Anglo-Saxon commonwealth. They added to it, they often enriched, but they did not make it, and they have not yet greatly changed it. We are determined that they shall not. It is a good country. It suits us. And what we assert is that we are not going to surrender it to somebody else or allow other people, no matter what their merits, to make it something different. If there is any changing to be done, we will do it ourselves.

Similar sentiments were often expressed. Several congressmen insisted that the national origins basis for selection did not imply superior or inferior nationalities, but properly gave great weight to a common culture as the indispensable cement of any nation. Here the immigration reformers of the 1920s greatly missed the presidential leadership that progressives had enjoyed in virtually all their campaigns, from antitrust to conservation to railroad and banking regulation. Harding was incompetent, and Calvin Coolidge a disengaged man of few words and no passion for change, though he agreed that it was time for immigration to be limited. Teddy Roosevelt, who died in 1919, had a remarkable gift for urging immigration restriction while appearing to have confidence in assimilation and an inclusive, immigrant-embracing message (which in his case even extended to the Japanese, though not to the Chinese, let alone to Africans). He might have kept more Republicans, at least, on that more positive message. The congressional leaders of the restriction campaign had no such help from the White House. The ideas they wanted to express, of ethnoracial discrimination based not on invidious discrimination and bigotry but on national cohesion, were in the contemporary air, but scattered. A *New York Times* editorial attempted to make the point:

> It is both natural and wise that the American race wishes to preserve its unity and does not wish to see its present blend greatly changed [because it] prefers immigrants who will be easily absorbed and . . . it strenuously objects to the formation of alien colonies here [and not because it] adheres to silly notions of "superior" and "inferior" races.

Chicago lawyer Edward Lewis offered a term for this guiding idea. He called the concept of basing future immigration on the national origins of the American people an indispensable search for "like-mindedness." In his *America, Nation or Confusion?* (1928) he wrote,

> Nations come of slow growth and long travail, that they depend on like-mindedness and . . . if the United States becomes a hodge-podge of a score of races, no one of which is dominant, it will lose its unity and become like Metternich's idea of Italy, a geographical expression.

"Like-mindedness," an idea explored by the influential contemporary philosopher John Dewey, was language expressing the importance of non-racial, cultural principles of selection in order to maintain national unity. One of the more influential contemporary statements of this argument came, ironically, from an American of Italian descent, Gino Speranza, whose series of articles in *World's Work* in 1923–1924 argued that the spiritual unity of the nation depended on the continued cultural and ethnic homogeneity of a nation founded by mostly British settlers. Speranza had good company. Thirty-four biologists and other scholars from Yale, Harvard, and Princeton urged Congress to endorse national origin–based legislation to provide "basic homogeneity" without which "no civilization can have its best development." Many found this argument compelling, agreeing that what was at stake in a regime of unlimited mass immigration was the eventual destruction of a working American nationality. To them, the acceptable alternatives were either an end to immigration or immigration flows shaped to match the nation's existing ethnocultural patterns.

Unfortunately, many of the nation's intellectuals had been going into print for years with harsher reasons for restriction. Rita Simon's survey of leading magazines from the 1880s through the 1920s turned up opinions on both sides of the question of restriction, but many writers on the restrictionist side went beyond the "these new groups are difficult to assimilate" logic to hierarchical judgments. For example: *North American Review*, May 1915, "Immigrants from most of the world . . . are inferior. They threaten our vitality and our intelligence"; *Saturday Evening Post*, April 28, 1923, "If America doesn't keep out the queer alien mongrelized people of Southern and Eastern Europe, her crop of citizens will eventually be dwarfed and mongrelized in turn." Writers such as Lothrop Stoddard and Madison Grant have been much quoted, but they had precursors and imitators who, like them, had for years been free with terms like "unfit" and "mongrelization" that implied a fixed racial hierarchy and presumably mobilized ethnoracial contempt. Joining Congressman Johnson in his complaint against this sort of language, restrictionist Henry Pratt Fairchild regretted that it was "furnishing ammunition to the opposition, when it was possible to make out an amply convincing case on the basis simply of race differences, without any imputation whatever of respective superiority and inferiority."

Choosing what it hoped would be taken as positive language, the House immigration committee in 1924 reported a bill with the statement: "If . . . the principle of individual liberty . . . is to endure, the basic strain of our population must be maintained and our economic standards preserved." They moved the base year to 1890 and lowered the numbers to 150,000, cutting the proportion of immigration to base population to 2 percent. "With full recognition of the material progress which we owe to the races from southern and eastern Europe, we are conscious that the continued arrival of great numbers tends to upset our balance of population, to depress our standard of living. . . . Late arrivals are in all fairness not entitled to special privilege over those who have arrived at an earlier date and thereby contributed more to the advancement of the nation," the committee argued.

Then a new idea emerged, apparently first (there are other claimants) from Henry Curran, commissioner of immigration at Ellis Island, according to historian Stephen T. Wagner. "It has always seemed to me," Curran testified before the Senate immigration committee, "that the most assimilable and the best kind of immigration we could get would be that which is most nearly like the 100 million Americans who are now here." Why not design

"each annual installment" as "a replica according to the different constituents of stock who are now here?" This concept won over Senator David
Reed of Pennsylvania on the spot, who inquired about possible charges of
discrimination. Curran: "I think there is not one iota of discrimination. If
we let in every year the percentage that is already here of any nationality,
nobody can object to that." So instead of basing immigration on some percentage of the foreign-born in some arbitrary year, as in the 1921 law, the
basis would become the national origins of the current nation of Americans.
Whites only. The latter assumption was not debated.

Reed, convinced that the artificiality of the selection of the 1890 census
would place restriction on a shaky basis, took control of the legislation and
enthusiastically endorsed the new concept. It proved to be a magnet drawing supporters. "If one were to imagine all the immigrants from other countries in a given year congregated on board a single vessel," said another Senator, "the ship's company . . . would be in microcosm the United States of
America in its racial distribution." It would take some time to make the calculations about the national origins of Americans in 1920, Senator Lodge
commented, but after that "there can be no question then of discrimination, because it will treat all races alike on the basis of their actual proportion of the existing population." In this way, argued Reed, the discrimination built into the 1921 law and the House's Johnson bill—in that they
disregarded the American-born in calculating quotas—would be eliminated. To some Senators, the important point was to lower the numbers,
and Reed's bill did this in the most acceptable way. "If we will only check
the tide of immigration and give free play to all the assimilative forces of our
national life," said the Senator from Maryland, the Italians, Poles, and Russian Jews of Baltimore would surely contribute in time to the nation's welfare, just as had the British.

The House held to the formula of foreign-born in the 1890 census, but
Reed's Senate version rested on a stronger argument and was chosen by
the conference committee and then, overwhelmingly, by both houses.
"The national origins basis for immigration gives every national group as
many immigrants to this country as that national origins group has contributed to the population of the U.S.," stated the Senate Judiciary Committee, "and . . . it is founded, not on a foreign-born basis or on a native-
born basis, but on an all-American basis" and "without discrimination
against either foreigners or Americans." The law would annually bring, one
supporter said, "an installment of European immigration reproducing in
miniature the American composite." Migration from the Western Hemisphere remained essentially unregulated. Asian immigration was limited to

immediate family members, which kept it to minimal levels, by existing legislation affecting the Chinese and by adoption in the new bill of language barring immigration of "aliens ineligible for citizenship," determined by the Supreme Court to be those not white, black, or "Indian." Some critics made the astute prediction that the national origins of the ("white") population of the United States in 1920—the base year—would prove impossible to accurately determine, but all substantive and procedural objections were overridden by huge votes—323 to 71 in the House, 62 to 6 in the Senate. The Johnson-Reed Act was adopted on May 26, 1924, signed into law by President Coolidge.

John Higham described the winning coalition in this way: "Most of the support" came from "the common people of the South and West," and labor unions loaned their modest strength in defense of the working American. The Midwest should be added to the coalition geography, for support for the 1924 law was virtually unanimous there. Higham adds that, at the margin of politics, support came from "Patrician race thinkers" who offered "a stream of books and articles" on the "eugenic implications of immigration policy." Whatever their impact on public opinion, many congressional sponsors of the legislation emphatically separated themselves from arguments in favor of "Nordic supremacy," which were sometimes put into the record by their opponents. Only the ethnic politicians from the urbanized Northeast stood in opposition to immigration reform. There was essentially no party division over this immensely popular measure.

The immigration reform law of 1924 was a milestone, and both simple and complex. A new system of immigration policy had replaced no real policy at all—something the progressive generation had also done in other areas, such as monetary policy (with the Federal Reserve Act of 1913) and monopoly (the Sherman Act of 1890, the Clayton Act of 1914). The number of immigrants to America was to be sharply restricted, national quotas to be capped at a total of 155,000, plus several categories of nonquota slots that proved more expansive than intended. The selection of immigrants was determined by nationality (actually, country of birth, sometimes not the same thing), but inside national quotas certain skills useful to the United States were given preference, along with family ties. The goal was a small amount of annual immigration that would basically replicate the nation rather than transform its ethnocultural or nationality base into something else. "America must be kept American," as President Calvin Coolidge had put the sentiment, in his message to Congress on December 6, 1923.

But if the goal was clear, the means to the end were not yet in place. The stop-gap measure of 2 percent of the foreign-born recorded in the

1890 census would govern until a Cabinet committee certified the "national origins" of the American people in 1920, when a recent census offered the best and latest data available. A panel of experts reported in 1927 and stirred up an unexpected storm among the older immigrant groups, or "Nordics." The English quota was too high, the Scandinavian and German too low, came the angry complaints. Decades of heavy immigration had indeed given the country and its politics a tribal cast, one of the not-so-welcome "immigrants' gifts." A confused period of ethnic antagonism ensued, both political parties and their 1928 presidential nominees wobbling about between the 1920 national origins idea and the 1890 foreign-born quota idea. The skillful lobbying of John Trevor's Immigration Conference Committee, combining the effort of thirty-three patriotic societies, made the difference. President Herbert Hoover announced that the new quotas would go into effect on July 1. "For a decade or more," John Higham observed of the restrictionists' victory, "the country had needed an effective numerical restriction to protect the living standards and the bargaining power of the American working class." The last progressive reform was in place.

II

BENEFITS AND EROSION OF THE NATIONAL ORIGINS SYSTEM

7

IMMIGRATION RESTRICTION: RESULTS AND REFLECTIONS

The United States from the early nineteenth century to 1930 absorbed 60 percent of the huge surge of Great Wave immigration. As the United States finally decided in the 1920s to limit its intake, the other four major immigrant-receiving countries of the neo-Europes—Canada, Argentina, Brazil, and Australia—were taking similar measures. Canada discontinued all immigration but from the United Kingdom and France (with skilled worker exceptions), Argentina and Brazil established preference systems for the nationalities of the early settlers, chiefly Portuguese, Italian, Spanish (and with Argentina, German and Swiss), and Australia established a "white Australia" goal with preferences for those of British or American stock. Thus all five, Anglo-Saxon and Latin-dominated alike, opted for selection systems (of varying degrees of effectiveness) designed, in different ways, to replicate the nation's structure of nationalities as historically understood.

Restriction brought the numbers entering the United States down sharply, though a powerful force working in the same direction was the collapse of the American (and global) economy into the Great Depression lasting from 1929 to 1940 and after that the hazards of international travel during World War II. Recorded immigration to the United States averaged 305,000 per year from 1925 to 1929, under the interim quotas, then dropped sharply in the 1930s to an average of 53,000 a year that hides a virtual negative immigration in 1932. In the 1940s, immigration averaged about 100,000 a year, but with an upward trend after the war. Writing after the 1924 system had been in place for nearly twenty-five years, William S. Bernard estimated that, subtracting emigration, only 1.7 million people had migrated to the United States in that period, the equivalent of two years' arrivals prior to restriction.

The demographic consequences of ending the open door policy cannot be known with certainty, because no one can be sure what immigration would have been in the absence of restriction. Demographer Leon Bouvier has estimated that, assuming no restriction and prewar levels of one million a year for the rest of the century, the American population would have reached 400 million by 2000. This would have meant 120 million more American high-consumption lifestyles piled on the roughly 280 million reported in the census of 2000, making far worse the dismal figures on species extinction, wetland loss, soil erosion, and the accumulation of climate-changing and health-impairing pollutants that are being tallied as the century closes. The immigration reformers had not made the connection between immigration's contribution to population growth and other worrisome problems their generation's conservationists had thought of separately, such as depletion of forest reserves, rising pollution levels, and the extinction of species symbolized by the deaths of the last passenger pigeon and Carolina parakeet in the Cincinnati Zoo in 1918. But the connection was there, and restriction was a demographic blessing, slowing population growth rates that were at the base of the problem of resource and habitat depletion. In 1933, with immigration almost halted by a combination of restriction and economic depression, the President's Committee on Social Trends predicted that U.S. population would reach a peak in 1980 somewhere between 145 and 190 million, probably closer to the lower figure, and then begin to decline. These totals, especially the lower one, are not far out of the range of most estimates of permanent carrying capacity. Good news, to which immigration restriction contributed.

The chief goals of policy reform, to shrink the incoming numbers and to tilt the sources of the immigration stream back toward northern Europe, were less decisively achieved. Numbers entering legally but outside the quotas ("nonquota immigrants," mostly relatives of those recently arrived and Europeans entering through Latin American and Caribbean countries) surprised policymakers by matching and in time exceeding those governed by quotas. Yet with numbers so low, ethnic composition did not agitate the public. International economic maladies, war, and the new American system of restriction had thus combined to reduce immigration numbers to levels more in line with the long course of American history and to some observers seemed to have ended the role of immigration as a major force in

American life. Apparently the nation would henceforth grow and develop, as Thomas Jefferson had preferred, from natural increase and the cultural assets of its people.

The Great Wave, like all immigration, had deposited both benefits and costs. The arduous, unskilled work of our industrial expansion found willing hands. New ethnic communities brought many immigrant gifts, beyond enumeration. Cuisine was diversified, the American wine industry based in California established an international position due to Italian and Hungarian immigrants' skills and tastes. The Great Wave brought America the creative talents of Fiorello LaGuardia and Robert Wagner, Frank Sinatra and Maria Callas, Irving Berlin and Jerome Kern, George and Ira Gershwin, and Leonard Bernstein, Saul Bellow, and Lionel Trilling. No one can fully enumerate these positive contributions.

But a sentimentalist view of immigration is this era's clouded lens. Mass immigration from Europe's fringes brought high costs—wage depression, urban crowding, disease, illiteracy, cultural resistance to progressive projects such as the emancipation of women and environmental protection. It brought international crime syndicates and a cadre of violent criminals—McKinley's assassin Czolgosz; the Italian mobsters Charles "Lucky" Luciano, Frank Costello, and Al Capone; their Jewish counterparts Bugsy Goldstein, Phil Strauss, and Rich Cohen; two of the plotters of the deadly East Coast bombings of 1919, Sacco and Vanzetti; the kidnapper and murderer of the baby son of Anne and Charles Lindbergh, George Bruno Hauptmann; and the assassin of Robert F. Kennedy, Sirhan Sirhan. Immigrants are like the rest of humanity, in Thomas Jefferson's phrase, made of equal parts of poetry and mud.

Some of the costs of an era of unrestricted immigration were much clearer when it was curbed. In local and national politics the virtual disappearance of immigration from the agenda of American politics removed (with the regional exception of Mexican agricultural labor in the Southwest) a contentious and divisive issue from the center of American life.

Many employers in both manufacturing and agriculture had predicted economic hardship due to labor shortages, but as restriction shrank the incoming foreign labor pool in the 1920s and after, the economic results appear to have been beneficial in all directions. Tight labor markets in industry stimulated capital investments and operating efficiencies that raised productivity 40 percent across the decade of the 1920s. Economic historians include the role of immigration restriction as one of the factors producing the wage gains of industrial labor and the reduction in income inequality that occurred in the interwar decades. Economist Paul Douglas found that annual manufacturing-wage growth in the United States was 0.32 percent from 1890 to 1914 but an astonishing 3.3 percent from 1919 to 1926, strong evidence of immigration's wage-depressing effect. Reviewing the data from before and after restriction, Harvard economist Claudia Golden concludes, with many others, that the perceived injury to American wages posed by the Great Wave had been a real one. The impact on native workers' wages was "generally negative and often substantial." "The [immigration] laws are on the books and are very advantageous to labor," wrote the authors of a text on labor relations in 1947.

This was especially so for unskilled American workers with rural backgrounds, and chiefly for blacks. "The decline of European migration, coupled with the increased labor demands brought on by World War I, opened the doors of Pittsburgh's mills to incoming blacks," concluded historians of the effect of tight labor markets on black labor in a city typical of the industrial centers of the East and Midwest. Commenting in 1960 on evidence of the accelerating absorption of wage earners "into what was commonly called the middle class," labor historian Foster Dulles concluded: "This process was aided by the curtailment of immigration."

Ironically, one benefit of restriction—the successful and surprisingly rapid assimilation of the New Immigrants—was in time and with much irony interpreted to mean that the reformers had been wrong to fear national fragmentation. The curbing of the Great Wave created a forty-year breathing space of relatively low immigration, with two effects favorable to assimilation. The pressures toward joining the American mainstream did not have to contend with continual massive replenishment of foreigners, and immigrant communities realized that the sojourner-and-return pattern followed by the non-Jewish elements of the wave was untenable. Writing of Italian Americans, sociologist Richard Alba concluded that "the shutting off of the immigrant flow made clear to the second and third generations that their future lay in the new society." The result, to condense a complicated story, was that the squalid ghettos of the turn of the century thinned out, and the New Immigrants and their children moved rapidly toward the mainstream of American society.

For the desire to become American was very strong among most of the New Immigrants, especially after the imposition of controls ended the easy way back and forth between homelands. To be sure, in all ethnic groups there were anti-assimilationist pressures—strong residual loyalties to the mother culture, deployed especially by clergy, ethnic leaders and politicians, and some parents and most grandparents, who were heavily invested in the maintenance of cultural solidarity. But the desire and practical need to affiliate with this robust, Anglo-dominated America were stronger. Ethnic histories abound with the evidence of this restless, sometimes painful Americanization, a process in which the immigrants were caught but in which they were also aggressive actors—adding words to the language and other cultural elements to American life, changing names, embracing the public schools, moving out of ethnic ghettos, intermarrying. A survey of children of Polish immigrants in the mid-1920s found that most preferred "American" to "Polish American" as an identity. The League for Latin American Citizens (LULAC) formed in the 1920s in the Southwest, conducted all of its meetings in English and stressed the importance of learning U.S. ways. In this era of intense American nationalism, the New Immigrants, incessantly bruised by remarks that they were still foreigners, tended to accept these terms and move toward the mainstream.

The magnet was the world's highest standard of living, social acceptance, and mobility.

This invigorated assimilation process was, of course, vastly easier for the large majority who were of European descent, harder for the Asians and Hispanics, and extremely difficult for Caribbean blacks. Even for the Europeans, not all of them fully melted in one generation after restriction of the numbers, as Nathan Glazer and Daniel Patrick Moynihan pointed out in *Beyond the Melting Pot* (1963). Nonetheless, the rapid acceleration of assimilation permitted by the new controls on immigration presented Adolph Hitler, not even a generation after the Johnson-Reed Act, with an American nation far more united and formidable than the "motley," "mongrelized," and splintered America he confidently expected to meet in the great test of nations he launched in 1939. Without restriction, the American story through the middle decades of the twentieth century might plausibly have been one of rising levels of social segmentation and conflict, rather than of a remarkable and swift if incomplete consolidation. A vital next step toward national consolidation had to await the Civil Rights movement; immigration control could not bring it, though it had the capacity to contribute toward it by shielding the American labor market from low-wage foreign labor.

*   *   *   *

A policy that had so many beneficial economic, social, and demographic impacts, especially on the American working class, immigrants in America, and African Americans, might expect favorable treatment in the history textbooks. This was so for a time, but histories written since the 1950s have been uniformly disapproving, condemning the new restrictions enacted in the 1920s without proposing any alternatives. The 1924 law "caused America to sacrifice something of its tradition of freedom and opportunity, as well as its future ethnic diversity," concludes one popular college history text. Restrictionists in contemporary textbooks are described as nativists motivated entirely by bigotry and usually discussed on the same page with the reviving Ku Klux Klan.

Why this condemnation? The restrictionist reform impulse comprised two interwoven strands. One was a realistic calculation that the common good of the people already here was being eroded in multiple ways by something new in American history, the unregulated and sustained mass flow of migrants from poorer societies on the perimeters of Europe and Asia. The other strand was a defensive and by World War I an increasingly pessimistic sense that the existing society, built on a British heritage and superior to any on earth, had little to gain and much to lose from amalgamation with inferior cultures and races, many of whom could never or only with difficulty rise to the American standard.

The first impulse was sound, and was one foundation for eventual policy reforms that were extensively debated in public channels, desired and approved by the majority of the American people from both parties and from left to right, and led to results beneficial to the nation. Yet this impulse, and the beneficial results, have been all but entirely eclipsed in historical accounts of immigration reform by the second, which often expressed itself in the racially charged language of an era in which theories of racial superiority—based on permanent, immutable traits—were almost unchallenged in American life and thought. When revisiting that era, all that most historians in and after the Civil Rights movement can hear are the discordant, contempt-breeding distinctions so often made between preferred and—by implication or assertion—undesirable nationalities or ethnic groups.

This narrowed focus on one aspect of a complex policy issue serves an important contemporary purpose. Historians living in a world in which racism is not entirely extirpated and could conceivably have resurgence, want to send a signal to society that there will be no compromise with it. Thus when racist assumptions are found woven into a past social problem or the reform movement the problem generated, the good will not be accepted with the bad, lest it soften our stern judgments. We seem to feel that we do not yet live in a time when it is safe to muddy the moral waters with historical narratives in which people were doing the right thing, some of them for the wrong reasons.

The wiser of the immigration reformers anticipated this vulnerability, and they were thinking not of the judgments of historians but of the democracy around them. They argued that restrictionism was and should be justified economically as protecting American labor standards and socially by the desire for cultural like-mindedness. It did not rest on invidious distinctions directed toward those who came from strongly divergent cultures. Enlightened restrictionists of this sort could not prevent some people from doing the right thing—curbing the numbers according to some rationale supported by public opinion—while expressing the wrong reasons, reasons that the passage of time has allowed us to see as profoundly odious.

The restrictionists' low standing in modern history textbooks is thus in part an artifact of changing social mores with respect to race and the intensity of our contemporary revulsion from what was done in the name of racial exclusion in central Europe in the 1930s and 1940s and in the American South. This has made a balanced appraisal virtually impossible since mid-century. My own assessment in the preceding pages finds that restriction of the numbers of immigrants was an important goal of the progressive era reform efforts and brought public benefits. But every effort in public policy is flawed to some degree, as was this one. Apart from being too long delayed, was there a better way to bring immigration under control so as to promote the national interest? An earlier reform strategy was to allow admission on the basis of individual merits, the literacy test. When this appeared, on very short trial, to be ineffective, there was no real interest in stiffening the tests. Their next idea, stipulating a smaller immigration stream and establishing national quotas so that it would match the ethnicity of the foreign-born population of 1890 (or 1920), was so intellectually indefensible that it attracted trouble rather than consensus. No other alternative came forward except for the conception of selecting on the basis of matching the national origins of the "American people," and this came late in the game, in 1923. This was immediately and widely popular, as it made a certain sense. Keep America American, as Calvin Coolidge captured it. Some people at the time and many more today might raise objections to this logic for an immigration policy, but it mobilized huge majorities in policy circles and with the public, which is one test of public policy. What cannot be defended, along the way, is the verbalization by some restrictionists of bigoted generalizations about certain ethnoracial groups, who were repeatedly chided by other restrictionists that this sort of talk was unnecessary and a large mistake. To be critical in this way is not tantamount to demanding of people long ago that they hold ideas that no one held at the time.

And what of the policymakers' decision, as they formulated the definition of "the American people" in the base year 1920, used to apportion quotas, to exclude descendants of American aborigines and slaves, aliens ineligible for citizenship or their descendants, and immigrants and descendants from the Western hemisphere? This has seemed to later generations a rigidly racist "whites only" policy, reminiscent of the openly "white Australia" policy adopted there a few years earlier. But U.S. policy as formulated in the 1920s fell short of that. This "whites only" American people in the base year 1920 was used only to design "quota immigration," estimated at about 150,000. "Nonquota" immigrants could be of any nationality—Haitian, Jamaican, Brazilian, even Japanese—and those numbers, expected to be small, soon ran larger (mostly from eastern Europe) than those entering under the quotas. Of course, most of these were "white," but people of any color could legally immigrate to the U.S. under the national origins system, and the Mexican flow was fast-growing. Still, Congress and the president had established a national policy that defined an "American people" as the basis for selecting a large segment (soon less than half) of immigration, and it excluded nonwhites. There was almost no criticism of this at the time, and one might say that Congress here was quietly (there was sparing use of the word "white," and no debate over it, to my knowledge) doing what the vast majority of American voters wanted, which is what democracy tends to produce. But the public can sometimes be led, and one might wish that there had been a more robust critical discussion of the merits of building the national origins quota system, presumably the heart of the new policy, on the entire American population base, regardless of slave or "Indian" heritage (i.e, color). No indigenous people were trying to immigrate to the United States, so explicitly excluding them had no practical effect. The Supreme Court had just ruled that Asians were inadmissible to citizenship, and as long as that ruling held up, quotas for Asian countries, most would say, made no sense. This left a large group of Americans, descendants of slaves, officially cut out of "the American people," though they had a major hand in building America. Quotas for them would have meant some flow of immigrants from Africa, but as long as the overall immigration was small, those African numbers would be small, and U.S. immigration policy would indeed be aimed at producing "a mirror of America," and not altering the current makeup. Those with a sense of history may say that such a debate in the 1920s over the inclusion in an immigration formula of descendants of slaves would have been short and possibly unpleasant. But airing that issue would have given national expression to some dissenting voices on race relations, how not for the better?

The handling of the issue of the Japanese was a plain error with no mitigating excuses. The 1908 Gentlemen's Agreement effectively limiting Japanese immigration was unwisely repudiated and replaced in 1924 by the

explicit bar to aliens inadmissible to citizenship, despite abundant testimony before Congress that in addition to being unnecessary this move was
seen by Japanese Americans and the Japanese people as insulting on several
levels. The goal could have been achieved without this affront. A quota of
250 for Japan had been attached to the legislation, and while this gesture
satisfied the Japanese government, their ambassador in Washington unwisely wrote a letter to Secretary of State Charles Evans Hughes warning
of "dire consequences" if the new law did not contain the quota and drop
the language ending the Gentlemen's Agreement struck with Roosevelt
years before. Hughes unwisely sent the letter to the Senate, where indignant Senators warmed up the night with denunciations of Japanese meddling in America's internal affairs—and out came the quota. It was doubt-
less a sound policy to discourage the immigration of groups whom the
Supreme Court had ruled ineligible for naturalization, but the Gentleman's
Agreement already achieved this purpose. The words in the 1924 act,
"aliens inadmissible to citizenship," could be heard as code for only one nationality, the Japanese, since Chinese, Koreans, and Asian Indians had been
excluded earlier. The law implied that Japan was not carrying out her part
of the earlier arrangement and Congress must step in to exclude the Japanese also. Because Japanese immigration continued but at a low level under
both the Gentleman's Agreement and the 1924 act, nothing was gained by
the legislative rebuff, itself a result of minor mistakes and senatorial posturing. But beneath it lay a central flaw of progressive era thinking and policy on immigration, judging it not just from our own time but within their
context, the refusal—despite strong counterarguments made at the time—
to expand citizenship to all those allowed to reside in the country, whatever
their nationality. Limitation of foreign population flows was a proper goal.
Barring from citizenship any group legally and permanently in residence,
long after citizenship was extended to blacks by the Fourteenth Amend-
ment (1867), was a sad error of most reformers (and the courts), headed
otherwise in the right general direction.

Legislation, like sausage, has unsavory ingredients. Immigration restriction, with its flaws, was one of the many positive if imperfect measures of
the progressive reform era, which sought—with considerable success—to
bring costly and disruptive social forces under democratic control. Its suc-
cesses in hastening inclusive assimilation, in reducing population growth
rates and thus environmental damage, and of removing a contentious issue
from the political agenda, have tended to be forgotten in the zeal of we
racially enlightened contemporaries to condemn utterly all the works of our
ancestors who were so often not.

8

REFORM OF THE REFORM?
GATE-WIDENING COUNTERATTACK
QUIETLY BEGINS

The new immigration system was widely popular, and the immigration committees of Congress quickly became backwaters of minor tinkering or inactivity. The 1930s arrived with vast and chronic unemployment, and the American people wanted nothing from immigration. War in Europe would bring unprecedented refugee issues, as we shall see, but dealing with these—or avoiding them—did not require any rethinking of the basic system for deciding on the few thousand people who would be given immigration papers.

But American immigration policy had a small but dedicated body of opponents. These were composed of elements of the religious and political leadership of ethnic communities associated with the New Immigration, especially Jews from Central and Eastern Europe who were deeply concerned with the rise of fascism and anti-Semitism on the continent and eternally interested in haven. Unable to interest politicians or the media in the settled issue of America's immigration law, these groups hoped for new circumstances in which restrictions could be discredited and the old regime of open doors restored.

One campaign of immense importance in this direction had already been launched. In 1886 France gave a gift to America, a symbol of friendship between two republics, in the form of a gigantic statue, sculpted by Frederic Auguste Bartholdi and named by him *Liberty Enlightening the World*. It was shipped to New York (Philadelphia narrowly missed out) and, erected in the harbor, was as a symbol of America as a model to inspire other lovers of freedom. A proposed link to immigration had, ironically, been rebuffed. The secretary of the treasury, searching for a site for a federal immigration inspection depot in 1891, proposed locating it near the statue on Bedloe's Island, and retreated in the face of spirited objections. "The Goddess of Liberty would gather up her skirts in disdain," and would be "contaminated" by the flow of immigrants off the boats. The depot went instead to Ellis Island.

But that was not the end of that. A temporary art and literary exhibition had earlier been organized to raise money for the statue's pedestal that France was not supplying. Emma Lazarus, a young Jewish woman from a well-assimilated New York family, shocked by news of violent pogroms in Russia, submitted a poem entitled "The New Colossus." The poem concluded

> Give me your tired, your poor,
> Your huddled masses yearning to breathe free,
> The wretched refuse of your teeming shore.
> Send these, the homeless, tempest-tost to me,
> I lift my lamp beside the golden door.

It was read (along with other entries) at the opening of the exhibition in 1883, and then both poem and Miss Lazarus, who died in 1887, were largely forgotten.

In 1903 a friend of Lazarus gained permission to place a small bronze tablet containing the poem on an inside wall of the pedestal. This, too, went largely unnoticed. The arrival of millions of immigrants whose first view of America included that statue in the harbor generated among them a certain mythology of welcome and asylum around the upheld torch—the Lazarus interpretation of the monument—but to most Americans the statue was a local curiosity, or a proud acknowledgment that liberty did indeed enlighten the world.

This would begin to change in the 1930s, as journalists and history textbook writers began to link the statue not with liberty but with immigration. Franklin Roosevelt made the first presidential link between the statue and immigration in a 1936 birthday celebration on the island. Tourists began to crowd the ferries running from Manhattan to Bedloe's Island, and the language of Park Service interpreters and the national media began a long-term shift of the meaning of "Lady Liberty"—and thus, America—from spreading freedom by example to offering unconditional asylum. It is not clear why this happened, but it happened without commentary or complaint. There were groups dedicated to reversing the immigration reforms of the 1920s who liked the Lazarus poem when they learned of it (wincing, of course, at the "wretched refuse" part). Talented writers such as the Yugoslav-born journalist Louis Adamic devoted his prolific writings to the importance of the poem. The transformation of the mythology of the statue from liberty enlightening the world to mother of exiles seemed to have legs of its own, and probably reflected a desire among the intellectual elites to signal to the millions who had come during the New Immigration that they were now welcome and an essential part of America. In any event, if America's symbol was Bartholdi's statue, and if the meaning of the statue was now to be unconditional asylum rather than an exemplar of liberty, the restrictions on the books were at odds with the country's core identity. Thus the popular, politically unassailable reform system of 1924–1929 had developed by mid-century a formidable potential adversary—a new myth about national purpose and identity embodied by a statue in New York harbor, no longer liberty enlightening the world by example but now increasingly interpreted as the beacon guiding the world's huddled masses to a place of eternal asylum.

THE 1930s: DOING WITHOUT IMMIGRANTS

The collapse of the American economy that began in 1929 was severe and relentless, darkening every year of the 1930s and generating a considerable internal migration of forlorn, desperate Americans in search of work. Every job was precious and every worker shadowed by the unemployed. In those circumstances, observed one scholar of American immigration patterns, "we might say that for all practical purpose we have become opposed to immigration on a selective or any other basis." "I concluded," wrote President Herbert Hoover in his memoirs, recalling 1930, that "in view of the large amount of unemployment at the time . . . directly or indirectly all immigrants were a public charge at the moment—either they themselves went on relief as soon as they landed, or, if they did get jobs, they forced others onto relief. I, therefore, stopped all immigration with some minor exceptions as to tourists, students, and professional men and women, and I made the order apply even to non-quota countries."

The virtual moratorium on immigration that came with the 1930s seemed to some observers welcome for reasons quite apart from the issue of unemployment. "I am [now] against mass immigration," wrote immigrant

Louis Adamic who had been instrumental in having Emma Lazarus' poem
attached to the pedestal of the Statue of Liberty, because

> America needs to give herself a chance, to take time to merge and integrate
> her population, study herself and determine what she really is, and gain some
> control over her cultural destiny. . . . Let the European masses for the time
> stay where they are . . . and solve their problems while we work out our own.

The pause from the long binge of mass immigration was thus seen by
some in the interwar years to have benefits apart from the job-protective
imperatives of a depression era. In any event, the combination of the stern
restrictionism of both the Hoover and the Roosevelt administrations and,
more important, bad news traveling along the immigrant kinship networks
about America's dismal employment prospects, cut overall legal immigration virtually to the vanishing point in the first half of the 1930s. The Great
Wave subsided in a tiny ripple. End of an era.

From another direction, an estimated five hundred thousand Mexicans
(no one knows exactly) crossed the border into El Norte in the 1920s to
work in the expanding irrigation-driven agricultural economies from Texas
to California, as well as the industries of the Midwest. This forth-and-back
but mostly settlement-making human movement into and through the arid
Southwest was not yet recognized as what it was, the Mexican harbinger of
a new chapter in U.S. immigration history, the Second Great Wave.

9

FORTIES AND FIFTIES: REGULATED IMMIGRATION—POPULAR, AND UNDER GLOBAL PRESSURE

After a decade the new American immigration policy system—assisted by the economic depression stretched across the 1930s—was achieving its goals of much lower numbers and selection tilted somewhat more toward nationalities of familiar cultural heritage. Not all progressive reforms were such clear success stories. The social costs of unregulated immigration were lowered, and the diminished problem made space on the stage of American politics for other concerns. If the country was somehow harmed by the lower numbers of immigrants, no one made the argument. President Franklin Roosevelt captured the new situation in remarks at the Statue of Liberty in 1936: "A steady stream of men and women" had immigrated here over three centuries" and "made the New World's freedom safer, richer, more far-reaching . . . [but] we have within our shores today the materials out of which we shall continue to build an even better home for liberty."

Even then, the new restrictions had critics. The system was not prepared for two sorts of immigration events that the future would increasingly produce— sustained agricultural employer demands for temporary workers, and refugees seeking asylum from real or anticipated persecution.

World War II mobilization, especially the draft, produced a domestic agricultural labor shortage, but in no region so keenly felt and so close to an apparent remedy as in the Southwest. Congress responded with Public Law 45 of 1942, inaugurating the Bracero Program of temporary admission of Mexican agricultural laborers. This was not intended or expected to have anything to do with immigration. After the war, southwestern growers told Congress that American labor did not seem abundantly available to perform seasonal, transitory farm labor at Third World wages, and a new guest-worker program to benefit U.S. agribusiness was concluded with the Mexican government in 1948 and extended periodically. Criticism mounted over the years, and the Kennedy-Johnson administration allowed the Bracero Program to end in 1964 in view of resistance from the AFL-CIO and various Mexican American community groups who had long been concerned about the impact of contract migratory workers on American labor. At the program's peak, almost 500,000 Mexican *braceros* were employed in the Southwest; a total of 4.7 million Mexican workers learned how to move north and find employment during the life of the program. It was a fantasy that a guest-worker program could produce field armies of "temporary" male workers who would disappear after harvest and never bring families or put down roots—that is, become immigrants. There was always leakage from the program, and mass deportations between 1950 and 1955 did not much interrupt the process of the so-called temporary workers coming north. After termination of the program, Mexican workers came again in the spring of 1965, now a stream of illegal aliens constituting a new front in the coming wars over immigration. Policymakers who legislated this twenty-one-year subsidy to growers in the Southwest were producing a history lesson in the dynamics of guest-worker programs—they drive out domestic labor, develop momentum, and create immigration streams. The lesson did not sink in.

A European refugee problem developed over this same mid-century period, a very different issue but equally stretching the boundaries and agitating the politics of national immigration policy. The trickles of immigration characteristic of the 1930s broadened as Germany's Nazi dictatorship under Adolph Hitler displayed a relentless hostility to Jews and other minorities, annexed Austria and Czechoslovakia, ignited another European war by invading Poland, and by 1940 established fascist control over all the continent. Hitlerian Germany was giving the world, among other agonies, a grim new experience with unprecedented population expulsion, followed by the supreme horror of an organized effort to exterminate entire peoples, what would later be called the Holocaust. Sensing ruthless repression, though not the unimaginable disaster that lay ahead, opponents of Nazism of all faiths and sectors of society, but especially Jews, began to leave Germany in mounting numbers, generating at the end of the 1930s refugee pressures that caught all countries of potential refuge unprepared, reluctant, and to some degree incredulous.

U.S. immigration law contained no specific provisions for refugees, despite a vague heritage of asylum for the politically and religiously oppressed. Ten million Americans were unemployed in 1939, and in the United States there was no sympathy for and much resistance to the idea of America becoming again the destination of millions of Europeans. President Franklin Roosevelt ordered the State Department to ease the rules for screening applicants for immigration visas, and in fact one-quarter of a million refugees from Europe entered the United States between 1932 and 1944 (100,000 of them Jews). They included physicists Albert Einstein, Enrico Fermi, and Leo Szilard; philosophers Paul Tillich and Hannah Arendt; musicians Arturo Toscanini and Bela Bartok; writer Thomas Mann; and other talented people who could have continued to enrich European life in saner times.

The ghastly discoveries of the death camps by advancing Allied armies in 1945 led some in retrospect to suggest that the United States should have accepted every boatload of fleeing Europeans in the late 1930s or have organized some sort of international sharing, thus preventing the Holocaust. This is a retrospective wish, not a historical option. Close to 75 percent of Germany's Jews did relocate to other countries before the war, and after Hitler's stunning conquests made another seven million Jews his wartime prisoners, there was no practical prospect for rescuing them (and others) from whatever the dictator had in mind—itself not clear until well into the war and hard to believe even then. In the 1930s, an immediate open door for millions of Jewish refugees in a decade of massive unemployment, long before the Holocaust was more than a faint and unbelievable rumor, was not even proposed by American Jewish leadership, which was split between one wing urging some relaxation of regulations and another wary that Jewish refugees would spark American anti-Semitism. And "few Jews of any persuasion," historian David Kennedy writes, "in America or elsewhere, including Germany, and few gentiles either . . . as yet fully comprehended the force of the systematic onslaught against Jewry that Hitler would soon unleash. How, indeed, could it be comprehended?" Whatever Jewish opinion might have been, some sort of mass asylum in America (or anywhere else) was a political impossibility in all countries nominated by other countries as places of refuge.

Even if such a policy course had been somehow constructed on a multinational basis, such a response would have encouraged Hitler and all other "ethnic cleansing" leaders in the future to expel undesirable populations as a matter of international routine. It is a hard truth that countries that generously accept refugees encourage the production of more refugees, creating another problem as they attempt to solve one. The core problem was

the behavior of the German regime and the absence of international sanctions on absolutely impermissible actions such as mass population expulsion
or extermination. The terrible events of the 1930s and 1940s revealed the
necessity of resolute and early international measures against regimes guilty
of the barbarisms that launch massive flight from homelands.

The troubling refugee question emerged again as the war ended. Millions of Europeans displaced by wartime forced-labor assignments or finding themselves living inside the war-expanded boundaries of a Russian
Communist empire faced the choice of submission, rebellion, or flight.
Many chose flight, in the direction that history had taught Europeans to
flee—to the West, to the neo-Europes. Counting potential refugees is impossible, but official estimates ran from eight to twenty million displaced
persons in Europe in 1945, with 1.9 million living in Allied camps.

The Congress of the United States would not normally have focused on
this distant problem, but the White House and foreign policy establishment, energized by Franklin Roosevelt's activist style, was keenly aware of
its new role as the managers of America's leadership in world affairs. Concerned with European stability and America's "world image," and not unaware that liberalized immigration rules translated into voter expansion in
the Democratic Party's northeastern urban base, President Harry Truman
continued FDR's pattern—the president wresting the lead in immigration
policy from (an often resentful) Congress. The Cold War was emerging as
the new challenge to American security, and the executive branch realized
that expanded immigration visas to the United States could become a foreign policy tool, and one with no visible budgetary consequences. Truman
ordered that refugees be given priority within quotas in 1945 and pressed
Congress to pass the first refugee policy measure in U.S. history, the Displaced Persons Act in 1948, allowing 250,000 visas over two years. Federal
funds were appropriated for refugee relocation within the United States
and disbursed to religious and civic voluntary agencies (Volags), which were
becoming an increasingly potent lobby for expanded refugee programs. Extended in 1950, the Displaced Persons Act eventually settled in the United
States 450,000, or 40 percent, of the one million Europeans who were relocated to 113 countries. Most of them would have been ineligible under
the laws of the 1920s.

The acceptance of large numbers of refugees to the United States looked
like extraordinary and temporary measures to deal with a one-time war-
driven crisis. But they were also a sign of a political shift affecting future immigration. Voluntary nongovernmental associations had always participated
from time to time in American politics, and in immigration matters organ-

ized labor and the patriotic societies had often matched the energy and influence of ethnic lobbies.

There emerged during the 1940s the outlines of a new political alignment. The patriotic-society Volags were losing influence, while those of ethnic and religious groups became more active and skilled. The reversal of the Chinese Exclusion Act in 1943 demonstrated the new lobbying muscle of the latter, and the displaced persons refugee measures of the 1940s and 1950s had the additional effect of building a refugee resettlement industry around the federal funds appropriated for this purpose. One-time adjustments to unprecedented events of a world war began to accumulate as a permanent new and significant feature of American immigration policy, and opened a major breach in the quota system enacted in the 1920s. One-time exceptions kept repeating themselves in an unstable world in which communism was expanding and American governments were eager to portray their society in a favorable light. The pro-Western government of China fell to revolutionary forces in 1949 and sixteen hundred Chinese students and professors were given visas. Nearly thirty thousand Hungarians were admitted after the Russian military repression of the Hungarian Revolution of 1956. In this instance, President Dwight Eisenhower opened a major loophole in immigration law by using the Attorney General's recently invented "parole authority," which had been intended for use only for individuals. The 215,000 Cubans who crossed to Florida in 1959 were admitted under the same rubric, unchallenged by Congress. President Eisenhower persuaded Congress to pass refugee acts in 1953 and 1957, enlarging the stream of refugees and shifting their points of origin from Europe to Asia, the Middle East, and Africa. Charging refugee numbers to future quotas had long since been abandoned as a fiction, and quotas were essentially ignored. Human traffic around the national-origins system was increasing as the executive branch reshaped immigration policy piecemeal toward larger numbers from more parts of the world, to the consternation of some congressional leaders.

IMMIGRATION POLICY SYSTEM REAFFIRMED: 1950–1952

One of these, Senator Patrick McCarran, son of Irish immigrants and chairman of the Senate Judiciary Committee that had immigration under its charge, sponsored an extensive study and review of immigration issues in the late 1940s, as it became evident that European refugee improvisations by the executive branch were destabilizing the system built in the 1920s. The resulting report (Senate Report 1515) represented a serious effort to defend the national origins system while attempting to correct the features that were beginning to draw attack as "racial discrimination." Explicitly disavowing "any theory of Nordic superiority," the report forthrightly endorsed the national origins system, affirming that Americans at the time of its adoption "were fully justified in determining that the country was no longer a field for further colonization." Our law "gives every national group as many immigrants to this country as that national-origins group has contributed to the population of the U.S." Yet there remained on the books the Asia-Pacific Triangle with its token quotas, and the language excluding "aliens not eligible for citizenship." The Senate committee was aware that these attracted international criticism and provided fodder for communist propaganda in the Cold War struggle. The report's recommendations included the removal of all exclusion categories based on race or national origin.

Senate Report 1515 was also notable among all the literature on American immigration policy for its demographic focus and insight, apparently owing in part to the presence on staff of a talented demographer, Dudley Kirk. The report established as essential background the remarkable and unprecedented expansion of global human numbers. If world population continued to grow as it had from 1900 to 1940, the planet's human population would reach twenty-one billion by 2240. The report was not the first publication to call public attention to these numbers and their consequences. Two best-selling books on the issue were published in the year the work on Senate Report 1515 began, 1948. Fairfield Osborn's *Our Plundered Planet* was a measured but urgent exploration of the environmental implications of the growth ahead, while *Road to Survival* by William Vogt (who testified before the Senate committee) predicted Malthusian doom for the poor of the world whose reckless fecundity had brought this trouble on themselves. Senator McCarran's 925-page Senate Report 1515 was no best-seller, but it marked a beginning in thinking about U.S. immigration policy in the context of global demographic trends. It found at mid-century signs of a "rising tide of immigration" because of population growth in Latin America and Asia, a tide that "might well again attain the proportion of the early years of the twentieth century." This came at a time when "certain nations of the world have already exceeded their optimum population" in relation to resources. Though the "economically optimal population" for the United States was "a controversial question," some experts told the Senate committee that "we have long since passed it," becoming one of the world's crowded and resource-constrained countries and thus had an interest in curbing its own immigration-induced population growth.

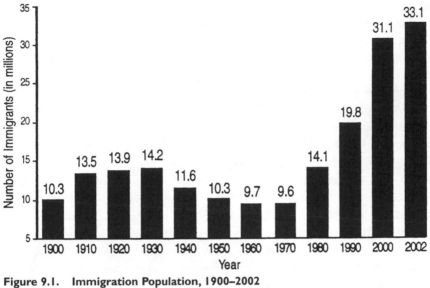

Figure 9.1.   Immigration Population, 1900–2002
Source: Center for Immigration Studies.

Senator McCarran's population concerns were far ahead of his time, but they were not primarily what brought him to immigration reform. His principal interest in taking the lead in rethinking the immigration system was two-fold. McCarran was a passionate enemy of communism and wanted stronger controls against the entry into America of her ideological enemies. And he shared the congressional desire to counterattack against the executive branch's repeated postwar forays around and outside the boundaries of the complex immigration regime as a new front on which to wage foreign policy. McCarran and other key congressional policymakers sensed a legislative mood to reaffirm the restrictive tilt of the national origins system, while the executive branch now saw immigration expansion as a foreign policy tool in the Cold War, especially in the Third World. McCarran, joining forces with Representative Francis Walter, submitted legislation in 1952 to clarify American immigration and naturalization laws, an effort to reestablish congressional control of policy that had slipped away toward the White House. The McCarran-Walter bill retained the same totals as the 1924 law, and affirmed the national-origins quota system as "a rational method . . . to best preserve the sociological and cultural balance" of the American population. It continued an easing of the bars against Asians that had started during the war, when, under pressure from religious and business groups, Congress in 1943 had repealed the Chinese Exclusion Act ("We can correct an historic mistake," President Roosevelt said in his message endorsing repeal) and established an annual quota of 105 for China, repeating this action for India and the Philippines in 1946. McCarran-Walter went farther, allowing immigration—usually at a minimal level of 100—from twenty-one countries or areas in what had once been called the "Asian Barred Zone," a phrase mercifully retired but replaced by another ghetto characterization, the "Asia-Pacific Triangle." With these small quotas for formerly excluded Asian nationalities, racial discrimination in immigration policy was ended, advocates claimed, clearly stung by what was becoming the central theme of critics of the 1924 system. The proposed reform bill still favored applicants from northwestern Europe but excluded no race or people entirely. McCarran, like much of the country worried about Soviet espionage, saw to it that the legislation established a five-year registration system for aliens and strengthened deportation procedures.

This round of immigration legislation, while producing a reaffirmation of restriction in general and the maintenance of American national identity through selection by national origins, stood in sharp contrast to the cycle of the 1920s. The center of passion seemed to have shifted from the side of those who, like McCarran and Walter, favored the national origins system and restrictionism in general, to those who wanted a larger flow representing more nationalities. Importantly, nativism made no appearance in the legislative discussion, either in fact or by allegation. "Stripped of its intellectual respectability," wrote historian David Bennett in his history of nativism, "increasingly irrelevant in the modern world of commerce and the professions . . . lacking the focal point of massive new immigration and its social problems, the old anti-alienism was over."

Indeed, the invidious name-calling came mostly on the other, expansionist side. Critics described McCarran's consolidation of the national origins system as "racist, fascist, reactionary, bigoted . . . xenophobia at its worst," by one account. The proposed legislation once again gave some nationalities preference and was thus "a barely disguised restatement of a thoroughly exploded racist theory" that "persons of Anglo-Saxon birth are superior to other nationalities [that] . . . was inexcusable at the time of its adoption" and is "outrageous now," in the words of a spokesman for the American Jewish Congress. Some proposed, unsuccessfully, to shift the base year for quotas to 1950, which would have increased allocations for eastern and central Europe but kept the mirror of America concept intact.

The McCarran-Walter legislation, reaffirming while modestly reforming the system of the 1920s, passed overwhelmingly. As a benchmark of the shift of the executive branch toward opening the borders, it was vetoed by President Truman. His veto message staked out presidents' special interest in the issue by pointing out that "immigration policy is . . . important to the conduct of our foreign relations." He then used the stern words that "the basis of this quota system was false and unworthy in 1924" and is "a slur on the patriotism, the capacity, and the decency of a large part of our citizenry." The politics of the veto message had two components—the old tradition of pandering to ethnic voters, at which the Democrats had always outperformed the GOP, and the newer Cold War interest of the executive branch in the use of opening American borders as an off-budget way of making international friends and embarrassing countries with walls around them.

The veto was overridden. Yet the wording and tone of Truman's objections indicated that immigration politics was slowly taking on a new alignment. Mass immigration pressures at the turn of the century had given rise to restrictionist reformers in both parties, right and left of center. The ensuing reforms that curbed mass immigration grew in part out of progressive and socialist concerns about threats to American wage levels, urban disorder, and political corruption, though the legislation also was a response to anxieties about national cohesion and identity that are conventionally thought of as conservative issues. Immigration reform had historically been bipartisan, drawing strength, and opposition, from across the political spectrum. By the time of Truman's veto of the McCarran-Walter bill, however, New Deal liberals were increasingly lining up, as their progressive predecessors had not lined up, as strong critics of the reforms that had curbed the Great Wave. Liberals were the dominant intellectual and political force in American politics at mid-century, despite losing the White House to Eisenhower in the 1952 election, so the power and rhetoric shifted in their direction. McCarran-Walter reaffirmed the reform system of the 1920s. But was a different, open-the-borders reform cycle somewhere in the wings?

ASSAULT ON THE NATIONAL ORIGINS SYSTEM

As they revised and refined the basic national origins system, McCarran, Walter, and the large majorities that endorsed their work could not know how the tides were turning against them. They were intimately familiar with the ethnic, religious, and interested professional lobbies who had always testified against restriction in general and national origins as a formula—groups like the Common Council on American Unity, the Association of Immigration and Nationality Lawyers, the National Catholic Welfare Conference, and the American Jewish Congress ("professional Jews," Rep. Walter had angrily called the

latter group, and the rest were "professional immigrant-handlers.") These lobbies did not know exactly what they wanted in replacement of national origins
restriction beyond more of their own kin (except for the Jewish groups, who
aimed not just at open doors for Jews but also for a diversification of the immigration stream sufficient to eliminate the majority status of western Europeans so that an anti-Semetic facist regime in America would be more unlikely.) They were united in their rejection of the national origins system, but
for decades their cause had no resonance in public opinion. Yet far-reaching
political changes were at work. The new immigrants and their children had
moved into the Democratic Party in the 1920s because of its ethnic outsider
image and its historic resistance to the moral reform agenda of Yankee Republicans. The presidential nomination of Catholic Governor Al Smith of New
York in 1928 accelerated this alignment, and both the liberal social policies and
the inclusive ethnic style of Franklin Roosevelt's New Deal pulled the urban
ethnic vote into a New Deal coalition that would dominate American politics
through the 1960s. Harry Truman understood the political potential, in Northeastern cities pivotal to carrying the most populous states, of an attack on the
existing immigration policy for being somehow unfair to Poles, Jews, and Italians (i.e., the New Immigrants, now voters). There seemed to be no political
costs to be paid for offending the broad public, who were passively in favor of
the system in place and unaware that it was under attack.

More important than ethnic coalition-building, Truman and younger liberal
Democrats such as Minnesota's Hubert Humphrey realized that their party
had a historic rendezvous with racial discrimination, especially as entrenched
in the South in the Jim Crow system. An assault on racial discrimination began to make sense to far-sighted Democrats for several reasons—out of self-
interest given the growing black vote in urban precincts, out of concern for
Third World opinion in the Cold War, and out of common decency. Truman
was a cautious friend of the gathering Civil Rights movement, friend enough
to have caused a southern Dixiecrat third-party revolt from his party in 1948.
He was an even more vigorous denouncer of discrimination against foreigners:
"The greatest vice of our present quota system," he had written in his veto
message, "is that it discriminates . . . against many peoples of the world." This
was 1952, a year in which he had nothing at stake in view of his decision not
to run and could explore the potential of the language that would power the
future: antidiscrimination. Immediately after his veto was overturned, Truman
appointed a Commission on Immigration and Naturalization, whose report
(*Whom We Shall Welcome*) proposed abolishing the national origins system
and replacing it with a larger number (250,000, with an added annual 100,000
political asylum seekers for three years) chosen by an independent commis-

sion on the basis of asylum, family reunification, and "needs in the U.S." Mc-
Carran and Walter were angrily negative, and Truman dropped the issue, having staked out the new liberal position.

It began to concern friends of the restriction regime, however, when
Dwight Eisenhower, no active opponent of racial discrimination but keenly
interested in America's image in Third World countries who were pawns in
the Cold War, referred in the 1952 campaign to "unfair provisions" of the
basic immigration law. As president he also sponsored enlarged refugee exceptions, recommended immigration reforms in his 1956 State of the
Union address, and sent down legislative proposals to move the census basis from 1920 to 1950 and distribute the larger numbers on other than national origin grounds. Francis Walter, in a 1956 Memorial Day speech, defended the "nondiscriminatory" policy in place and warned that reformers
were bent on trebling the number of allowable immigrants just at a time
when world population growth was accelerating, most importantly in non-
quota-controlled Latin America. He and others sensed a fundamental
challenge to U.S. immigration policy from liberal reformers.

What do the opponents of our national origins quota system want? asked
former State Department Visa Office head Robert C. Alexander in an article in the *American Legion Magazine* in 1956. "When they glibly advocate
action which would result in a change in the ethnological composition of
our people . . . perhaps they should tell us, what is wrong with our national
origins?" In a memo to colleagues in the American Jewish Committee, Sidney Liskofsky candidly remarked that the question was "a tough one to answer." Is there a justification for "a cultural-ethnic criterion for the admission of immigrants to the U.S.," or not? We open-immigration reformers
think not, but the American people apparently think so, Liskofsky reflected.
Alexander's question shifted the burden of proof from defenders of national
origins to those who would end it. Do we propose to go back to free immigration? He called attention to a recent article by sociologist Nathan Glazer,
who pointed out that those who want to go back to free immigration "write
as if immigration had no effect on America except to make it bigger, better
. . . more of the same." But a "sense of history" tells us that "the greatest migration in history" has also made America "different." Do we "want to become even more different, or are we satisfied with what we are? In 1921,
the American people decided they wanted to stop. . . . Nations have rarely
been faced with deciding their ethnic makeup, but the United States was. I
think the racist thinking that accompanied that decision was reprehensible.
The decision itself, however, one can understand. America had decided to
stop the kaleidoscope and find out what it had become."

This brief volley of ideas was a remarkably candid and perceptive statement of the issues involved in overturning the national origins regime. The earlier free immigration system had been changing the country, and the American people had clearly decided to curb immigration so that it annually supplied a small mirror of America, giving time "to find out what it had become." Reformers of that policy decision were developing a strong critical argument, but might also need a persuasive answer to the question, What is wrong with America that you would fix with a new (or restoration of the old) immigration system?

Publicly, the discussion of immigration policy was still a very minor, indeed, usually nonexistent, theme in national politics. Both parties in the 1956 election adopted platform statements vaguely decrying "discrimination" in the immigration system, but neither Eisenhower nor Adlai Stevenson injected the issue into the campaign. Nor did immigration surface in the 1960 presidential campaign. It would be, however, one of the agenda items for the liberal reformers who took over in 1961, and the ground was prepared in the 1950s. The Civil Rights movement surged into national news and consciousness in 1955–1956 with the Montgomery, Alabama, bus boycott and the emergence of Reverend Martin Luther King Jr. For the next decade the discriminatory Jim Crow legal regime of the South came under a furious assault in southern streets and schools, in national channels of news and opinion. The moral fervor of this crusade was so intense that it fanned into new life similar antidiscrimination movements among Native Americans and other ethnic minorities, feminists, and homosexuals. The enemy at the bottom of virtually every national blemish seemed to be Discrimination, the historic, now intolerable, subordinating classification of groups on the basis of inherited characteristics. The nation's national origins–grounded immigration laws could never have escaped an assault by these reformist passions. In retrospect, at least, the only question was: Who would lead, and formulate what alternatives?

Massachusetts Senator John F. Kennedy cautiously stepped out on the issue in the 1950s, sensing that a liberalization stance would gather vital ethnic voting blocs for his long-planned run for the presidency. His work on a refugee bill caught the attention of officials of the Anti-Defamation League (ADL) of B'nai B'rith, who convinced Kennedy to become an author of a pamphlet on immigration, with the help of an ADL-supplied historian, Arthur Mann, and Kennedy's staff. The result was *A Nation of Immigrants*, a 1958 bouquet of praise for the contributions of immigrants and a call for an end to the racist, morally embarrassing national origins system. The little book was initially ignored, but its arguments would dominate the emerging debate. The ADL, part of a Jewish coalition whose agenda had for decades included opening wider the American gates to increase U.S. ethnic heterogeneity and reduce the chances of a populist mass movement embracing anti-Semitism, had made a golden alliance. John F. Kennedy was no crusader on immigration (or anything else), but he was an young activist president by 1961, comfortable with immigration reform as part of his agenda and elected on a party platform that pledged elimination of the national origins system.

III

SECOND GREAT WAVE AND THE RETURN OF MASS IMMIGRATION

IMMIGRATION REFORM AGAIN:
ROAD TO THE 1965 IMMIGRATION ACT

House immigration committee leadership and staff, in preparation for what was to become the landmark Immigration Act of 1965, commendably began with an inquiry in 1962 including a series of hearings and reports assessing the global population prospect and its implications. Rep. Francis Walter's subcommittee invited the nation's top demographers to provide testimony leading to a special series of seventeen reports in 1962–1963. They were asked to talk about the human population future, with special attention to anticipated immigration pressures from Mexico, Central America, and the Caribbean. The immigration policy implications "would be worked out later," Walter said. They never were. These hearings should have served as a valuable foundation for linking U.S. immigration policy to global and national demography, which in the early 1960s meant maintaining strict limits on incoming numbers, whatever reforms were contemplated. Policymakers and the press ignored this early activity, and global demographic trends were little mentioned in subsequent debates.

Whatever Congress might have had in mind on immigration, it was understood that real action waited on the president's agenda. Since Kennedy's 1960 victory had been narrow, he moved very slowly on sensitive issues, especially those where he expected formidable resistance. That would come from, among others, Francis Walter. Walter's death in May 1963 came just as Kennedy was finally moving on Civil Rights legislation, and it seemed natural to link the two causes whose joint target, by long agreement among liberals, was "discrimination." Kennedy sent a special message on immigration to Congress in July, asking for repeal of a policy that "discriminates among applicants for admission into the U.S. on the basis of the accident of birth," and because the basis in the census of 1920 is "arbitrary" the entire system is "without basis in either logic or reason." The Asia-Pacific Triangle limits should be abolished at once, national origins quotas ended in five years and replaced by a selection system based on individual skills and family reunification, "first come, first served." There would be a minimal increase in total numbers—from 157,000 quota immigrants to 165,000. Reform *never* meant increased numbers, as the reformers constantly assured the public.

This initiative, along with the rest of the Kennedy program, was inherited by Lyndon Johnson after Kennedy's assassination. He also inherited Kennedy's determined reformist advisers on immigration, among them Myer Feldman, Norbert Schlei, and Abba Schwarz. The latter convinced the new president to endorse reform in his 1964 State of the Union address and to hold a meeting with ethnic leaders where Johnson repeated the key slogan of the attack on the national origins system: "We ought to never ask, 'In what country were you born.'" Still, expansionist reformers privately were pessimistic. In the words of the American Jewish Committee's lobbyist in Washington, "there is no great public demand for immigration reform," which "is a very minor issue."

It was indeed a minor issue to the public, not on the radar screen in a decade overheating with social movements and an escalating war in Southeast Asia. Liberal reformers discovered after Kennedy's assassination that legislating social change could be accomplished even when only the policy elites, if not the larger public, recognized a problem needing a solution. There was emerging on the immigration question a pattern in public debate that could be found on many issues: elite opinion makers selected a problem and a liberal policy solution, while grassroots opinion, unfocused and marginalized, ran strongly the other way. Editorials in papers like the *New York Times* and the *Washington Post* or in national magazines such as the *Saturday Evening Post* denounced the national origins system as the equivalent of Jim Crow, and endorsed repeal of it, saying little about an alternative. As historian Betty Koed observed in her history of the 1965 immigration act, editorials and letters to the editor "in smaller cities and towns" revealed "widespread condemnation of the new immigration bill" and of the idea of "liberalizing" immigration policy.

Legislative hearings began in the House in summer 1964, while the Senate was engaged in something more pressing but closely related—passage of the 1964 Civil Rights Act, which barred discrimination on the basis of race, creed, religion, sex, or "national origin." This language attracted frowning attention to the immigration status quo. How could the United States exert world leadership, Congressman Emmanuel Celler asked, if our current immigration system was "a gratuitous insult to many nations" because of its race-conscious basis? The national origins system was not based on race but nationality, but in the intense climate of the Civil Rights crusade the two were easily elided into equivalent evils, impermissible factors in decision making. The law treated nationalities unequally, Senator Paul Douglas said, and while "it would be impossible to draw up a law restricting immigration without discriminating somehow between those who are admitted and those who are not," we should end the "basically unjust criterion of national origin" for a more "equitable formula," presumably discrimination on some more defensible basis. Preference categories for professionals and relatives seemed to him more equitable. We need "an immigration policy reflecting America's ideal of the equality of all men without regard to race, color, creed, or national origin," said Senator Hiram Fong of Hawaii when the Senate opened hearings in 1965. "Theories of ethnic superiority" must no longer be the basis for our immigration law, stated the bill's chief Senate sponsor, Philip Hart of Michigan. Against such sentiments, an American Legion spokesman countered that "it is in the best interest of our country to maintain the present makeup of our cultural and social structure." In the context of Cold War and the Civil Rights struggle, there seemed considerably more energy and pertinence in the reformers' arguments. The national origins system was on the defensive now, ironically joined at the hip with Jim Crow.

Yet how could immigration reformers change a policy regime that was widely popular? A Harris poll released in May 1965 showed the public "strongly opposed to easing of immigration laws" by a 2 to 1 margin (58 percent to 24 percent). This must have discouraged immigration liberalizers, but they knew of the burst of Great Society legislation was beginning to pour through Congress in the mid-1960s, most of it not generated out of public demand or even understanding but out of the unique circumstances created by Kennedy's death, Johnson's legislative skills, and the intellectual and political collapse of American conservatism.

And the defenders of the national origins system—those who understood its complexities—conceded some of its flaws. Up to two-thirds of the immigration flows after World War II had come outside the quotas, as entrants from the Western Hemisphere and refugees. The system had become a swiss cheese of loopholes, with the result that annual numbers had been rising and the cultural background of immigrants was not what the system was designed to produce. Complex maneuvering produced a House version of the administration's legislation that ended national origins quotas and shifted to a system of preferences based on family reunification and skills.

Senator Sam Ervin of North Carolina was the only member of the subcommittee on immigration defending the national origins system during hearings. Ervin met every administration witness with the argument that you could not draft any immigration law in which you did not "discriminate," in that you favor some over others. Why not then discriminate, as the McCarran-Walter Act did, in favor of national groups who historically had the greatest influence in building the nation? "The McCarran-Walter Act is . . . based on conditions existing in the U.S., like a mirror reflecting the United States." To put all the earth's peoples on the same basis as prospective immigrants to the United States, Ervin argued, was to discriminate against the "people from England . . . France . . . Germany . . . Holland" who had first settled and shaped the country. Unfortunately for Ervin's cause, these first settlers and shapers were no longer voters, and their descendants were not paying close attention to immigration reform. On the Senate floor, Senator Robert Byrd (among others) supported Ervin: "Every other country that is attractive to immigrants practices selectivity and without apology," including Australia, Japan, and Israel, Byrd said. Our system is "just and wise," since "additional population" from western European countries is "more easily and readily assimilated into the American population. . . . Why should the U.S. be the only advanced nation in the world today to develop a guilt complex concerning its immigration policies?"

Whatever the merits of this defense of the existing system made by a handful of legislators, it confronted a large political problem. The American population who would have approved of this argument were mostly dead, and those living had, in contrast to their ancestors in 1921 to 1928, little interest in immigration issues or knowledge of what was being proposed. The patriotic societies, the American Legion and the Daughters of the American Revolution, joined by obviously marginal groups such as the Baltimore Anti-Communist League and the League of Christian Women, presented their traditional opposition to enlarged and non-European immigration but did not seem to exert much influence over the average legislator—especially when so many of these groups showed little knowledge of the legislation and seemed mostly concerned with the threat of communist subversives slipping across national borders. It was evident that the restrictions of the 1920s had lost important elements of their core support. A chief sponsor of limiting immigration had been organized labor. But in the 1950s AFL-CIO leadership—though not, apparently, the rank and file—had begun to shift its ground on immigration, and by the economically robust 1960s no longer expressed concerns about job and wage competition of an earlier era. The same was true of another component of the potential restrictionist coalition. African American leaders in the 1960s were beginning a move toward political solidarity with all the world's "people of color" and could not be counted on to take the restrictionist positions staked out by Frederick Douglass, Booker Washington, and A. Philip Randolph.

Even leaders of the patriotic societies seemed to sense the inevitability of some sort of retreat from national origins, and their opposition was not strenuous or skillful. The Senate floor manager of the bill, Senator Edward Kennedy, reported that in his meetings with several patriotic society representatives they "expressed little overt defense of the national origins system" and indicated their willingness to consider a new framework so long as the numbers were not enlarged. Kennedy assured them that this was not the reformers' intention, and it is clear from the legislative record that "the reformers consistently denied that they were seeking to increase immigration significantly," in the summary of Steven Wagner. Both historians of the legislative background of the 1965 act, Wagner and Koed, decline to call this outright deception, believing instead that the reformers had not given much thought to the system they were putting in place, for they "were looking backwards more than forwards." Their "main impetus . . . was not practical, but ideological." They were expunging what they took to be a legislative blot on America's internationally scrutinized record on human rights, more intent on dismantling an inherited system than in the careful design of a substitute.

These assurances left the oddly enfeebled opposition unable to take aim against larger numbers and different source countries because these were not being proposed, and perhaps not even anticipated. There seemed to be a universal miscalculation of the results that would follow from the new emphasis given to family reunification in the new preference system. Everyone appeared to agree with the view of the *Wall Street Journal* that family preferences "insured that the new immigration pattern would not stray radically from the old one." It is hard in retrospect to see why it was not obvious that few American citizens had immediate relatives abroad, so that this feature of the new selection system would build streams of family flows from a base in the most newly arrived, which meant Mexicans and whatever new refugees might arrive in an unpredictable future. Family preference was leverage for newcomers and left long-term residents with diminished influence over immigration streams shaping the nation's future.

A formidable coalition had mobilized behind repeal of the old law and for a vaguely defined "liberalization." The coalition included the numerous

Volags from religious denominations along with those organizations claiming to represent the ethnic groups associated with the New Immigration, strategically placed politically in Northeastern and Midwestern urban states. Joining them were business leaders and organizations, including Western "big agriculture." Sympathetic to these lobbying groups with a reasonably direct stake were most liberals, for whom immigration reform had surfaced as a smaller theater of the Civil Rights movement and one that did not involve the dangers of marching in Mississippi.

Ervin attempted to get the best bargain possible under the circumstances. "Congressmen don't want to look like racists," a *New York Times* reporter said, recording the intellectual victory of the reformers. Ervin asked pointed questions of administration witnesses about the legislation's impact on overall numbers and their composition and was given reassuring and (as it turned out) alarmingly wrong estimates. Administration witnesses predicted that the bulk of new immigrants would come from large backlogs in Italy, Greece, and Poland and that annual numbers would increase only a modest 50,000 to 75,000. On the question of Latin American immigration, Attorney General Nicholas Katzenbach was obviously ignorant of the testimony in the population hearings of 1963 in which experts had testified that Mexico's population had nearly doubled between 1940 and 1960. In the last decade, 400,000 Mexicans had migrated to the United States as three million *braceros* crossed the border seasonally. Yet Katzenbach, ignorant of all this, stated that "there is not much pressure to come to the United States from those countries."

Senator Ervin saw the opportunity. Was it not "discrimination" to leave the entire Western Hemisphere without limitation, implying "they were the best peoples of all," and hurting the feelings of those in the Eastern Hemisphere? The administration reluctantly agreed to a 120,000 "ceiling" (a leaky ceiling; immediate-family and refugee admissions were uncapped) on Western Hemisphere immigration. In 1978, separate hemispheric ceilings were merged into a worldwide fake number of 290,000 that legislators persisted in calling a "ceiling" but historians and others should not. It was merely the capped component of a system with no upper limit.

The law of unintended consequences was about to produce a major case study. Reformers were putting in place a new system under which total numbers would triple and the source countries of immigration would radically shift from Europe to Latin America and Asia—exactly the two demographic results that the entire restrictionist campaign from the 1870s to 1929 was designed to prevent. Yet the two core ideas of the restrictionists, that modern America was better off without large-scale immigration and that the existing ethnoracial makeup of the American people should be preserved, had not been directly challenged. Indeed, they were explicitly reaffirmed. Attorney General Robert Kennedy said in Senate hearings in 1964 that abolishing the restrictions on the Asia-Pacific Triangle would result in "approximately 5,000 [immigrants] . . . after which immigration from that source would virtually disappear." As a senator in 1965 he testified that abolishing the European tilt of the national origins system and placing emphasis on family reunification would maintain the status quo as to nations of origins. "The [proposed new] distribution of limited quota immigration can have no significant effect on the ethnic balance of the United States," and "the net increase attributable to this bill would be at most 50,000 a year." "Our cities will not be flooded with a million immigrants annually," prophesied Senator Edward Kennedy: "Under the proposed bill, the present level of immigration remains substantially the same." No one openly recommended what would turn out to be the bill's two chief results, increasing the volume of immigration back to the million-a-year range before 1920s restriction or the idea that it was time for the nation aspiring to lead the world to be ethnoracially altered so as to resemble that world rather than the nation that had grown out of thirteen British colonies augmented by African labor. This latter may be a splendid idea, the grandest of the last half-century. We have yet to seriously debate the wisdom of it, for when our national craft was turned in that direction, there was no discussion of the new course. It remains a suppressed topic.

The Senate bill passed by a vote of 76 to 18, all but two of the negative votes coming from southerners. The South–West coalition of the 1920s had shattered. The West abandoned the restrictionist system it helped build forty years earlier. The South, obsessively defending Jim Crow, was politically isolated and on the losing side of every national issue. Congress had decisively repudiated the old system for managing immigration, replacing it with what turned out to be an unpredictable and radically new regime. The Hart-Celler Immigration Act of 1965 ended the national origins system, with its 1952 improvements. That older system had served the nation well by inaugurating a needed and popular restriction of immigration. But its principles of selection had come under criticism as world politics and domestic attitudes toward race relations changed profoundly. In the new system of 1965, an inherited factor, nationality, still functioned as an element, but, reading the law, it seemed that no nationalities had a favored position at the outset. Lyndon Johnson had said, "We ought never to ask, 'In what country were you born?'" but of course we continued to ask, and the answer could matter. Your nationality could keep you out in any year that your nation's applicants exceeded 20,000, the limit for all countries (after revisions made in 1976.) Still, "discrimination" was supposed to be thankfully gone, because all nations could send some migrants and the principles of selection did not at first glance seem to have any direct connection to nationality. To select those chosen for entry the law established a new set of preference categories that represented a major retreat from the historic emphasis in American immigration policy on labor-market and skills criteria (only two of the seven in the new system) and toward kinship relations said to promote "family reunification" (four of the seven; the last category was for refugees, 17,400 slots). The national interest took a back seat, as selection criteria were shifted strongly (70 percent of the total) toward the private, kinship interests of citizens who had relatives abroad—or, recent immigrants.

In any event, "discrimination" proved hard to shake. The new system surprisingly "discriminated," as Senator Ervin had predicted, but now "against" citizens of western Europe and the British Isles, including Ireland, "in favor of" Latin Americans and Asians, because it gave special influence to kinship—or, nepotism. Ervin and a handful of others had anticipated large population pressures from these regions, and the North Carolina senator prevailed in the negotiations on one point, insisting that Western Hemisphere immigration for the first time be placed under a cap of 120,000 (the Eastern Hemisphere quota was 170,000). But the cap was made in Congress, which meant that it was not a cap, as it did not include spouses, minor children, and parents of U.S. citizens.

With adoption of the 1965 act, legal immigration began a striking rise from both Latin America and Asia. In the decade of the 1970s, Europe and Canada sent 20 percent of legal immigrants, Latin America and Asia 77 percent. This reflected push factors of poverty below the Mexican border and in Asia, whereas Europe bustled with prosperity. The new system clearly favored those with immediate family ties in the United States, which western Europeans and residents of the United Kingdom could rarely show.

Table 10.1. Regional Origins of Immigrants to the United States, 1951–2000

Country of Birth	1951–1960	1961–1970	1971–1980	1981–1990	1991–2000
Europe and Canada	70.2%	45.9%	20.4%	11.2%	17.1%
Latin America and the Caribbean	22.5%	39.0%	40.3%	47.2%	47.2%
Asia	6.2%	13.4%	36.4%	38.4%	30.7%
Africa and other	1.1%	1.8%	2.8%	3.2%	5%

Source: Statistical Yearbook of the Immigration and Naturalization Service, 2001 at www.ins.usdoj.gov/graphics/aboutins/statistics/IMM01yrbk/IMM2001.list.htm.

The new law also contained an unsuspected feature that gave it a conveyor belt quality, soon called "chain migration." Historian David Reimers has adroitly sketched the process. An Asian male comes to the United States to study, gets Labor Department certification allowing him to take a job, becomes an official immigrant and then decides to "reunite his family." To do this the simplest way would be to return home, but instead he petitions under the 1965 law's second preference for his wife and children to join him. The couple become citizens and then petition for their parents and brothers and sisters—all outside the numerical quotas. The brothers and sisters then petition for their own spouses, children, parents and siblings. In an example set out by Reimers, ten years after the Asian student arrived, nineteen persons have immigrated to the United States. "No wonder the 1965 Act came to be called the brothers and sisters act," Reimers remarks. Such human chains, widening from our original Asian male, were rarely formed after 1965 from the United States back to western Europe or the United Kingdom, as the original immigration chains were mostly old and broken. Few parents or brothers and sisters of American citizens remained in Naples or Dublin. Rep. Emmanuel Celler, one of the strongest supporters of the 1965 law, was astonished by what he called the "unintentional discrimination" of the law he had cosponsored. He unsuccessfully attempted to increase special visas for Europe that would not require family ties. It is not recorded whether or not Senator Ervin enjoyed the moment.

The new system, like the old, was also flawed by its rigidity. Congress wrote immigration law as if its judgments should endure for decades. But immigration is a labor flow that should be meshed with the changing needs of the national economy, and a demographic nation-shaper that should be harnessed to national population goals. Recognizing at least the former, Celler pressed for restoration of a feature of Kennedy's original bill, an independent immigration board to recommend annual readjustments of skills-related preference categories in light of changes in the economy. This good idea was lost in the shuffle. The system was not open to administrative realignment in response to economic cycles or demographic trends. Even if it had been, family ties abroad greatly outweighed skills needed in the United States. The law represented "the transfer of policy control from the elected representatives of the American people to individuals wishing to bring relatives to this country," according to Senator Eugene McCarthy's rueful and later judgment. "Virtually all immigration decisions today are made by private individuals."

"The bill that we will sign today," said President Johnson, "is not a revolutionary bill" and "does not affect the lives of millions." What it did, he thought, was essentially moral and symbolic. It ends "the harsh injustice of the national origins quota system," which was "a cruel and enduring wrong." Journalist Theodore White offered a better interpretation, when, years later and with hindsight, he called the new immigration law a "noble, revolutionary—and probably the most thoughtless of the many acts of the Great Society."

SECOND WAVE FINDS AN OPENED DOOR: THE LEAKY SYSTEM OF 1965

Revolutionary? But the 1965 Immigration Act was not given much contemporary attention in a decade of social upheaval and a war in Vietnam, was not mentioned by Lyndon Johnson in his memoirs, and is routinely allotted one or two sentences in history textbooks.

This emphasis will change, and attention to the 1965 Immigration Act will grow, for White's word "revolutionary" identifies a demographic turning point. With all due respect to the epochal and invaluable changes made in America when the Jim Crow system was killed by the Civil Rights Act of 1964, the passage of time may position the 1965 Immigration Act as the Great Society's most nation-changing single act, especially if seen as the first of a series of ongoing liberalizations of U.S. immigration and border policy extending through the end of the century and facilitating four decades (so far) of mass immigration. For the 1965 law, and subsequent policy, shifted the nation from a population-stabilization to a population-growth path, with far-reaching consequences, overwhelmingly negative. It bids to be seen as the largest, if most slow-moving, of the reforms of that liberal era. Demography is destiny.

Like many of history's cascading events, the essential context for immigration policymaking in the 1960s is evident in hindsight but was missed by all but a handful of intelligent policymakers of the era. Despite (poorly attended and mostly unreported) hearings in the House in 1962–1963 on world demography past and future, lawmakers essentially ignored the implications of a quiet global transformation, what economic historian Walt Rostow recently called *The Great Population Spike* (1998). An unprecedented and ultimately tragic event in human and planetary life, the surge of Homo sapiens numbers from one billion in 1830 through today's six billion to the expected nine to eleven billion, came in a mere instant of two and a half centuries out of humanity's thousands of years on the globe. This upward spike in human population is a combination of a success story—economic and social modernization that lowered death rates as it improved standards of living—with a disastrous inability of humans to understand the need to lower their birth rates as quickly. The results of this stupendous failure of culture and intelligence have been and will be exploding populations becoming too large for the carrying capacity of environments and socioeconomic systems—hence billions of humans fated to live with malnutrition, starvation, disease, and wars over resources. These combine to produce the push factor in immigration, and policymakers vastly underestimated it in the 1960s. Rostow, optimistic about human ingenuity in the long run, sees the period from the 1990s to about 2025 as "a period of maximum strain on resources and environment when global population is still expanding . . . a global crisis of Malthusian consequences" made worse by the unknown strains of global warming. Another sophisticated observer, Hamish MacRae, in *The World In 2020* (1994), sees a turbulent era of water and oil shortages, relentless habitat destruction, and international conflict over transborder pollution and for basic resources.

Another by-product is mass migrations surging out of overcrowded, environmentally decaying, economically impoverished societies toward regions known to offer a better life. The first massive and concerted flow generated by this upward spike of human numbers was the Great Wave, washing out of that part of the world—Europe—that first experienced the modernization-driven explosion of human numbers. That European wave, as we have seen, headed west to the neo-Europes, dragging millions of enslaved Africans with them for a short time.

In the United States, the 1965 Immigration Act widened the American gate just as the population spike was sending a Second Great Wave of human migration surging out of Latin America and parts of Asia, with eddies out of the Middle East, Russia, and North Africa. This second vast human migration continues as this book is written and will extend deep into the twenty-first century. As it gained momentum, policy reformers in the United States unwittingly gave the nation a new, more porous immigration system and "asylum as the meaning of America" ethos. They thus facilitated and encouraged a new era of large-scale and nation-changing immigration to the United States, without either expressed intention or democratic consent. To this we now turn, and to the complex question of its continuing impacts.

II

MASS IMMIGRATION BUILDS MOMENTUM: REFUGEES UNLIMITED

The new immigration regime quickly ushered in a vast change. Legal immigration from Europe shrank from 113,000 in 1965 to an average 65,000 a year by the late 1970s. By 1970 migrants from Latin America had risen 30 percent from 1965 and during the 1980s brought 3.5 million, or nearly half the decade's total. Asian immigration surged to 36 percent of total legal immigrants in the 1970s and accounted for almost 3 million in the 1980s. So much for the predictions and promises of Washington policymakers in the 1960s. They had underestimated the push factors in Third World nations, and entirely failed to foresee the development of chain migration, which built on a growing base within the United States of recent Latin American and Asian immigrants and refugees, a base that Europe no longer possessed.

The new law was bypassed before it was a year old, in order to expand immigration as a weapon in the Cold War. Cuba's communist dictator Fidel Castro, facing political turmoil in the fall of 1965, announced that any Cuban wishing to leave was free to do so. To embarrass Castro, President Johnson began using his "parole power" (in quotation marks, because many in Congress felt they had never granted presidents the sort of blanket admission authority utilized by Eisenhower and his successors) to admit any Cuban who reached the United States. Congress quickly passed the Cuban Refugee Adjustment Act of 1966, placing all arriving Cubans in their own special category, effectively granting them all refugee status on arrival. This was "discrimination" in favor of a particular nationality, but it seemed that "good" discrimination raised no objections. By the time Castro reversed policy in 1973, 270,000 Cubans had entered the United States—677,000 since 1959, when Castro took power. Thousands of Cubans stormed the Peruvian embassy in Havana in 1980 seeking asylum. Castro opened the port of Mariel for departing boats, and 125,000 Cuban "Marielitos," many of them the discharge of Cuba's prisons, sailed to Florida with President Jimmy Carter's hearty welcome. Public opinion had generally approved of the first wave of Cubans, but by the time of the Mariel influx polls showed strong hostility to the Carter administration's open door for Cubans (800,000 in total), and for some reason disapproval was higher among blacks (73 percent/15 percent) than whites (68 percent/24 percent). Disapproval might have been stronger had the public known the extent of government payments to refugees in general and the private agencies that had grown up to settle them within the country.

Other large migratory flows had nothing to do with making points against communism and further exposed the confusion in American refugee and asylum policy. Impoverished, overpopulated Haiti entered a period of acute political instability in 1971, and Florida's beaches received sixty thousand Haitians in the 1970s (perhaps that many died at sea), with irregular large flows through the 1980s and 1990s. These were not refugees fleeing a Hitler or Stalin, it was pointed out, but "economic refugees," that is, not refugees by any legal definition. A Marxist takeover of Nicaragua in 1979 and civil wars in El Salvador and Guatemala produced streams of migrants into the United States during the 1980s, few of whom could demonstrated direct political persecution. Were all people fleeing from poverty or civil strife in their home country to be considered refugees and resettled in the United States? President Ronald Reagan justified his interventionist Central American policy in part by producing the figure of 2.3 million "refugees" ("foot people") who would be created if communism took over in the region, and a prominent historian estimated that by the 1990s there were two million Central American "refugees," or one of eight people in the region, though most of these millions had not yet left.

Clearly, American refugee policy was in disarray, jerked about as international political events dislodged millions. U.S. military intervention in Indochina ended in defeat and withdrawal in 1975, and at least 130,000 Vietnamese, Cambodians, and Laotians immediately fled the victorious communists, some Vietnamese clinging to the wheels of U.S. helicopters evacuating the embassy in Saigon, most fleeing the country in boats. These had been our allies, and their lives were certainly in danger as communist rule began. If many or all were genuine refugees from almost certain political persecution, how many of them should the United States take? Monthly flows reached 14,000 in 1980–1981, 550,000 in all within seven years, 1 million Indochinese by 1991. Whether or not the increasingly familiar sight of people fleeing communist dictatorships to live in the United States embarrassed Red regimes, it was expensive to the United States in dollar terms. Resettlement costs were disguised and not well publicized but have been estimated at $1.4 billion for Cubans even before the Mariel exodus; Vietnamese relocation costs as of 1978 were conservatively reckoned at $1 billion, a figure that has mounted in the years since.

Painfully aware of the incoherence of U.S. refugee policy and irritated that the White House and State Department had usurped legislation prerogatives, Congress passed the Refugee Act of 1980, which adopted the UN definition of a refugee as "any person who is outside any country of his nationality . . . and who is unable or unwilling to return . . . because of persecution, or a well-founded fear of persecution, on account of race, religion, nationality, membership of a particular social group, or political opinion." The definition was a small step toward policy clarity, but of little help in setting U.S. policy. The worldwide number of refugees by such a definition was variously estimated from ten to twenty-four million people in the early 1980s, a number easily multiplied many times if, as some refugee relocation activists urged, one included as "persecution" a country's cultural hostility to homosexuals, China's one-child policy, which forced some parents into sterilization or abortion, or cultural sanction in Africa and parts of the Islamic world for female genital mutilation. The category "refugee" thus has proved elastic and potentially infinitely expandable.

To establish the American annual commitment, Congress resorted again to what it is congenitally incapable of doing, setting an immigration ceiling. The 1980 Refugee Act replaced the 1965 act annual quota for 17,400 refugees with the higher figure of 50,000 as a "normal flow." The president was authorized to exceed that number after consultation—which made it no ceiling at all. The number 50,000 was exceeded; the numbers ranged from 67,000 to 217,00 over the next ten years. This total does not count the Cubans, who enjoyed special status until 1994 (when President Clinton limited the range of the Cuban adjustment act by directing that Cubans intercepted at sea and found ineligible for refugee status would be returned to Cuba). Unpredictable large pulses of Cold War refugees continued— among them a quarter of a million Iranian students unwilling to return home when the Shah was overthrown in 1979 and thousands of Russian Jews arriving in the 1990s from the former Soviet Union. Acceptance of some proportion of the world's "refugees" had become an important part of U.S. foreign policy, as it seemed a cheap way to embarrass communist regimes and depict the United States as a compassionate nation. Setting limits, however, was beyond the policy system's abilities.

12

ILLEGAL IMMIGRATION: "PEACEFUL INVASION" AND POLICY INEPTITUDE

Annual totals of legal immigration, which had averaged 178,000 over the duration of the national origins system, rose to 400,000 by 1973, to 600,000 by 1978, reaching 1 million by 1989 and hovering in that range through the 1990s. These figures exclude illegal aliens, refugees who have not filed for permanent status, and an estimated half-million "nonimmigrant" aliens working in the country at any given time. By the 1990s, immigration was adding between 1 and 1.5 million persons (nearly 500,000 of that illegal) to the American population every year, and accounting for 60 percent of America's population growth, a proportion steadily rising.

And the source nations of the new Americans were no longer England, Germany, Ireland, Italy, and Poland but (the top ten, as of 1990) Mexico, the Philippines, Vietnam, China and Taiwan, the Dominican Republic, Korea, India, the USSR, Jamaica, and Iran. Across the 1980s and 1990s, 82 percent came from Latin America and Asia, 13 percent from Europe.

By the 1970s these changes began to gain media and political attention, as we should expect. Historian John Higham reminded us of the starting point in understanding immigration when he wrote that "immigrants are an unsettling force wherever they appear," especially in large numbers from culturally diverse backgrounds and over an extended time. The numbers were startlingly large and rising, and it was the numbers of immigrants, not where they came from, that first generated concern and, in the late 1970s, the beginnings of a new restrictionist reform effort.

A pioneering first (and thus far, only) Commission on Population Growth and the American Future, chaired by John D. Rockefeller III, reported to President Richard Nixon in 1972 that "in the long run, no substantial benefits will result from further growth of the Nation's population, rather that the gradual stabilization of our population would contribute significantly to the Nation's ability to solve its problems." Thus we should "welcome and plan for a stabilized population," which meant bringing immigration policy into alignment with that goal. The commission recommended controlling illegal immigration and capping legal immigration at the current level of four hundred thousand annually (a minority of the commission wanted a smaller number). When the commission also recommended liberalized abortion policies and birth control, President Nixon sensed a political liability and rejected the entire report.

Some environmentalists persisted. National Parks and Conservation Association (NPCA) president Anthony Wayne Smith said in a 1978 editorial in *National Parks and Conservation Magazine* that "the pressures of a steadily rising population preclude adequate long-term solutions to conservation issues." What with the domestic birth rate below replacement level at a total fertility rate (TFR, or average number of live births per woman) of 1.8, the 400,000 legal plus 800,000 illegal immigrants entering the United States annually matched, and doubled, natural increase. Startled and alarmed by these numbers, the NPCA in 1978 formed a coalition of labor and environmental groups to press for measures to control illegal immigration.

In this, the organization moved against the shifting tide. Though the population-growth impacts of the post-1965 immigration system were rising, willingness to discuss population issues was fading. The environmental and labor groups briefly convened in NPCA's coalition soon concluded that calls for immigration reform would get them attacked by Catholic, Jewish, and Protestant church leaders and civil rights activists as somehow anti-immigrant, which might mean anti-Mexican, which might mean "racist," a risk these organizations, overwhelmingly run by liberal Washington-based staff, were afraid to take. The immigration–population growth connection was factually unassailable and growing stronger, but the topic was thought to be taboo. The nation's foremost organization working for population stabilization, Zero Population Growth (ZPG), opposed the suggestion from its president (1975–1977) Dr. John Tanton, and others, to make immigration control a permanent part of ZPG's lobbying program. Frustrated at the organization's reluctance to address the part of population growth directly assigned to governmental control, Tanton, a Michigan ophthalmologist and environmental activist, joined with other environmentalists and populationists (with ZPG's blessing) to launch a small organization in Washington in 1978, the Federation for American Immigration Reform (FAIR). FAIR provided the organizational beginnings of what became known as the "new restrictionism."

Critics of the status quo first raised questions not about the immigration flows permitted by existing policy but illegal entries around it. NPCA president Smith's editorial had mentioned the figure of eight hundred thousand illegal aliens annually, and here he touched an issue of rising public concern, even if his numbers were only an educated guess. Large-scale illegal entry into the United States, a wealthy country with a generous welfare state whose lowest wages were ten times those in the Third World, should have been anticipated at the southern border. Mexico's population was rapidly growing, its economy erratic. The Bracero Program had built enormous immigration momentum by offering seasonal agricultural jobs and building family networks in the United States. Ending the program in 1964 did nothing to alter the allure of a migratory relationship that looked like low-wage workers to American growers and jobs at high wages to Mexicans. The Immigration and Naturalization Service (INS) reported the annual apprehension and removal of five hundred thousand illegal aliens in the late 1960s, most from Mexico but many from Central America and the Caribbean, and INS commissioner Leonard Chapman, a retired Marine Corps general, spoke of an "invasion."

By the mid-1970s illegal immigration had become what journalist Roberto Suro called "a hot second-tier issue." Visual and print media conveyed pictures of illegal aliens, overwhelmingly young males, climbing fences or sprinting through highway checkpoints at the U.S.-Mexican border in California and Texas. Estimates of those entering the United States illegally ran from two hundred thousand to one million a year. Corrective reform efforts seemed inevitable, as public opinion ran strongly against a large-scale, illegal human invasion that displaced some American workers at the bottom of the wage scale, exerted downward pressure on wages in affected industries and amounted to a government subsidy to large growers in the Southwest, encouraged the development of criminal rings for smuggling, and created a growing class of underground noncitizens in the country who had little recourse in the law. In the words of economist and secretary of labor (1977–1981) Ray Marshall, the deal offered to the United States by access to illegal Mexican farm workers is that "there is more product, it costs less to produce, and the only losers are low-income American citizens with Hispanic names." California labor leader Cesar Chavez and his United Farm Workers agreed that a porous border and "floods of immigrants from Mexico" undercut the economic and social gains of Americans of Hispanic descent, and in the word's of his biographer, Chavez "tried in vain to stem the tide of undocumented workers." University of California, Davis, economist Phillip Martin observed that "this immigrant labor subsidy encourages the expansion of an industry in which the majority of workers earn below-poverty-level incomes," and "holding down food prices by holding down farm worker wages . . . is morally wrong." It was also saving consumers very little—tomato prices would rise 3 percent if illegal workers were removed from the fields, according to a Center for Immigration Studies (CIS) report. Illegal Mexican workers brought larger problems than lowered wages, Hispanic writer Roberto Suro argued. Their presence in Latino communities created permanent tensions with the larger society. "Latinos will always be handicapped so long as a large proportion of the Latino population is made up of people who have no legal standing in the United States."

Astonishingly, illegal entry and workforce participation had defenders. The term should not be "illegal aliens," it was argued, but "Undocumented Workers," recognizing their service to America. Entering illegally was not really illegal, if we recognize a higher human right to "feed families" and "have a better way of life." They did work "no Americans will do," and most returned to Mexico at the end of the growing season—an argument reflecting the old dream of cheap, docile workers who did not really live here. A few economists offered a more interesting view. Illegal immigration from Mexico and elsewhere was a natural and unstoppable part of the inevitable economic integration of the Western Hemisphere, they insisted, and the United States was schizophrenic in attempting to promote that integration through the North American Free Trade Agreement (NAFTA) while preventing it in terms of labor markets.

To most Americans, however, free trade in goods might (in most cases) make overall sense, but this did not apply to people. The arguments against tolerating the large and growing flow of illegal labor were politically as well as intellectually overwhelming, and no government could long ignore them. In the early 1970s congressional liberals mounted a drive to repeal the "Texas Proviso" and make employing illegal aliens a crime, but they were blocked by powerful conservative Senator James O. Eastland of Mississippi, a large-scale farmer intensely interested in cheap agricultural labor. President Gerald Ford felt the popular alarm at illegal entries, and turned to his chief law officer, Attorney General Edward Levi. Sensing what might lie ahead and, as a Jew, "particularly troubled by [the anticipation of] identity cards and roundups," in Suro's telling of it, Levi appointed a committee and stalled. The election of 1976 took Levi and Ford out of the picture, and the problem was passed to

Jimmy Carter. The new president made some reform suggestions that received little support on the Hill, whereupon the issue was passed to a congressional Select Commission on Immigration and Refugee Policy headed by Notre Dame University president Father Theodore Hesburgh. The commission's 1981 report noted opinion surveys showing public opposition to current high levels of immigration, both legal and illegal, but affirmed the positive value of legal immigration and proposed that "closing the back door" of illegal immigration was required in order to preclude a public backlash against all immigration. Since illegal immigrants came for jobs, the "jobs magnet" must be cut off. This magnet was in the American workplace, where employers were free to hire illegal immigrants under a little-noticed "Texas Proviso" of 1952. Enact penalties on employers of illegal aliens, the commission recommended (an idea first put forward by liberal Senator Paul Douglas in the 1950s), and the flow northward will abate.

Public and editorial opinion was strongly supportive of action on the problems of illegal immigrants, and two legislators, Senator Alan Simpson (R-Wyo.) and Congressman Romano Mazzoli (D-Ky.), stepped forward to sponsor reforms. Simpson quickly became the central figure, a respected legislator who brought a certain passion to the issue of repairing an intolerable system: "The American people are so very fed up from being told—when they want immigration laws enacted which they believe will serve their national interest and when they also want the law enforced—that they are being cruel and mean-spirited and racist. They are fed up with efforts to make them feel that Americans do not have that fundamental right of any people—to decide who will join them here and help form the future country in which they and their posterity will live. . . . It is time to slow down, to reassess." He and Mazzoli had intended to pursue changes in both the legal and the illegal components, but the Reagan administration, reluctant players on the issue, produced a task force report in summer 1981 aiming only at illegal entry. Simpson and Mazzoli felt pushed into a focus on one part of the immigration problem at a time and introduced their own bill aimed at reducing illegal entry. They proposed what Simpson called the "three-legged stool"—improved border enforcement, penalties for employers who hired illegal aliens, and a counterfeit-resistance identification system for workers.

Thus the first serious legislative proposal to deal with illegal immigration moved in 1981 out of committees and reached the floors of Congress, a decade after the problem broke into the national media. Though the thing to be stopped or curbed was illegal, it turned out that there were many who would vigorously oppose measures required to bring it under control. A strange coalition came together, built around constituencies that benefited from the northward (with some seasonal southward return) flow. Large-scale perishable crop growers, especially in the West where Mexican field labor had a long history, came together with Latino activists, church groups engaged in human rights and refugee issues, and the civil liberties lobby objecting to worker-identification proposals. The coalition opposed employer sanctions as administratively burdensome and tending to invite discrimination against American Latinos and quickly attached to the legislative package the idea of an "amnesty" to solve the problem with a stroke of the pen, a solution far preferable to the specter of mass deportation (which no one was proposing) of an illegal population now estimated between three and five million.

Public opinion was strongly supportive of any necessary measures to end illegal entry and was opposed to an amnesty. A Gallup Poll in the fall of 1977 found 77 percent in favor of an employer-sanctions law, and a 1980 poll found that 66 percent endorsed halting all immigration if unemployment rose above 5 percent. These numbers held through the 1980s. But public opinion does not testify before Congress, and the only organized support for effective controls came from FAIR, a small and fledgling lobbying group urging lower overall numbers and an end to illegal entry—and no amnesty. Weakened by successive compromises and given only lukewarm and intermittent support by President Reagan, the Simpson-Mazzoli measure passed the Republican-dominated Senate twice but was held up by liberal leadership in the House. Both parties were wary of the issue, unwilling to become identified with any particular solution before the 1984 election.

In 1986 Congress passed and President Reagan signed the Immigration Reform and Control Act (IRCA), in retrospect a public policy failure of major proportions. Sanctions on employers of illegal aliens entered American law, where they should have been all along, but a proposed system of worker verification based on a computer registry of Social Security numbers was defeated by objections to "a national ID card" (which was never proposed), and the claim that Hispanics would be "singled out" for special scrutiny. The final measure allowed employers to accept as proof of legal residence any two of a wide range of documents, most easily counterfeited. "The change in the farm labor market made by IRCA," wrote economist Phillip Martin, "is the switch from undocumented workers to falsely documented workers." For this toothless provision, Congress traded an unprecedented amnesty for illegal aliens who had been in continuous residence since 1982, plus a special program to legalize already present illegal agricultural workers. The double amnesty was justified on the theory that blanket legalization was preferable to mass deportation, and that the problem would not build up again because the magnet would be inactivated.

Almost nothing promised by the legislation turned out as expected. The amnesty covered only 60 percent of the illegal population, but this amounted to 2.7 people who could then apply for visas for their relatives. Demographer David Simcox estimated that federal assistance, welfare benefits, and costs of schooling the children of amnestied workers added up to $78.7 billion, or a subsidy of nearly $30,000 for each legalized alien.

For illegal aliens who were ineligible for amnesty, enforcement by INS of the ban on hiring them was spotty, and document fraud quickly became almost universal. The Border Patrol reported that illegal entries dropped off in 1987, as the networks channeling cheap Third World labor into the United States (Mexico was the staging ground and chief source country, but in any given week the Border Patrol at San Diego arrested nationals from over one hundred countries) waited to see if the United States was serious about curtailing illegal immigration. It was not. Driven by a Mexican economic crisis and civil wars in Central America and lured by a magnet of jobs in low-wage industries from agriculture to food service, lawn-home maintenance to child care—and, some said, also welfare benefits, free public schooling, and free hospital emergency room care—illegal immigration rose above former levels and continued as a heated topic of immigration debate.

Historian Reed Ueda rightly calls IRCA "the most generous immigration law passed in U.S. history," with "novel and generous provisions for the legalization of illegal aliens and [enlarging] a host of quota allotments based on special needs and status." It conferred legal status on millions who had, in the critics' terms, "butted in line" ahead of other millions abroad who were on waiting lists for visas, and it allowed the flow of illegal immigrants to continue at levels estimated by the INS at five hundred thousand annually by the mid-1990s—approximately half of legal immigration itself, which had reached levels matching the flows prior to World War I.

IRCA proved to be no aberration. As policy decisions in the following years would prove, American immigration policymaking had entered a long era of permissiveness toward massive legal and illegal entry, policymakers repeatedly in the 1980s and 1990s expanding the opportunities and inducements to migration. This occurred in spite of public opinion polls showing the American public in all parts of the country and across all racial and ethnic groups opposed to such high numbers and especially angry about illegal entry. The Border Patrol was underfunded no matter which party was in power. One in three (estimated) illegal border crossers who were apprehended were penalized by only a bus trip back across the border, free to try again.

CASE FOR RESTRICTION: ECONOMICS

Sustained illegal immigration, spasmodic refugee crises, legal immigration pushing upward through the 1990s to around one million a year—these were the large openings in the American immigration system through which surged the Second Great Wave. The United States accepted more immigrants than any country in the world by a large margin, but the wave washed across multiple national boundaries, especially drawn to Europe, Canada, and Australia. In all immigrant-receiving countries there were rising levels of criticism and debate.

Policy debate in the United States in the 1980s centered initially on economics, a focus chosen in part because academic and public policy specialists were less comfortable with the other, "softer" dimensions of immigration's impacts. But in a basic sense immigration would tend to be seen first as an economic issue because it *was* a labor supply, and most of us spend most of our lives either as labor or hiring it. Some Americans needed no debate on this topic. On the one side, employers in the United States knew what the southern plantation lords, the factory titans of our industrializing decades, and the builders of the transcontinental railroad links in the West had known, that a replenishing flow of foreign labor was a very good thing for their part of the economy, from the bosses' point of view. These big employers were joined in their positive assessment of the economic aspect of the sort of immigration America was getting after the 1960s by millions of homeowners who could not imagine doing without that Latino cook, nanny, or industrious gardener. Immigrant workers, even the professionals and certainly the field hands and hole diggers, were cheap, usually uninterested in unionization, and applied downward pressure on American workers' wages. On the other side, the workers of America in industries exposed to foreign labor had their own view of the economic dimension of mass immigration—wage competition, displacement, and lowered standards.

These opposing perspectives and convictions were not equally represented in the public discussions of the economics of immigration. The mass media, attuned as always to American sentimentalism, saw the story of immigration as thousands of stories of individual immigrant's economic contributions—the loyal housecleaner, the uncomplaining guys who pick the artichokes and tomatoes, the Korean shopkeeper, the Indian motel owner. The central theme in most journalistic accounts was immigrants willingly doing menial, low-paying labor that Americans will no longer do or immigrant entrepreneurs supplying energy that Americans seemed to be losing. The media told of the revitalization of entire neighborhoods—rebuilt and thriving sections of the formerly devastated Bronx or Brooklyn in New York, vibrant Koreatown in Los Angeles—stories rooted in a widespread, unproved, and somewhat odd assumption that American entrepreneurialism was somehow always depleting and required periodic revitalization from abroad. The media had far less interest in the cost side: social services to low-skilled people with high birth rates. Either way, journalism traveled on isolated stories, preferring inspiring ones.

Such anecdotes, sentimental or sordid, made flimsy arguments. For serious policy discussion it is necessary to call in the experts. Economists tried to measure labor-market impacts, and an old and durable argument was heard again: mass immigration of low-skill, low-wage labor harms American workers and adds to poverty. "Post-1965 immigrants," Cornell economist Vernon Briggs wrote, most of them "coming from the poorer nations of the world, where average education, wages, and skill levels are far below those in the United States, are suppressing the wages of all workers in the lowest skill sector of the labor market." The economic logic was compelling, but early metropolitan studies on wage suppression by immigrants were inconclusive.

By the 1990s, the picture had clarified. Economists such as Harvard's George Borjas had been documenting a steady decline in what economists called the "social capital endowment" (or sometimes, in the blunt language of economics, the "human quality") of immigrants. Starting in the early 1970s, immigrants on average showed declining educational levels and low social mobility (the key word is "average"; the shape of immigrant skills resembled an hourglass, economist Phillip Martin pointed out, with a large low-skilled bottom, a thin middle, and a small bulge at the top of computer programmers, doctors, and other professionals). By the late 1990s, a RAND Corporation researcher told Congress that the share of immigrants with less than twelve years of education had steadily increased since the 1970s, rising from 15 percent in that decade to 40 percent in California and 50 percent in Texas in the 1990s.

In 1997 the National Research Council (NRC) published an analysis of the accumulated evidence on immigrants' economic impacts, *The New Americans* (1997). Its conclusions were at first reported in the media as documenting a net positive contribution to national economic life by immigrants. Two Harvard economists who worked on the study, George Borjas and Richard Freeman, wrote to the *New York Times* accusing the study's director of falsely portraying immigration in a press conference on the report as a "free lunch." To the contrary, Borjas and Freeman noted, the study found that immigration may have produced a tiny net gain in economic output, perhaps as small as $1 billion or as much as $10 billion, an insignificant sum in an $8 trillion economy. This was offset by an estimated $15 to $20 billion fiscal drain from relatively heavy immigrant use of welfare and social services.

Borjas and Freeman pointed out that a chief economic impact of immigration was on low-skilled high school dropouts who were forced to compete with them directly. The result: twenty million American low-skilled workers saw their average hourly wage drop 30 percent from 1979 to 1995. Half of this drop was due to immigration. "Immigration creates winners and losers," Borjas and Freeman continued: "Low income workers and taxpayers in immigrant states lose; those who employ immigrants or use immigrant services win." The impact was substantial, because the scale of immigration pushed the foreign-born population to nearly 10 percent of the population, almost one in every eight American workers, as measured by the 1990 census. The NRC study itself concluded that "the magnitude of the current flows—and the flow's disproportionate share of poorly educated immigrants . . . has increased the costs of immigration, and harmed many native-born workers."

The study was far less interested in demography than economics. Immigration, *The New Americans* acknowledged, would play "the dominant role" in U.S. population growth for at least the next half-century. In that fifty-year period the American population would grow by an additional 124 million if immigration remained at present levels, 80 million of them attributable to immigration. The NRC authors had nothing to say about the environmental implications of such population growth, pleading lack of expertise and that it was not their charge.

In his 1999 book, *Heaven's Door*, Borjas found that previous social science researchers had "greatly exaggerated" contemporary mass immigration's economic benefits and looked away from its costs. Himself an immigrant from Cuba, Borjas charged that those defending the immigration status quo were in effect "supporting an astonishing transfer of wealth from the poorest people in the country, who are disproportionately minorities, to the rich." "Immigration is an income redistribution program" inside America, he bluntly concluded, "a debate over how the pie is split." The wage drag of low-skilled immigrant labor shifted about $160 billion from workers to users of immigrants' services—employers in low-wage industries, consumers of cheap strawberries and tomatoes, hirers of nannies and gardeners.

That the losers from the immigration status quo were "low income workers and taxpayers," in Borjas and Freeman's words, suggested that the policy would be hard to reform, as these losers were politically weak. It was often said that if half of the million-plus immigrants arriving each year were lawyers, immigration restriction would be enacted overnight. A small version of that scenario of professional-class competition with immigrants emerged in the 1990s as high-technology companies in California's Silicon Valley and elsewhere were charged with laying off high-wage American computer programmers and replacing them with cheaper and more pliable "temporary" foreign workers—"indentured servants," FAIR's Dan Stein called them—brought in under the controversial H1-B visa program designed to supply U.S. employers with skilled employees.

A more potent constituency for immigration reform was taxpayers, who might be mobilized by mounting evidence about the fiscal burden of immigration. A war of studies raged through the 1970s and 1980s over whether immigrant families were heavy users of the public schools and welfare and thus cost state and local governments more than they paid in taxes. The NRC study, examined closely, confirmed the fears. In California, where 43 percent of the school-age population (5–17) were children of immigrants (the national figure was 16 percent), education and other social services imposed a fiscal burden on California taxpayers. This was but one part of the glum news about the costs of what marxists once called the hard-to-calculate "social wage"—the expenditures that society is forced to make to supplement the low wages employers enjoyed as a subsidy. These included public schools for immigrants with their larger-than-average families and lower-than-average incomes, special language programs, emergency room medical treatment mandated for the indigent (whatever their legal status), courtroom and incarceration costs for immigrant criminals. The NRC report found that in California the average immigrant-headed household used

$3,463 more in services than it paid in taxes, costing the state's taxpayers an immigrant subsidy of $1,178 per household. In New Jersey, a state with more modest social services, the net fiscal burden of immigrants was less—$232 per native household. A 1999 study by Steven Camarota of the CIS confirmed Borjas' findings that immigrants' share of the total poverty population had grown 123 percent since 1979, the rate among immigrants now roughly double that of natives. For the most immigrant-impacted state, California, a RAND study in 1997 found that unprecedented heavy immigration of poorly educated people was imposing "a growing strain on public services," while exerting downward pressure on the wages of the less-skilled U.S.-born workers. In California, the cost-benefit "balance is shifting to the cost side," Kevin McCarthy and Georges Vernez concluded, recommending, among other things, a reduction in legal immigration to the United States.

"The fact that immigration hurts the poor and benefits the rich doesn't necessarily make it a bad thing," observed John Cassidy in reviewing the NRC report and other scholarly studies in *The New Yorker*, but "these are worrisome findings" and "the new economic research suggests that the intellectual case for immigration needs bolstering." This was especially so when it was realized that among the working-class Americans most harmed by economic competition with immigrants were African Americans whose well being was assumed to be a special national concern. Black complaints about immigrant job competition were over a century old but were heard again as mass immigration surged through the 1980s and 1990s. "They brought in all these Guatemalan and Mexican workers," said a black worker at Case Farms poultry plant in Morgantown, N.C., "because they figured they'd work for nothing," and before long the plant workforce was virtually all Latino. Los Angeles writer Jack Miles, struck by the anger and violence directed against recent Latino and Asian immigrants by blacks during the 1992 riots in Los Angeles, concluded that "America's older black poor and newer brown poor are on a collision course." Blacks were being displaced on the lower rungs of the economy by browns, because "nonblack employers . . . trust Latinos. They fear or disdain blacks. . . . By an irony I find particularly cruel, unskilled Latino immigration may be doing to American blacks at the end of the twentieth century what the European immigration that brought my own ancestors here did to them at the end of the nineteenth century."

But something had changed, some thought—the blacks themselves, or at least the younger urban males. Latinos in Southern California told journalist Roberto Suro that the blacks had only themselves to blame, for they are "lazy, defeated, and corrupt, . . . jerks who stand on the street corners all day," while "we have a work ethic." Suro agreed that Latinos "colonize whole factories" and occupations, but only with the silent collaboration of white employers. University of Chicago sociologist William Julius Wilson was astonished in interviews in the late 1980s to hear Chicago employers talk in a negative way about blacks, seeing them as lazy, dishonest, and without a work ethic. They vastly preferred Hispanic and Asian workers. Miles did not think blacks should be blamed. "People do not blow into our country like the weather," Miles wrote: "We let them in, and we have reasons for doing so. . . . In my city, on my block, in my own house, I have seen the Latino alternative chosen over the native black one."

The irony was even deeper. Latinos themselves, once gaining a foothold in the United States and becoming Cuban Americans or Mexican Americans, expressed opposition to illegal immigrants from Mexico and Central America, primarily on the ground of labor-market competition. Polls reported consistent Latino support for lower levels of immigration, beginning with a pioneering Hart-Tarrance poll commissioned by FAIR executive director Roger Connor in 1983. A Latino National Poll of 1992 confirmed this and other earlier polls—that 75 percent of Hispanics feel that too many immigrants are entering America. Presumably, their own ethnicity protected them from being accused of motivation by "nativism," or mere antiforeign prejudice. This left only concrete economic and social conflict as a basis for their attitudes. This was evidence, hard to dismiss, that immigrants were in many respects (unwittingly) imposing costs on the natives. John Higham half a century ago bluntly stated the basic dynamic: "If anyone had cause for complaint against the foreign-born on grounds of substantial self-interest, it was the American hand who did much the same work, served the same boss, and often lived in the same neighborhood."

14

CASE FOR RESTRICTION: CONCERNS OVER NATIONAL COHESION

The restrictionist reform movement of the first part of the twentieth century was one aspect of a vigorous American nationalism that, among other things, assumed and asserted the superiority of the dominant culture. Yet at that very time American intellectuals, always attracted to the subject of American identity, began to argue that it ought to be reconceived. A body of ideas that would be called "cultural pluralism" was given a foundational statement in a 1915 essay by Horace Kallen, augmented by the wartime and postwar writings of Randolph Bourne and others. They argued that America ought to abandon all efforts and hopes of being a melting pot producing Anglo Americans or even Anglo plus a few other European things. It should instead see itself as a place where every culture that immigration brought to these shores (plus the Native American culture almost extinguished) should be allowed to sustain itself within the larger society—because all were equal and valuable. As some envisioned it, America would not be a pot to blend all cultural inputs but instead a salad bowl (a term invented a bit later) to preserve all of them. Kallen imagined a very different America, "a federation of distinct nationalities . . . an orchestration of mankind."

Melting pot imagery and the desirability of rapid Americanization persisted for decades in mainstream society, but cultural pluralism or cultural relativism was increasingly popular among intellectuals. As in so much else, the 1960s were a watershed in the evolution of thinking about American identity. The revolution in thinking about race relations fatally undermined older conceptions. If African Americans were human equals to be treated as social equals, who could still maintain that some cultures were preferable to others? Cultural relativism was triumphant everywhere, and the ideal of "Anglo-conformity" was increasingly denounced by intellectuals, including those who wrote the history and social science texts for the schools and the larger society. An "ethnic revival" surged through the nation's emotional life, or was at least summoned and touted by books like Michael Novak's *The Rise of the Unmeltable Ethnics* (1972). "The spirit of ethnicity . . . begs for reawakening," said Congressman Roman Pucinski of Chicago in 1972 as he sponsored federal support for ethnic heritage studies in the schools, because "there is a growing sense of sameness permeating our existence." Writers, members of Congress, and other shapers of the social discourse urged all non-WASP ethnoracial groups to hold firm to and accentuate their differentness, and federal money flowed into this project.

What followed from such ideas was the growing conviction that what America needed was more ethnoracial and cultural diversification away from the WASP norm, which itself was increasingly seen as tainted by association with a racist and indigenous-people-exterminating history. In the 1950s and 1960s this impulse toward nation-broadening took the inclusive form of integrating the African American minority into white society. In time that goal expanded and took on the name "multiculturalism," a term that one scholar found in forty newspaper articles in 1981 and eleven years later, in two thousand, a fifty-fold increase. The term means more than one thing, but it may be called the belief, among other things, that American life should welcome and embrace other cultures, and the more distinct and different they are, the better. This romantic sentiment and body of ideas, ultimately centrifugal in its thrust, is more a critique of American life and history than an affirmation of anything in particular beyond unfailing cultural tolerance. It had no goal but more diversity, unless one can make sense of such passages as this from Michael Novak: "Struggling to be born is a creature of multi-cultural beauty, dazzling, free, a higher and richer form of life." Still, cultural pluralism in the form of multiculturalism remains perhaps the strongest current running in the great river of American thought and emotion in the last third of the twentieth century.

These currents of thought and feeling did not produce the 1965 act, whose architects had explicitly denied any intention to revise America's cultural makeup. Multiculturalists nevertheless welcomed the results of the leaky system of 1965, which became the great demographic engine of their project. It was fateful for discussion of immigration policy that multiculturalism set the tone for American intellectual life as the Second Great Wave of migration arrived. It meant that, while the economic and fiscal impacts of immigration might be legitimate subjects for policy debate, questions about cultural impacts were met with enormous resistance and even hostility. While mass immigration always generates concerns about social cohesion, those who voiced such concerns were immediately said to be dealing in the old superiority–inferiority poisons, stigmatization of the Other, bad nationalism. "We seem incapable yet of addressing the important issue of what holds this society together [and therefore what needs attention and nurturing]," wrote sociologist Charles Keely. "When raised, the question usually seems to have a bigoted tone." Surely he meant that those who raised "the important issue of what holds this society together" were *said* "to have a bigoted tone" by those who would prevent critical debate on the "diversity" agenda.

While this was true for the 1970s and 1980s, the taboo on discussion of whether endless cultural diversification might possibly have unfortunate consequences or necessary limits lifted somewhat in the 1990s, as the immigration debate entered its third decade, for several reasons. Multiculturalism was increasingly identified with the arrogant thought-policing of political correctness, and this association of extreme multiculturalism as "left-wing McCarthyism" encouraged dissenters who had earlier been intimidated. Disturbed by certain social trends, many within the United States began to complain of the fragmentation of society—along sharper class lines as the gulf between rich and poor seemed to widen, and along tribal lines as groups asserted their distinctiveness, separateness, and grievances. Historian Arthur M. Schlesinger, Jr. in a best-selling book, *The Disuniting of America* (1991), called attention to signs of social division and found as their chief source "a new conception . . . of a nation of groups, differentiated in their ancestries, inviolable in their diverse identities." This was multiculturalism, initially a welcoming spirit toward ethnic and racial diversity, but growing into an almost anti-American critique of assimilation and the denial of a shared national history and identity. "Something good— movement towards a more inclusive society and broader concepts of what an educated person should know," wrote Robert Pickus of the World Without War Council, "is producing something bad—the disuniting of America."

What Pickus called "the profound erosion of common ground in America" concerned many people in the 1990s, and of course radical multiculturalism was by no means the only contributor. He offered a list that included "Duke's English Department, corporate America . . . religious decay or religious assertiveness, Hollywood, the media," just some of the "separatist realities in American life." Schlesinger added to the list contemporary historians, or many of them, who were no longer presenting or the schools teaching a common history but in its place celebratory stories of America's separate races and ethnic groups. "The balance," he said, "is shifting from unum to pluribus" across the entire range of American thought. Writer Michael Lind argued that America, once the Anglo American republic (1789–1861) succeeded by the Euro-American republic (1875–1957), had been pushed by mass immigration into a new group-organized, multiculturalism-celebrating society, the multicultural-American republic (1972–present). This third republic had the outward trappings of a nation-state, he argued, but no common story and a bleak future menaced more by "Brazilianization" along class lines than by balkanization along ethnoracial lines. Historian John Higham noted in 1997 that "ethno-racial tensions are acute and in some ways growing. Are we witnessing an approaching end of nation-building itself? . . . An erosion of the nation-state, as its capacity to maintain national borders and an effective national center weakens?"

Outside America, as we have seen, recent world history seemed a tale of nations breaking apart into their separate religious or ethnocultural elements, or engaged in bloody wars inside old borders. The world, including again and in an especially violent way the Balkans themselves, seemed to be balkanizing on a rising curve of ethnic group–nationality animosity. Could even America be vulnerable? Journalist Kevin Phillips had written an article in 1978 entitled "The Balkanization of America." By the 1990s, Schlesinger, with his *Disuniting*, led a growing list of those who saw in the United States a widening of class gaps as well as the centrifugal internal forces of multiculturalism, bilingual-education-supported language maintenance, racial-preference entitlements for favored groups, and the writing and teaching of a new American history in which a national narrative had been dissolved into subgroup celebrations. Senator Moynihan noted in his 1993 book *Pandaemonium* that the splintering of nations would perhaps form 50 to 150 new countries in the next fifty years. "Some of them in North America? Possibly." Among the sources of a national fragmentation that was now taken seriously by American intellectuals, mass immigration over three decades, most of it from Latin America and Asia, could not be forever ignored as an important, perhaps the preeminent, source of challenge to national cohesion and traditional identity.

The immigration debate expanded to address these questions. Was E pluribus unum—out of many, one—still working in the late-twentieth-century mass-immigration era? Or was immigration contributing its part, along with other forces such as globalization, to a cultural and class fragmentation of America, transforming it into who knew what?

These questions, put forward by many writers and speakers in different ways, were in reality a rebirth of a controversy, absent from America since the beginning of the twentieth century. Was the nation holding together or dividing, its common culture and history core enriched or diluted? "If the American people truly want to change their historic European rooted civilization into a Latin-Caribbean-Asian 'multi-culture,' then let them debate and approve that proposition through an informed political process," wrote Lawrence Auster. "And if Americans do not want their society to change in such a revolutionary manner, then let them revise their immigration laws accordingly." That reasonable point was clouded, some thought, by the excess in the title chosen for Auster's book, *The Path to National Suicide* (1990). New York economic writer (and recent immigrant) Peter Brimelow, in *Alien Nation* (1995), was another author who shared the conviction of many restrictionists of a century earlier that American nationality was not independent of but bound up with not only a specific historic culture (Anglo European) but also "blood," ethnoracial nationality, or a "white majority" seeing itself as a nation. Auster and Brimelow made no claims about group racial superiority or inferiority. To them it was Anglo European cultural hegemony that had made America a place of unmatched and expanding freedom, democracy, and high levels of social trust and cooperation. Brimelow agreed that small numbers of Chinese, Mexicans, and other non-Europeans had before the 1965 act assimilated nicely and "disappeared" into America—leaving the country still a biracial nation composed of a Europe-descended majority and an Africa-descended minority. Mass migration from non-European sources after 1965, however, was transforming the United States into something else—and, they seemed to think, something ultimately unworkable. Brimelow approvingly quoted *National Review* editor John O'Sullivan: "It is commonly said that America is more than a nation; it is an idea. My thesis . . . is the precise opposite: America is more than an idea; it is a nation." Immigration waves were changing that. "There is no precedent," Brimelow wrote, "for a sovereign country undergoing such a rapid and radical transformation of its ethnic character in the entire history of the world," and he argued that history delivers a mostly negative verdict on whether multiracial societies (America had been biracial) work. What should be done? "Americans ought to be asked" about this risky and unprecedented experiment. Brimelow was confident that there was little public support for an undeclared and government-engineered project of demographic transformation, and therefore the numbers must come down (he did not seem to care if the immigrants came from Europe or the nonwhite world, so long as the numbers were so small that demographic transformation was prevented.)

Racist stuff, some reviewers wrote, perhaps hoping to squelch any debate on the nation's ethnocultural transformation. A better description of *Alien Nation* is race-conscious when pondering the cohesive ties of nationality. Brimelow did not propose a racial test for admission and expressed the conviction that current patterns of mass immigration threatened the gains made by black Americans especially. On the fundamental question of what makes and perpetuates a nation, *Alien Nation* gave an out-of-fashion (to say the least) ethnoracial-historical answer, one that pointed immigration policy back toward the "like-mindedness through national origins preferences" logic of 1924, or at the least toward very small incoming numbers.

To some others who agreed that immigration levels were far too high, this form of concern over immigration's sociocultural impacts was misplaced. It implied the necessity of a permanent white-European majority for a working national cohesion. But why must this be so? America had always been a society in ethnic and racial transformation away from an English core, wrote CIS Director Mark Krikorian, one of those on the reform side who believed in the "America is an idea" thesis. An American could be made out of anyone of any color or culture who accepted the Idea. Krikorian's center declared itself "pro-immigrant" but also "pro-lowering of the numbers," because, in Krikorian's words, we *do* have a problem, "the difficulty of assimilating large numbers of foreigners into a society that promotes ethnic division and snickers at the idea of Americanization." Restrict the inflow, and work harder at Americanization, he and others urged. Leon Bouvier and Lindsey Grant agreed that current immigration posed cultural problems, but these had nothing to do with color and everything to do with rates of cultural assimilation to American norms and allegiance in areas of highest immigration. Worrying that the "glue of a sense of community" was giving way to "belonging to subgroups," they vaguely urged "a move toward a more communitarian mode of social interaction"—and reducing immigration to two hundred thousand a year.

These concerns were broadly shared as the century moved toward a close. Even President Clinton admitted some uneasiness about the scale of immigration over which he would preside for two terms. Speaking at Portland State University in 1998, he said that "a new wave of immigration larger than any in a century, far more diverse than any in our history," means that there will be "no majority race" in California in five years and in the United States in fifty. "No other nation in history has gone through demographic change of this magnitude in so short a time," and "unless we handle this well, immigration of this sweep and scope could threaten the bonds of our union." Clinton had nothing to say about how to "handle this well," but the U.S. Commission on Immigration Reform recommended in 1997 reducing immigration levels to about 550,000 per year, along with measures to shut down illegal immigration. With lower numbers, the commission endorsed what they called an "immigrant policy"—stronger Americanization efforts by governments and private groups. "Americanization," Barbara Jordan wrote in a *New York Times* op-ed, "that word earned a bad reputation when it was stolen by racists and xenophobes in the 1920s. But it is our word, and we are taking it back" to help "those who choose to come here . . . embrace the common core of American civic culture." Reform convictions had taken hold at the highest levels of deliberative policy-making.

Having a president and a national commission express concern over the cultural assimilation of immigrants and recommend (in the case of the commission) lower numbers represented a setback for the defenders of continued mass immigration. They fell back on an old argument, an appeal to history. "The U.S. has experienced these effects over and over again from previous waves of immigration," insisted Sidney Weintraub. "In each case, the wave was accompanied by dire predictions of the economic, political and social consequences on the U.S., only to be contradicted in practice." Our successful, even triumphant national story makes such worries seem silly, even reprehensible. In this view, the nation's assimilative engines—a potently attractive popular culture, the world's most successful economy, a compelling core ideal called by Swedish sociologist Gunnar Myrdal (and others) "the American creed," intermarriage—had arranged more than sufficient national unity out of earlier massive immigration flows to allow a cohesive America to lead the West to victories over fascism in the 1940s and communism thereafter. Our national culture had not been splintered and weakened by the earlier period of mass immigration, though people then, as now, had predicted that it would be. Instead, we were immensely enriched while remaining cohesive. Why should the present and future be any different? Besides, the foreign-born percentage of the population was still below the levels of 1900 or 1910.

History lessons of this kind settle arguments only when none of the facts have changed, which is next to never, and not in this case. Critics of the immigration status quo pointed out that everything was wrong with this historical analogy. Assimilation of the First Great Wave was greatly facilitated by the sharp curtailment brought by war and then a restrictionist policy, providing a "breathing space" of forty years of very low levels of immigration during which the forces of assimilation regained the upper hand. There was no prospect on the horizon of this sort of reform-generated breathing space in the 1990s, as mass immigration entered a fourth decade, and the foreign-born percentage of the population had reached 25 percent in California, 20 percent in New York, 16 percent in Florida.

The post-1965 immigrants also came into a very different America, which lacked the strong integrationist institutions and occasions of a century before—a powerful, confident host culture based on English beginnings with European borrowings, a culture firmly insisting on assimilation to American norms, a strong public school system that conducted its business in English, and the unifying experience of total war in the 1940s, followed by a period of universal male military service.

MEXICAN DIFFERENCE

And the Second Great Wave had another new characteristic: one broad ethnic group, Hispanics (admittedly quite diverse within the language group), made up more than half the total immigration and had the highest fertility rates. The Puerto Rican, Cuban, and Caribbean components were separated from their cultural base only by a journey over coastal waters. Mexico

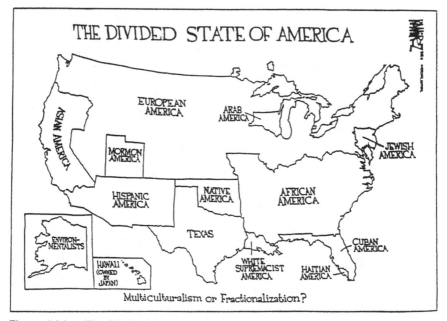

Figure 14.1. The Divided State of America

Table 14.1.   Leading Immigrant Groups by Nation of Origin, 2000

Country	Number of Immigrants	Percent of Immigrants
Mexico	171,748	20.21
Soviet Union	43,807	5.15
China	41,861	4.93
Philippines	40,587	4.78
India	39,072	4.60
Vietnam	25,340	2.98
Haiti	22,004	2.59
Canada	21,475	2.53
Jamaica	15,654	1.84
United Kingdom	14,532	1.71
All others	413,080	48.61
Total	849,807	100.00

Source: Statistical Yearbook of the Immigration and Naturalization Service, 2000, at www.ins.usdoj.gov/graphics/aboutins/statistics/IMM01yrbk/ExecIMM01/Table2.xls.

represented a special case. Among Latin countries exporting population to the United States in the Second Great Wave, Mexico was by far the most populous and shared a two-thousand-mile border with the United States. This land boundary presented a staging ground for Mexican, Central American, and Latin American migration (and a growing number of Middle Eastern and Asian illegal migrants) but also allowed a reasonably quick and constant replenishment of Hispanic cultural influences, augmented by Mexican governmental efforts to manipulate the Mexican diaspora.

This southwest border was the new Atlantic crossing, except for the vital fact that it could be crossed and recrossed on foot or by vehicle, and without much initial investment. This stream of migrants presented something quite unprecedented, noted historian David Kennedy in a 1996 *Atlantic Monthly* article. More than a third of the immigrants to the United States now came "flowing into a defined region from a single cultural, linguistic and national source: Mexico." Some Mexican and Central American immigrants had always dispersed to other regions, the Midwest and Pacific Northwest, and in the 1980s and 1990s were moving in large numbers into the South. But in the Southwest the sheer demographic power of concentrated Mexican and Central American immigration—California contained half the Hispanic immigrants to the United States—created a new situation in a part of America that had once belonged to Mexico and had been lost by a war initiated by the United States.

Given these realities, the fast-growing Mexican presence in the second half of the twentieth century might have been expected to stir a sustained controversy, both in affected communities and nationally. There certainly had been such a controversy a century earlier as Mexico began its northward export of surplus population. The immigration debates of the 1920s included much blunt and, to the modern ear, coarse language about the laziness, uncleanliness, and general cultural backwardness of the average Mexican and the perils inherent in unchecked Mexican immigration. Along with this came offsetting salutes, from Southwestern employers especially, to the strong work ethic, family values, and pliant attitude that "docile, obedient, inherently honest" Mexican peasants brought into El Norte.

The closing years of the twentieth century saw more Mexican immigration but far less open discussion of it. Mexican migration was now massive and sustained, but despite this the public discussion of this major part of the Hispanic influx was surprisingly muted. The media occasionally carried stories that hinted at social friction—high Hispanic birth rates in local hospital emergency rooms, high rates of drunken-driving offenses among young Latino males, Hispanics leading other groups in high school dropout rates, and brown gang formation in Southern California schools and neighborhoods. These scattered news reports, especially in the major metropolitan media channels, came stripped of editorial comment or judgmental observations by journalists or public figures. The illegal part of Mexican and Central American immigration did generate heated debate in the 1980s and 1990s, as we have seen, but the complaints were about illegality along with neighborhood and labor market impacts of low-skilled males, not about Mexicanness or Latinization. Late twentieth century Americans did not, at least in public, have the sort of conversations about the characteristics of this nationality that their great-grandparents had about the Chinese, Japanese, southern Italians, Poles, Jews—and Mexicans—of the Great Wave. Public opinion polling, however, gave a glimpse of popular attitudes. In a 1986 poll the respondents were asked open-ended questions about their views of certain immigrant groups, and 59 percent of the responses about Latin Americans were negative (associated with "overpopulation," "drugs," and "illegal aliens") while only 39 percent of the responses about Asians were disparaging. When those polled are analyzed by social class, working-class and less-educated people were more likely to fear job competition from Latinos.

Yet polls are hardly a public discussion. Latin American migration on a large scale after the 1960s brought vast demographic and social change. When this happened with immigration from central and eastern Europe at the opening of the twentieth century, intellectuals responded with a vigorous discussion that included the characteristics of the new groups and what their arrival meant. Most but not all of the commentary was negative. Writers such as Edward A. Ross, John R. Commons, Henry Pratt Fairchild, and those scholar-presidents Woodrow Wilson and Theodore Roosevelt openly debated the merits of allowing mass migration of non-Europeans. Their debates shaped the policy changes that came in 1921–1929.

A similar debate did not happen during the four last decades of the twentieth century, with their growing deposit of Mexican nationals within the United States. Immigration itself was discussed, after a fashion. But the talk did not include attention to any particular group, including the largest group that steadily came from a large, growing, and very different society just over our southern border.

There seem many reasons for this conspicuously absent conversation. Our educators and religious and civic leaders have reasonably well communicated to educated people that the earlier national conversation over the characteristics of various groups of immigrants during the Great Wave had been too often fortified by racist assumptions and language. This bigoted element in American thinking and discourse contributed to social friction and the blatant discrimination encountered within America by the immigrant groups whose alleged negative or questionable qualities were being openly discussed. The history lesson seemed obvious. A country that does not discuss the cultural qualities of large incoming (or resident) groups of people in negative ways, indeed does not discuss cultural difference at all, is a healthier country that has learned from its past.

As a result of this lesson, the most politically incorrect language in America (as in Europe and Australia) is ethnic-group categorizing—unless it is favorably flattering or a part of some compensatory benefit. Violating this taboo brings savage retaliation. While we perhaps do not like to think of our country as requiring taboos to function, this one surely seems to most of us far preferable to the freedom that allowed our ancestors' occasionally bigoted expression.

Working in the same direction as this self-restraint on ethnic-group analysis is the dynamics of political democracy. Mexican Americans (and some Mexicans illegally here) vote, even though not at the rates of other Americans. Like all ethnic groups, Hispanic or otherwise, they are guarded by ethnic organizations deployed for self-defense, far more so than was the case one hundred years ago. Public figures and institutions must be wary of giving offense to alert ethnic defenders who know how to fight back.

Thus the Mexican component of the Second Great Wave generated almost no candid and critical public discussion of the group's norms and characteristics, in contrast to a century earlier. An admirable work ethic was universally conceded and commended, but this is hardly discussion of the cultural impact of a major immigration stream. If there were critics of Mexican or other Latino culture they were far out on the unheard margin. Polls showed a high and sustained level of public objections to the levels of immigration generally, illegal and legal. The Mexican or larger Latino part of immigration received almost no separate discussion.

A good case could be made that the absence of any debate focused on any national group was splendid news, even though one nationality for the first time stood out from the others, given its size and the propinquity of its social base and diaspora-manipulating government. Plainly, our immediate southern neighbor was exporting a profound demographic change to the United States, and how could significant cultural change not come with the numbers? If this was not discussed in a country whose mass media are perpetually starved for stories, the principal reason must have been that history taught that nothing but trouble could come from opening that Pandora's box.

Then, as the twentieth century gave way to the next, the discussion of the Mexican immigration stream broke through to the surface—not in the Southwest where the social transformation was most intense, but in Cambridge, Massachusetts.

Several scholars there had been slowly breaking away from postwar orthodoxy in the study of economic development, which held that a country's economic success or backwardness was explained by external factors. This orthodoxy, *dependencia* theory, found the key to economic and social backwardness in the structure of global capitalism. The capitalist world's "center" nations exploited and held down the "periphery" or Third World countries. By the 1990s, a Harvard-centered group of scholars including David Landes, Robert Putnam, Lawrence Harrison, and Samuel P. Huntington were offering a new explanation, one returning in spirit to the prevailing view of a century before, established by Max Weber's 1904 classic, *The Protestant Ethic and the Spirit of Capitalism*. Weber had been right to look inside societies for the roots of (in his case European) economic success. In an anthology of essays published in 2000, *Culture Matters: How Values Shape Human Progress*, Harrison and Huntington brought together a number of writers who explained Asian success and Latin American backwardness in terms of cultural factors internal to nations and societies.

This opened the way for a question of crucial importance up and down the Americas: Why doesn't Latin America work? One writer in 1992 summarized the new scholarly outlook in this way: Latin America's "chronic malaise of political instability, social inequality and economic backwardness" can mainly "be traced to cultural values—ideas, attitudes, prejudices and habits—bequeathed centuries ago by the Spanish and Portuguese colonists."

What does this have to do with U.S. immigration policy? The end-of-century intellectual openness to the discussion of cultural differences among nations and peoples, even at the risk of releasing into the air the outcast idea that some sets of cultural values were inferior or superior to others (participants in this discussion struggled to find alternative terminology for the comparative study of cultural values), opened the way for a small burst of attention to the worrisome implications of Mexican immigration to the United States, on cultural grounds. Harrison argued in a chapter in his earlier book, *Who Prospers?*, that Mexico's "failure to build solid democratic institutions, its slow economic development, and its extreme social inequalities reflect the Hispanic value system that has been the principal obstacle to human progress throughout Hispanic America," and that these values came north with Mexican migrants and played a role in retarding their assimilation and social progress toward American norms. He held back from addressing the implications of this concern for immigration policy, but his noted colleague Huntington was direct and blunt. "Why Mexico Is a Problem" was the subtitle of his December 2000 article in the magazine of the conservative think tank American Enterprise Institute. He argued that "Mexican immigration poses challenges to our policies and to our identity in a way nothing else has in the past." The numbers are and have been exceptionally high and persistent, their regional concentration is unprecedented, and the evidence on assimilation suggests colonization rather than Americanization. "Mexican immigration looms as a unique and disturbing challenge to our cultural integrity," he wrote, "our national identity, and potentially to our future as a country." The remedy, he insisted, was curbing Mexican (and overall) immigration along the lines recommended by the Jordan Commission. Without Mexican immigration, overall immigration would drop by a third, illegal immigration would be "relatively minor," the "average level of the skill and education of immigrants would be undoubtedly the highest in American history," and "the wage levels of less skilled Americans would rise." In the same issue, Linda Chavez agreed that only one-third of Mexican immigrants to the United States "are becoming American" and "America is becoming a dangerously balkanized country."

Thus a new question seemed to have broken through the intimidating layers of taboos against the critical scrutiny of ethnic others. Was Mexican immigration, that mix of legal and illegal entry, really a bargain, all things considered? Or was it not, to the United States (and possibly also to Mexico), and were changes in order? A 2001 study by the Center for Immigration Studies collected some economic facts that seemed to speak for themselves: two-thirds of Mexican immigrants do not complete high school, compared with less than one in ten natives, and the lower average educational levels of Mexican immigrants make them more than twice as likely as natives to be in poverty and give them a lifetime fiscal impact of a negative $55,200 (taxes minus services used). The report might easily have added to the evidence. Median family income for Asians in 1997 was $51,850, $46,754 for non-Hispanic whites, but $28,142 for Hispanics. The study's author, Steven Camarota, concluded: "Mexican immigration reduces wages for the poorest American workers and imposes significant costs on the United States." The report had nothing to say about the sources of this discouraging economic and social performance, but it did offer immigration policy recommendations: "Reduce unskilled legal immigration in general, including from Mexico," and eliminate the preferences for adult children and siblings so that skills would be given more weight in selection. Again, an endorsement of the Jordan Commission conclusions, so long ignored.

Just months later, the Mexican National Population Council released a report stating that, contrary to earlier reassurances, mass immigration to the United States would continue at between 3.5 and 5 million people for at least the next thirty years, even assuming strong economic growth and declining birth rates. The northern flow was inevitable.

This little burst of discussion may or may not mark the beginning of a substantial reexamination of the Mexican part of immigration to the United States, in recognition, finally, of its nation-changing potential. Not all of that discussion will have the sound of an alarm, for when there is candid scrutiny of this or any other ethnic group, there will be mixed evidence. There have always been those who have good things to say about the Mexican migrant, especially the seasonal sort that comes to work, then returns home where he and his family take part in Mexico's life. American employers at the end of the twentieth century could be heard paying the same tributes as had the agricultural bosses of the 1920s and 1940s, saluting the Mexican (and generally Latino) work ethic and willingness to do "the dirty jobs Americans won't do." This is widely acknowledged, not just in agriculture but in urban service sectors.

Ironically, this comes as a type of bad news—about American unskilled workers, and especially blacks. As we have seen, Jack Miles, Roberto Suro, and others wrote in the 1990s about the strong preference of the American employer, from agribusiness bosses to housewives and homeowners, for brown over black labor. With Latinos, a black real estate developer in California admitted, white employers know "that there will be less trouble, that more work will get done." Miles worried about the blacks, passed over for a preferred labor force without "attitude." But Suro worried also about the browns who had come a generation earlier, Mexican Americans (and other legal Latinos) forced to compete against the new regiments of illegal immigrants. Latinos lawfully in America "must accept the fact that a large-scale illegal influx is harmful to their long-term interests."

Mexican immigration ultimately poses a larger question that was never far from the surface: Was the Southwestern region of the United States experiencing Mexican *reconquista*? The picture was extraordinarily complex. Historically, the Mexican American population in California, Arizona, New Mexico, and Texas, though naturalizing at a lower rate than other immigrant groups, had aspired to be U.S. citizens and made an impressive record in that direction against considerable resistance. Mexican American leadership came together in 1929 in Texas to form the largest Latino civil rights group, the League for United Latin American Citizens (LULAC), stressing Americanization, participation in U.S. political life—and opposition to Mexican immigration. By the 1960s this strategy, combined with strong socioeconomic currents, had produced an encouraging record of the social integration of resident Mexican Americans, evident in English language facility among the young, in most places a daily community life in which cultural distinctiveness was diluted by economic and social mixing, upward mobility, and intermarriage.

But by the 1990s many things had changed. A large and growing population of Mexicans, who were not in self-identification or often even in law Americans, had built up in the Southwestern United States where Mexican American advocacy groups no longer spoke LULAC's earlier integrationist language. A new generation of activists emerged after the 1960s, attempting to speak for and to the Mexican diaspora as a permanent ethnic power base. Often (especially in California) calling themselves "Chicanos" rather than Mexican Americans, these activists embraced an open-border immigration position that Cesar Chavez had rejected in the 1960s as harmful to workers of Mexican descent who were now a part of the American working class. *Reconquista* by northward migration, not assimilation and integration, was in the air of politics and the media. Ambitious Hispanic politicians could not resist mobilizing their ethnic constituency, and a language of separatist nationalism came from the new generation of university-based and urban Latino activists in the 1980s and 1990s.

Encouragement for Mexican cultural maintenance and political identification with the homeland came from Mexican governmental officials through a new Program for Mexican Communities Abroad launched in 1990. The president of Mexico, Ernesto Zedillo, told a Chicago audience of the National Council of La Raza that "I have proudly proclaimed that the

Mexican nation extends beyond the territory enclosed by its borders and that Mexican migrants are an important, a very important part of it." "I think we are practicing La Reconquista in California," announced the Mexican consul general in California at a Los Angeles meeting in 1998. Occasional Chicano activists or politicians talked aggressively of irredentism, of reversing through massive migration the results of the 1848 war. "These population dynamics," said Henry Cisneros, former mayor of San Antonio and secretary of the Department of Housing and Urban Development in the Clinton administration, "will result in the browning of America, the Hispanicization of America. It's already happening and it's inescapable." "California is going to be a Hispanic state, and if you don't like it you should leave," said Mario Obledo of the Mexican American Legal Defense and Education Fund (MALDEF) in a televised interview. A 1994 parade of seventy thousand Latinos in Los Angeles protesting California Proposition 187 (a ballot initiative to deny public services to illegal aliens) was festooned with the red, white, and green flag of Mexico, with hardly an American flag to be seen. "Somos Mexicanos!," shouted Antonio Villaraigosa, the Speaker of the California state assembly, at a 1997 rally. "The question is not whether *reconquista* will take place, but how and with what consequences," wrote one journalist. "This constant influx from a single country is unprecedented in American history," writer Linda Chavez commented, and "is unquestionably a factor inhibiting the successful assimilation of Mexicans already here." In 1999, a Texas town passed an ordinance declaring that all city meetings and functions would be held in Spanish, and in 2002 Mexican consulates in the United States began issuing IDs to all those of Mexican heritage, including illegal immigrants, and several U.S. banks and local governments expressed the intention to accept them as valid. A respected Stanford historian connected the dots. "The possibility looms that in the next generation or so we will see a kind of Chicano Quebec take shape in the American Southwest," David Kennedy wrote in an article titled "Can We Still Afford to Be a Nation of Immigration?"

The *reconquista* rhetoric by some Southwestern Hispanic activists and the trends sketched here were an unpredictable mix of posturing and deepening cultural divisions in a border region absorbing a major impact of the Second Great Wave from south to north. Peter Skerry has cautioned against taking the statements of self-appointed Latino "leaders" as evidence of group sentiment, and this certainly applies to *reconquista* talk. Some observers remained sanguine about the assimilation issue in the region, arguing that Mexicans coming north quickly absorbed American values, as they always had. Others, like Californian Victor Davis Hanson, used the term

"Mexifornia" to describe a future "hybrid civilization" taking shape in that region in which "poverty becomes endemic" while the middle and upper classes constuct an apartheid system of residences and recreation. "Schools erode, crime soars, and integration and Americanization falter." There seemed a growing perception that the Southwest and especially California, the most immigration-impacted state, was headed toward something new, the "transnationalization" of the regional population—the term of University of California at San Diego historian David Gutierrez—rather than the ascendancy of either United States or Mexican identity, a population less nationalistic than oppositional and alienated. It seemed clear that history lessons about how easily America had resolved centrifugal forces a century ago had little relevance to today's realities.

15

CASE FOR RESTRICTION: IMMIGRATION'S POPULATION-ENVIRONMENT CONNECTION

There is simply nothing so important to a people and its government as how many of them there are, whether their number is growing or declining, how they are distributed as between different ages, sexes and different social classes and racial and ethnic groups, and again, which way these numbers are moving.

—Daniel Patrick Moynihan

The philosopher Immanuel Kant once observed that "all error has its origin in resemblance." On the subject of immigration, Americans who register alarm about our current era of mass immigration are often given the reassuring "historical perspective" that this has all happened once before, and the country prospered. Mass immigration in the form of the First Great Wave came to America one hundred years ago, this lesson tells us, bringing alarm that proved unjustified. Now it comes to the same country again. Ignore the alarms.

But it is not the same country, or in the same world, despite the superficial marks of resemblance. The context has changed in several fundamental ways, and at the forefront of these is the global demographic and environmental dynamic.

A strong case can be made that the twentieth century (and the twenty-first) will one day be described from a perspective that transcends what we contemporaries think to be the lead events of our era—savage world wars and the Cold War. Instead, the age will be understood as one whose central event was a sudden and unprecedented human swarming, when explosive population growth brought far-reaching habitat strains, amplified social conflicts, and raised fundamental questions about the goal of the human project. It will thus be seen as a time of formidable intellectual and moral challenge to entrenched assumptions, when the future of that "rogue mammal," Homo sapiens (historian J. R. McNeill's term), and that of many other species, depended on how quickly we comprehended our radical new circumstances and adjusted values, thinking, and behavior.

Human population growth in the modern era has no parallel and is almost incomprehensible. Homo sapiens numbers accumulated across all of human history to reach a global total of one billion circa 1800–1830. Then another billion was added in just one hundred years, another in thirty (by 1960) and another in sixteen (by 1976). The sixth billion was reached just before the century was out, when writer Bill McKibben pointed out that "the *increase* in human population in the 1990s . . . exceeded the *total* population in 1960," and "the population has grown more since 1950 than it did during the previous four million years."

But this is not the crest. In the 1970s and 1980s some experts estimated that the surge of human numbers would reach twelve to sixteen billion, but growth rates slowed. In the developing world, birth rates in nations like China, India, and Brazil had unexpectedly dropped so quickly that UN estimates in 2000 pointed toward a global plateau at eleven billion (the medium variant), not twelve or sixteen. Then in 2002 UN demographers recalculated their projections again and saw stabilization at ten billion by 2150, possibly earlier. If these hopeful forecasts prove correct, the results are still dire. Four billion more people will be added to this crowded world, most of them in impoverished and failing societies trying desperately to industrialize.

To add to the collision of unprecedented developments, as the world entered the twenty-first century a few demographers perceived there were or would soon be two population, or demographic, problems, not one. The first and far more serious was—still—rapid population growth, most of it in the developing world. The second was more an opportunity than a problem, the developed world's emerging demographics of aging populations, below-replacement birth rates, and prospects for eventually shrinking populations if trends in these nations remained the same. This recently perceived demographic megatrend—sometimes called subreplacement fertility, or SRF—should be taken, unlike the first, as fabulously good news. It means that in time, the human "too much" era will yield to a downward trend toward sustainable numbers, accompanied by an easing of crowding and environmental and resource strains. The few elderly males in charge of governments and the media who have heard of SRF and its apparent implications have responded with something near panic, foreseeing unprecedented ratios (one to one?) between dependent populations of old and very young and the productive labor force in between. Their concern is both premature and misguided. No country has yet begun to shrink (and the United States, alone among the developed nations, no longer has SRF, due to immigration). When shrinkage begins, as Lincoln Day has pointed out in an astute early book on the subject, *The Future of Low-Birthrate Populations* (1992), ecologically sustainable population size can be selected and then maintained by some combination of policy-encouraged fertility increases or immigration.

The awesome passage from one billion preindustrial humans in 1800 to ten billion industrialized humans somewhere toward the end of the twenty-first century is at the core of most of our fundamental difficulties. A mounting chorus of alarm, analysis, and policy advice has been gathering for fifty years in the West, based mostly in the scientific communities of biology, ecology, climatology, oceanography, and physics but also in the social sciences engaged with demography and environment. These disciplines have been expanding our understanding of the implications of humankind's mounting numbers and industrializing living patterns for environments, resources, and recently, social stability and international conflict. There is a broad consensus in these scientific communities, understood and shared in the universities, philanthropic foundations, environmental organizations, and some sectors of government, that the tragically expanding human family everywhere, in varying ways and degrees, moves ever deeper into an era of environmental difficulties suggesting the term "crisis." This scientific consensus was forcefully expressed in the 1992 statement of a group of fifteen hundred scientists, including ninety-nine Nobel laureates, in a "Warning to Humanity": "Human beings and the natural world are on a collision course," and a major driver behind it is unprecedented human population growth. Another statement of the consensus was expressed by environmental historian J. R. McNeill in his *An Environmental History of the Twentieth-Century World*. While "it is impossible to know whether humankind has entered a genuine ecological crisis . . . it is clear enough that our current ways are ecologically unsustainable," and "the probability is that sharp adjustments will be required to avoid straitened [*sic*] circumstances." "It is prudent to address the prospect sooner rather than later." Two government reports anchored the consensus that environmental degradation and population growth were connected—the Rockefeller Commission of 1972 and the Global 2000

Report of 1980. Not all who shared these concerns thought Paul Ehrlich's formula fully adequate, but it was widely quoted: I = PAT, where Impact of humans = Population times Affluence times Technology.

It was recognized that the "ecological crunch" ahead will be harder on the world's many poor and powerless than on the wealthy and powerful. One reason for this unfairness may be a particularly grim historical timing. "The Petroleum Interval" in human life began (it can be argued) in 1859 with Colonel Drake's discovery of how to pump oil fields in Pennsylvania. "It will be very brief," wrote petroleum geologist Walter Youngquist, lasting perhaps three hundred years. The peak of world oil production will come before 2010, after which there will be a "permanent global oil crisis." The cheap power of the petroleum interval will not be available to the developing hopes of "the oil-less people" in China, India, and much of Latin America.

No consensus in a free society is complete or static. Among those who have grasped the ecological implications of humanity's epochal swarming and industrialization (let us call them Greens), some have not always resisted the temptation to exaggerate the problems. After all, the public is demographically and environmentally ignorant. Those luckily more educated and consequently alarmed have sometimes given in to the temptation, for maximum wake-up effect, to speak of the ominous inevitability of mass famine, "ecological collapse," and other doomsday endings, while underestimating the capacities of science and technology and human ingenuity for ameliorative response. This sometimes led them to make gloomy predictions that often did not unfold as promised, because humanity deploys a lot of inventiveness in getting around resource shortages, especially when warned. Green "doomsaying" thus provoked a healthy and sustained controversy about the actual scale of "the population problem" and its environmental side effects, as well as the best policy responses. Writers like Aaron Wildavsky or Greg Easterbrook, while acknowledging environmental problems, emerged as sharp critics of much environmentalist assessment and prediction as systematically too pessimistic. When several environmental groups mounted a sustained attack on Easterbrook's *A Moment on the Earth* (1992), it did not seem that there was any Green consensus. But it is more useful to put the matter in the terms suggested by environmental historian Hal Rothman. There were Deep Greens and Pale Greens, occasionally fiercely disagreeing about the measurement of the harms done by a growing and industrializing human population and the prospects for remedies. In short, the consensus among those informed about environmental matters has always embraced sharply disagreeing optimistic as well as pes-

simistic Greens who agree in accepting the reality that the world even now
has too many humans undermining their ecological endowment, and urgently needs a transition toward lowering human numbers and fundamentally changed economic systems or, as some prefer, "lifestyles."

Having said this, informed citizens will be aware that there appear to be
strong voices outside this Green consensus. Sure enough, no consensus is
complete, but it is important to recognize who the dissidents are. The discussion of the issues of population and environment was joined in the 1980s
and after by the "Browns." Since the doomsayer voices of some Dark
Greens were especially insistent in challenging the gospel of "growth as
usual," they alarmed and aroused mortal enemies in business and conservative foundations and think tanks, who began in the 1970s to fund the writings of "Brownlash" policy intellectuals who began a broad assault on the
evidence and conclusions of the Greens. The most successful of the Brownlashers was a nonscientist, Julian Simon, an undistinguished marketing professor retooled as an environmental expert. Simon died in 1998. His apparent successor is another nonscientist, the young Danish statistician Bjorn
Lomborg.

As skeptics, these and other Browns found a place in the overall discussion, for good and bad reasons. They exposed the vulnerabilities of what
Lomborg in his book *The Skeptical Environmentalist* (2001) called "The
Litany," that pattern in Green communication—especially in membership-
driven environmental lobbying organizations—of over-emphasis on bad
news and neglect of good news. Ridicule for excess is good discipline for en-
thusiasts in an ongoing argument. Simon and Lomborg made impressive ex-
aggerations the other way, finding reassuring good news everywhere—
human life spans longer, air getting cleaner, resources more abundant, the
evidence for global warming dubious. They especially stressed the evidence
of progress in some forms of pollution control and the undeniable rise in
many measures of human well being over the two centuries of industrialization and population expansion.

Here the Browns' usefulness ended. The larger part of the message of
Simon and the Browns was to argue not just that there was heartening
progress in some places and that market forces deserved some credit, but
that there *was* no population or environmental problem. No one said this
more brazenly than Simon, from his first book in 1980 to his death in 1998.
He tirelessly asserted his preposterous view that there were not too many
people but not enough, that resources would never run out, and population
growth could continue endlessly. "There is no meaningful physical limit . . .
to our capacity to keep growing forever," Simon wrote, while still solving all

environmental and resource problems. "This is my long-run forecast in brief: The material conditions of life will continue to get better for most people, in most countries, most of the time, indefinitely."

This argument is so scientifically ill-informed and ideologically biased as to deserve the universal scorn with which it has been met. He was neither a scientist nor even a respected economist, and his views on population and environment issues were held in contempt among environmental and demography professionals, who attempted to ignore him and his clones such as journalist Ben Wattenberg and talk-show host Rush Limbaugh. The media, on the other hand, did not ignore the Brownlashers and especially the dramatic Simon, and he was frequently quoted as a respected authority. Two years after Simon's death Lomborg published *The Skeptical Environmentalist*, a book repeating Simon's cornucopian message that the environmental problem was essentially behind rather than ahead of us. This time the scientific community counterattacked in waves, charging Lomborg with repeated exaggeration, facts lifted out of context, and misrepresentation of scientific findings and controversies. Yet the media continued to cite both Simon (even after his death) and Lomborg as respected experts in their news stories, for it framed a better story to bracket news of some disturbing environmental or demographic development with a Simonite denial that population or environmental alarm was even justified. This fostered the impression that serious experts were divided on the existence of an environmental cluster of problems with a crucial population dimension. They were not, and obscuring that fact is a grievous harm.

IMMIGRATION CONNECTION TO ENVIRONMENTAL DEGRADATION

What does all this have to do with immigration, which is a matter of people changing where they live? We are still sorting out these new issues. There would be no relationship between immigration and the world's growing list of environmental problems if immigrants merely moved from one nation or place with a given "environmental footprint" to another with exactly the same. Most immigrants, however, especially in this era of global communication and enhanced mobility, move from poor societies to richer ones, intending to do what they almost always succeed in doing, take on a higher standard of living that carries a larger ecological footprint. This being the case, the logic of the relationship is straightforward. Population growth in both poor and wealthy societies, but especially in the latter, intensifies environmental problems. Where immigration shifts population numbers to wealthier societies, it does not leave global environmental damage the same, but intensifies global as well as local environmental degradation.

The first connection, between human numbers and environmental harm, emerged in the West in the late nineteenth century—Americans would nominate George Perkins Marsh's 1864 book, *Man and Nature*. This is still an upsetting idea to some, so it is not surprising that the second connection, between immigration and environmental harm, is resisted by many. They charge that it is not only an unproved novelty but an offensive effort to blame immigrants for something the locals were doing before foreigners came to help. Fortunately, serious study of both these connections has begun. One place is the Environmental Change and Security Project based at the Woodrow Wilson International Center in Washington, D.C., where the spur and the source of financial support was the further connection of population, environment, and immigration to national security concerns. The publications of this project have shown no interest in blaming anybody in particular, but focus on the analysis of hitherto unexplored linkages and their policy implications. Immigration, population, and environment issues have become joined, in a way that had not been perceived in mainstream policy discussions in the past.

As always, some people were mentally ahead of others in perceiving and exploring these connections. There was some attention to population futures in the McCarran-Walter immigration hearings of 1950–1952. Then in the 1962–1963 House hearings that led to the 1965 immigration act legislators were informed by demographic experts that global population growth in the twentieth century would swamp the United States with migrants if the restrictions of policy were not maintained and strengthened. One did not have to be a trained demographer to know that a surge of population growth in Europe in the nineteenth century had propelled the First Great Wave of immigration to the new world and that a Second Great Wave in the twentieth century from Latin America and Asia would inevitably press on the United States. The environmental implications of this went almost unmentioned and essentially unexplored.

Still, it turned out to be difficult to get a frontier-born nation to focus its attention on the possibility of American overpopulation, especially when Nevada seemed so empty. But the 1960s were a decade when many long-suppressed problems forced their way onto the national agenda. For the first time, the population issue came strongly to the surface. Stanford biologist Paul Ehrlich's *The Population Bomb* (1967) gathered sensational sales and attention. Ehrlich's focus had been global, but by Earth Day 1970, the

Sierra Club and other environmental organizations were talking about
American overcrowding. At an American campus gathering in 1970, the
British writer C. P. Snow was asked by the students, "What is the cause?"
He answered: "Peace, food, and no more people than the earth can take."

Reflecting these subcurrents of opinion was the 1972 report of the Commission on Population Growth and the American Future, which, as we have
seen, looked into whether America had a population problem, declared that
it did and urged stabilization. After stabilization, the Rockefeller commission
did not know what number of Americans to aim at. The few scientists who
have attempted "carrying capacity analysis" to determine optimal population
levels for the United States have differed on the desired levels but agreed that
there were already too many Americans. Paul and Anne Ehrlich, pointing out
that optimal population size depends on the technology and consumption
patterns of society, thought 75 million Americans about right. University of
Maryland's Robert Costanza preferred 85 million, at current consumption
patterns. Cornell ecologists David and Marcia Pimentel defined the range as
between 40 and 100 million for the United States. Others either arrived at
different numbers—always quite below current population levels—or
scoffed at the exercise as beyond rational calculation.

Uninhibited about the lack of rationale for any particular population level,
the Rockefeller commission had aimed at ending growth, early stabilization,
and then further studies. Along the way, it made an important connection. After tallying up the ill effects of mounting numbers, the commission pointed out
that a large and growing part of U.S. population growth—16 percent across
the 1960s, soon to reach 25 percent given current demographic trends—came
from just legal immigration alone. If ending national population growth was an
urgent goal, immigration must be held to current levels or reduced so that it
supported and did not work against that objective. This could be easily done
without the government intervening in any American's fertility choices. Immigration held the key. Incoming numbers should be kept at current totals of
four hundred thousand a year, and if this number produced growth (a minority of the commission thought that number too high), it should be lowered as
necessary to support the goal of population stabilization.

Suddenly, immigration policy had been placed in a larger policy context,
and gained a new rationale. Critics had long complained that the nation did
not know what it was trying to achieve with immigration, making policy aim-
less and irrational. If population growth was connected to environmental,
economic, and social costs (as the commission and many others believed) and
was itself partially driven by immigration, then immigration policy had a job
to do in the vital area of national goals. Keep America off the growth path.

This was a relationship between immigration and other national goals that had never been asserted. It suggested the role of a prophet for U.S. Immigration commissioner W. W. Husband, who in 1924 had said: "In my opinion, our immigration problem will soon resolve itself into the question whether or not the country needs additional population, and if so, for what purpose."

The Rockefeller commission's visionary call for an end to population growth, with the immigration policy coda, was not met with any form of rebuttal. There was no argument that the commission's numbers were wrong and that immigration had not become a powerful driver of U.S. population size. Instead, as we have seen, President Nixon, who had appointed the commission, criticized and shelved its report because of abortion issue contamination. Some commentary in the media welcomed this burial on more elevated grounds than Nixon chose, asserting that the government should never adopt national population goals. This high-minded absurdity should not have settled the matter for anyone, because the government already pursued population goals. Our immigration policy *was* our national population policy, aiming at a growing population without even a gesture toward a convincing rationale or open debate.

Over the remaining years of the twentieth century individual writers, immigration reform groups like FAIR and Numbers USA, and the occasional political figure like Senator Alan Simpson or Congressman James Scheuer have forcefully questioned the wisdom of this stealth national population expansion policy. Demographer Leon Bouvier noted that in the year of the Rockefeller commission report, 1972, the U.S. TFR for the first time dropped below replacement level (2.1), reached 1.7 by the end of the decade, and remained below replacement level through the 1980s and 1990s. The baby boom was over. The American people were choosing smaller families and, inevitably, an end to population growth (which would occur after fifty to sixty years of "population momentum"). Projecting these fertility rates, Bouvier estimated that U.S. population would have peaked at about 250 million by 2030 and begin a gradual decline—if immigration remained at "net replacement levels" or about 250,000, the number thought to leave the country annually.

But it did not, and writer Roy Beck correctly argued in *The Case Against Immigration* (1996) that Congress had quietly canceled the people's chosen demographic future. Americans through their fertility behavior after the 1960s were choosing a demographic future of a stabilized population at around 250 million by 2050. That path to population stabilization was radically altered by politicians in Washington, who enacted expansionist immigration policies that proved to be population policies in disguise. Immigration's contribution to

Table 15.1.   Immigration to
the United States, 1820–2000,
by Decade

Year	Number
1821–1830	143,439
1831–1840	599,125
1841–1850	1,713,251
1851–1860	2,598,214
1861–1870	2,314,824
1871–1880	2,812,191
1881–1890	5,246,613
1891–1900	3,687,564
1901–1910	8,795,386
1911–1920	5,735,811
1921–1930	4,107,209
1931–1940	528,431
1941–1950	1,035,039
1951–1960	2,515,479
1961–1970	3,321,677
1971–1980	4,493,314
1981–1990	7,338,062
1991–2000	9,095,417
1820–2001 Total	67,153,749

Source: Statistical Yearbook of the Immigration
and Naturalization Service, 2001, at www
.ins.usdoj.gov/graphics/aboutins/statistics/
IMM01yrbk/IMM2001list.htm.

population growth (immigrants plus births to foreign-born women), which had been 13 percent in 1970, rose to 38 percent by 1980, and to 60 to 70 percent, and rising, by the end of the 1990s. With immigration pushing the throttle forward, the American population grew by 81 million from 1970 to 2000, 33 million in the 1990s alone—the largest single-decade population increase in U.S. history. Two-thirds of that growth represented immigrants and their children. Census Bureau projections kept being revised upward. In 2000 the bureau for the first time projected U.S. population totals to 2100, and the medium assumption pointed to 571 million, if immigration (and fertility) trends were unchanged. Even these projections were thought by some to be too low, and the Census Bureau admitted that it had in recent years underestimated both legal and illegal immigration.

"Do we really want an America of 500 million people?," asked Colorado's former governor Richard Lamm. "How big a country do we want to become? What problem in America will be made better by continuing to add massive numbers of people? . . . Immigration will decide whether we stabilize or

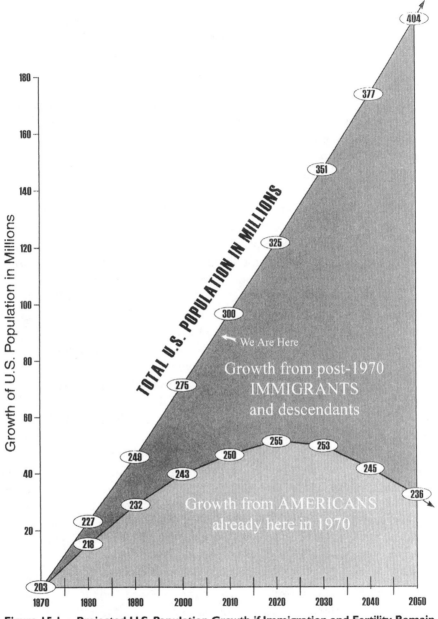

Figure 15.1. Projected U.S. Population Growth if Immigration and Fertility Remain Similar to Today's Rates
Sources: U.S. Bureau of Census Mid-range Projections (2000) and NumbersUSA.com.

whether we continue to grow." By 2040, concluded a California Department of Finance study, "California," the chief immigrant-receiving state, "will be twice as crowded as it is today." Throughout the second half of the twentieth century Americans saw suburbs sprawl out into farmland and Civil War battlefields, urban traffic become grid locked, water shortages mottle the national map, fragile beach ecologies besieged by coastal development, wildlife habitat invaded, and no one traced this back to their own government, which had shaped an immigration policy that drove 70 percent of the growth as one century gave way to another.

The critics of this immigration-driven growth path policy could not seem to get traction in the political process. Only occasionally would there be a connecting of the dots. President Clinton's Council on Sustainable Development concluded in 1996 that "we believe that reducing current immigration levels is a necessary part of working toward sustainability in the United States." This was an intellectual victory for critics of population growth through immigration, but one with no practical impact.

Surely the formidable environmentalist movement would offer strong support for the idea of ending population growth and then would recognize the corollary, that ending growth did not involve any coercion or even policy intervention among Americans, but could be done through downward adjustment of immigration numbers. Given the plain facts, weren't the Greens potential immigration reform advocates? This was a constituency of expanding political influence, and, as we have seen, in the 1960s had seemed to understand that a growing population of affluent Americans with their large ecological footprints intensified disruptive pressures on natural habitat, rising levels of atmospheric pollutants, mounting waste streams, species extinction, and other things they fought against. But the Green organizations moved away from the population stabilization emphasis in the last decades of the century (with the exception of the Wilderness Society), for reasons that are still not entirely clear. If they were now hesitant to raise the population issue, how to enlist them in the effort to uncouple the immigration engine from the population train?

Stunned by the ominous environmental implications of the projections of American population growth and aware that it made their mission to protect and restore the nation's environment more difficult if not impossible, a group of Sierra Club members in 1998 urged the club's national board to follow the logic of the club's thirty-year advocacy of population stabilization and reverse its 1996 stand that the club would take no position on the level of immigration to the United States. Instead, it would make immigration restriction a goal of the organization. Rebuffed by the board, they demanded a 1999 referendum, and an argument long simmering within the organization broke through to the surface, attracting widespread media coverage. The proposal to commit the club to immigration restriction was vigorously opposed by the board and staff and lost by a margin of 60 to 40 percent (only 14 percent of club membership voting).

The Sierra Club had long been on record for population stabilization in the United States, but in this dispute its officialdom argued that population was a global problem and should not be addressed from a national point of view, and that immigration did not belong on the club's agenda. This position took the club out of "the single most important environmental issue in the U.S.," in one member's words, and made it "part of the power structure and thus part of the problem." Current levels of immigration— "overimmigration" was environmentalist and former club executive director David Brower's phrase—prevented national population stabilization and made more difficult if not impossible the environmental protection that was the group's core mission. Club officials offered another argument, that any restrictionist position on immigration was "immigrant bashing" and would harm fundraising and alienate "people of color"—though polls consistently showed that the majority of Hispanics support immigration restriction— and generally make the club's political position weaker. Brower (and others) resigned from the club, accusing the board of inadequately responding to the crucial if politically sensitive issues such as overpopulation and immigration. The frustrated insurgents concluded that the Sierra Club officialdom were simply cowards who knew very well that immigration drove American population growth, which "moved back the goal posts" in the club's struggle to preserve nature against the human assault, but were afraid to take a "politically incorrect" position.

They were right. Club staff and board handcuffed themselves on the question of American population size because of a worry that criticism might come and might even aim the dreaded "R" word at this almost all-white environmental organization, as well as threatening its foundation funding. Neither side in the Sierra Club dispute paid enough attention to a bridging idea suggested by some, that nations (like the United States) that concluded that they must restrict immigration on (among other things) environmental protection grounds could also respond to their sense of moral obligation to humanity by devoting much larger resources to global sustainable economic-development efforts.

One did not have to be a Sierra Club administrator to have difficulty admitting to the obvious. The immigration connection to America's environmental problems turned out to be a difficult concept for otherwise intelligent people to grasp—or, more to the point, accept, lest one drift into the dreaded "anti-immigrant" category. Some, like Yale law professor Peter Schuck, seemed to have been "Simonized" into thinking that the environmental problem was well in hand. Immigration could not have been contributing to the environmental problem, Schuck wrote in 1995, because "the quality of the American environment today is vastly superior to its state in 1965." Simon's bad accounting had made its confusing mark among experts in fields far removed from ecological awareness. Even scholars who were not in the grip of Simonite environmental denial could somehow not take seriously the immigration–environment connection. Conceding that "there is no doubt some truth" in the argument that immigrants add to resource pressures and population growth, the distinguished Stanford University historian David Kennedy concluded there is not very much: "I do not think we would be appreciably better able to grapple with our thorniest environmental issues if we eliminated all immigration tomorrow," because "the kinds of lives that most immigrants lead" do not involve the levels of consumerism of the real culprits, the affluent natives. There is no doubt some truth in this, but not very much. Of course our environmental problems were mostly caused by the ways of living of we affluent, fossil fuel–devouring Americans. Yet the role of incoming immigrants cannot be dismissed. The "absence of immigration" in Kennedy's words (which nobody was proposing) or a substantial cut in the numbers (which many were proposing) would indeed make us "better able to grapple," as it would end population growth in the United States. The logic of this argument does not make immigrants "the problem." They are a part of the problem, and a crucial part. The rest, and the founding part of the problem, is American lifestyles. Kennedy acknowledged that immigration drove up U.S. population growth but thought this might be some sort of global environmental boon, as residence in the United States eventually dropped former third-worlders' fertility rates below what they would have been in Costa Rica or Bangladesh. But, as Bill McKibben points out, the Costa Rican who moves to the United States becomes one of the Americans who uses twenty times the energy he consumed in his native country, from Bangladesh, seventy times more than if he had not migrated. It is not a good idea for America, or for the world, for there to be more Americans, however they are acquired.

This sort of stubborn denial by otherwise intelligent persons of an immigration contribution to America's and the world's environmental problems could take even more tortured forms. Hal Kane, author (with Lester Brown) of the Worldwatch Institute's *Full House: Reassessing the Earth's Population Carrying Capacity* (1994), was heard at a 1995 conference in New York advocating moving *more* Third World immigrants to the United

States, because in America they would no longer be logging virgin forests in Brazil or Thailand. It was pointed out to Kane that they would then become Americans, eventually driving SUVs and in other ways adding to the world's most destructive ecological footprint. Kane squirmed and made no response. When the intellectual confusion and evasion is very deep among intelligent people, the mental virus of political correctness is usually at work, with its attached fear of criticism that one is somehow a racist. The thought-blocking formula is: Thou Shalt Not Link an Immigrant to a Negative Anything, Anytime, lest one be called awful names.

At the beginning of the twenty-first century, the basic demographic impact of current American immigration began to attract wider attention. "Apart from some business executives, I have never met anyone who favored doubling the population," wrote Harvard sociologist Christopher Jencks in a 2001 review of recent books on immigration. "The connection between immigration and population density hardly ever comes up." Jencks seemed to be thinking about all this for the first time, and recognized that such a doubling will involve substantial costs that ought to be discussed, not only such things as crowding and infrastructure needs and water shortages but costs to the rest of the world. As the American population grows, so do our greenhouse gas emissions. Philosopher Peter Singer nudged this discussion along in his 2002 book, *One World*, arguing that when an international bargain is seriously negotiated on control of greenhouse gas emissions the best choice will be to inaugurate "per capita national emissions allocations." For heavily polluting nations like the United States this will require difficult cuts in fossil fuel use, and every immigrant over the "net replacement" number (assumed to be around three hundred thousand) further shrinks every citizen's allowable allocation. The discussion of this arithmetic is just beginning.

The global population numbers are the drivers not only of demographic transformation but of a daunting tangle of ecological deterioration, resource shortages, and crowding foreseen by the Rockefeller Commission in 1972, by the Global 2000 report in 1980, and by a long list of scientific panels and individual authors. By the end of the century, the immigration connection was no longer a secret and could not be rebutted. Immigration policy had become America's unacknowledged U.S. population policy, and it had been full-throttle expansionist since the 1960s, on a road toward more troubles.

IV

STRANGE POLITICS OF POROUS BORDERS: PRESENT AND FUTURE

POLITICS OF IMMIGRATION—
THE 1990s

Historian David Reimers, in a chapter of *Unwelcome Strangers* (1998) titled "A Broken Immigration System," points out that while the 1965 law was responsible for a large increase in the numbers of legal immigrants, Congress, presidents, and courts continued for decades to turn up the volume. They did this with refugee and asylum "exceptions" on the legal side along with repeated amnesties, while they accepted the uncomfortable fact of porous borders to illegal immigration after the failed control effort of IRCA. Thus the immigration flood that surged through the 1990s and into the twenty-first century was the work of years of policy "liberalization" against a background of global migration pressures. Immigration builds momentum if uninterrupted, and U.S. policymakers through all these years periodically augmented and extended the momentum. Because the public, when asked by pollsters, repeatedly favored smaller numbers, there was some complex political dynamic at work that produced counter-majoritarian results, decade after decade.

This was evident again in 1990, when Congress, apparently responding to pressure from ethnic lobbying groups, widened the gates another time. A law of that year expanded per country limits, readjusted preference categories while leaving kinship as the chief ground for admission, and granted Salvadoran "temporary" illegal entrants a longer stay. Showing no shame, Congress once again created an artificial "ceiling" by establishing a "flexible cap" (seven hundred thousand). No immigration law in the twentieth century ever contained a serious "ceiling," any more than Congress puts a "ceiling" on what it will spend in any given year. The 1990 law, like all its predecessors, left several categories of immigrant outside the fig leaf of a cap. A "lottery" for "under-represented countries" was extended, visible proof that Congress had concluded that every nationality in the world had the right to send some people here. In time, it became clear that the 1990 law had expanded legal immigration by one-third. Astonished at the ease with which ethnic lobbies had secured larger numbers on top of the unprecedented large numbers of the 1980s, Raul Yzaquirre, President of La Raza (The Race), remarked that "Congress was clearly more liberal than the public." That it was, even the conservatives in that body. Yet, apparently uneasy with the one-sided changes it had just made, Congress added to the 1990 law a call for a commission on immigration reform—a title acknowledging a lack of confidence in the expansive and porous system national leaders had constructed and ineptly supervised.

The uneasiness was justified. Public frustration boiled over in the early 1990s. Grassroots citizens' organizations calling for immigration reform had been springing up in the most immigration-impacted states and cities, such as California, Florida, Texas, Miami, Los Angeles, New York. A few organized with the support and encouragement of FAIR, most independently. They increasingly made use of the new Internet e-mail capacities for quick communication. It was in California, caught in a severe economic slump, where the new grassroots restrictionism became the most potent political force. Most of the complaints came from residents of border counties where the illegal traffic was daily visible, but as many as forty groups were formed from San Diego to Marin County, protesting rising crime rates, crowded schools, and other fiscal impacts of a growing population of low-income illegal immigrants. Californians were also much agitated by the expansion of affirmative action, many outraged to learn that the program's preferential treatment in hiring, promotions, and government contracts now extended to four-fifths of arriving immigrants (legal or illegal). This was not because of any historic discrimination inside the United States but because they came from countries in Latin America or Asia that were being certified by federal bureaucrats as official minorities. "This meant that approximately 26 million immigrants coming to America since 1965," wrote historian Hugh Davis Graham, "could claim affirmative-action preferences on the basis of historic discrimination they had never experienced."

A group in Orange County, California, frustrated that writing letters to their representatives in Washington protesting illegal immigration produced no results, wrote Proposition 187, known as the Save Our State initiative to deny public services to illegal aliens. This popular idea was undercut for some by the proposition designers' decision to also deny public schooling to the children of illegal immigrants, who, if born in the United

**Table 16.1.   Immigrants as a Percentage
of U.S. Population, Selected Years**

Year	Immigrant Percentage of Total Population
1900	13.6%
1910	14.7%
1920	13.2%
1930	11.6%
1940	8.8%
1950	6.9%
1960	5.4%
1970	4.7%
1980	6.2%
1990	7.9%
2000	11.1%
2002	11.5%

Source: Center for Immigration Studies.

States, were American citizens. Controversy over the idea of state and local government engagement in immigration control was predictable, and the notion of schools as one enforcement point intensified it. Flawed as it was in design, Prop. 187 was increasingly seen by voters as the only option available to Californians to "send a signal" that they were angry at open borders and at America's policymakers who failed to control national borders. With little money, but with the help of a network of over forty groups statewide gathering the necessary signatures, Prop. 187 went on the ballot in 1994. It was vigorously condemned by well-funded opposition from ethnic lobbies, religious leaders, public school officials, social-welfare leaders, and the mainstream media, as "racist" and "divisive." Republican Governor Pete Wilson, in a tight race for reelection against the daughter of former governor "Pat" Brown, sensed the public mood and decided to support Prop. 187. Wilson emerged as a critic of illegal immigration who was skilled at directing his and the public's indignation against inept policymakers in Washington rather than the illegal immigrants themselves—though some of his TV spots showed illegal border-crossers climbing over fences or sprinting up the freeway north of the checkpoint at Chula Vista.

Prop. 187 passed by a resounding vote of 59 percent for and 41 percent against. Most Hispanic voters favored the measure in early polling, though only 31 percent voted for it after a long campaign in which Hispanic political leaders branded it as "anti-Hispanic." Geographer William Clark found that suburban Latinos joined all the state's ethnic and racial groups in favoring Prop. 187. Wilson was overwhelmingly reelected, while Prop. 187, having "sent a message" to politicians everywhere concerning the public sentiment on at least illegal immigration, was immediately tied up in court.

The 1994 election also gave Republicans control of both houses of Congress, and the events in California suggested that the moment might have arrived for restrictionist reform. In March 1995, the Commission on Immigration Reform, chaired by African American former congresswoman Barbara Jordan, made its first report, and finished its work in 1997. Jordan set the tone. Testifying before Congress, she began with the usual praise of immigration in general ("the United States has been and should continue to be a nation of immigrants"), then confirmed that reform was the message: "Legal immigration, however, has costs as well as benefits," and "our current immigration system must undergo major reform to ensure that admissions continue to serve our national interests." The commission recommended a cut in overall legal immigration to 550,000, or 40 percent, a shift of selection criteria toward skills needed in the United States, and an end to family chain migration by eliminating the preferences for brothers and sisters and adult children of new immigrant citizens. As for "unlawful immigration," it "is unacceptable," as was the idea of a large-scale agricultural guest-worker program. The commission asked for an increase in border security and pilot programs as stepping stones toward a national computerized registry based on Social Security data as a basis for an employment verification system for all citizens. Because Jordan was black, no one charged racism, or seriously disputed the commission's findings, which she presented in forceful terms: "Those who should get in, get in; those who should be kept out, are kept out; and those who should not be here will be required to leave." President Clinton, after a personal meeting with Jordan, issued a statement that the report was "consistent with my own views," and his press secretary promised presidential support.

Welcoming this call for reform, a Washington convocation of restrictionist groups from around the country circulated the statement: "We are not against immigration or immigrants. The issue is how many and who, which has always been the issue." FAIR's agenda for reform went farther than the Jordan commission. Total numbers, refugees and all, should be consistent with the overriding national goal of early population stabilization (which meant about three hundred thousand immigrants a year, matching outmigration). Selection should be shifted from family ties toward skills needed by the U.S. economy, possibly through a Canadian-style system of points for education, language ability, and skills; control of illegal immigration required a national system for worker verification. Of the dozen or so national and state immigration reform groups active at that time, none proposed ending immigration, though some urged a temporary moratorium (except for immediate family members) until illegal immigration was brought under control. Restrictionists struggled to convey their positive goals: "We want an America environmentally sustainable, uncrowded," said FAIR's director Dan Stein.

Congress seemed to move in the reform direction in 1995 with a Republican task force report declaring that "IRCA had failed" to deter illegal aliens and demanding, among other things, an end to the grant of "birthright citizenship" to "anchor babies" born on American soil to illegal immigrants. Chairman of the Senate Immigration Subcommittee Alan Simpson declared that "the American people are so very fed up . . . with efforts to make them feel that Americans do not have that most fundamental right of any people: to decide who will join them here and help form the future country." He concluded that "it is time to slow down, to reassess." Congressman Lamar Smith (R-Tex.), chair of the House subcommittee on immigration, submitted a comprehensive package of reforms of legal immigration. His measure would penalize long-term illegal presence in the United States, automatically deport noncitizens who commit serious crimes, and reduce annual numbers to 535,000. Other legislators put forward serious proposals for secure identification systems, and Texas Senator Kay Bailey Hutchison (R-Tex.) suggested a strong new disincentive on illegal entry when she urged fingerprinting all arrested aliens and denial of future U.S. citizenship for those caught entering more than once. The policy atmosphere seemed more full of resolution than posturing, unlike the final months of "reform" leading to IRCA.

The first battle front was a welfare reform bill moving through the House. It would limit welfare benefits for recently arrived immigrants, including recent immigrants' elderly parents who had never worked in the United States. In general, sponsors of new immigrants would become more responsible for their care should they become a public charge. President Clinton objected to these new rules but eventually signed a larger welfare reform law in 1996.

Almost at once, courts and state welfare officials called the measures into question. Congress soon restored most of the cuts affecting immigrants. The likelihood of legal-immigration reform began to fade, as the Republican Party's leadership as well as President Clinton began to respond to aggressive lobbying by business and ethnic forces (in Clinton's case, mostly to one wealthy Democratic donor, John Huang, claiming to represent Asian Americans). Thus the Illegal Immigration Reform and Immigrant Responsibility Act of 1996 was stripped of all but minor changes, and one of these, pilot programs for testing electronic employment-verification systems, was never implemented. "The pro-immigration coalition desired to preserve the current rate of legal immigration and did so," and thus "won the 1996 battle" while "restrictionists were thoroughly defeated," concluded historian David Reimers. "We kept them [the restrictionists] from getting almost anything," gloated Frank Sharry of the National Immigration Forum. "The deck was stacked in their favor, but we outfoxed them . . . an astonishing victory," and he was right.

The immigration reform impulse, Nathan Glazer observed, had been "remarkably muted and civil" in contrast to the 1920s, and was easily contained. In 1996, U.S. immigration policy admitted 916,000 legal immigrants joined by perhaps 500,000 illegal immigrants, the largest cohort since 1914. The booming American economy of the 1990s was a magnet drawing ever larger numbers of unskilled laborers across both southern and northern borders, while many of the skilled foreign computer programmers, doctors, nurses, and university students who came by air on temporary visas overstayed to blend in to American society until immigration lawyers exploiting loopholes or the option of marriage to an American brought regularization of status.

When the new century arrived, the Census Bureau's data gave a startling picture.

The U.S. population in the 1990s had grown by 32.7 million (to 281 million), the largest gain in history and the equivalent of adding the entire population of Canada. Immigrants were 13 to 14 million of that and, if one added the children born to them once in the country, the immigration-added total was 20 to 21 million, or two-thirds of the growth (in California, 96 percent). Since 1980, the United States had added 55 million people, or the equivalent of the population of France. The United States in 2001 contained more foreign-born residents than ever before (10.4 percent of the total population), and one in five Americans was either born abroad or to parents born abroad. Estimates of the illegal population ranged between 7 and 11 million. Census Bureau middle projections, which many experts thought too low, pointed to a U.S. population in 2100 of 571 million, and slight increases in expected fertility along with longer life spans could push that number to 1.2 billion. The gates were widely open and the flow of humans, legal and illegal, had four decades of momentum. The INS quietly gave up on interior enforcement of employer sanctions before the middle of the decade, with no congressional or public outrage. Increased border security in the San Diego region showed that illegal entries could be substantially reduced, but the well-organized northward flow out of Mexico then shifted to more remote (and more dangerous to both immigrants and the Border Patrol) sectors in Texas and Arizona.

END-OF-CENTURY CRITICISM OF THE
IMMIGRATION STATUS QUO

The quick collapse of the energetic 1992–1996 efforts to curb immigration was hard to explain. Public opinion recorded a high point of disapproval in 1996, when a Roper poll reported a new high—83 percent—in support for reducing immigration. Then some opinion polls in 1996 and after showed a slight drop in the negative reactions to the immigration status quo, though majorities still supported lower immigration levels. This slight dip in intensity of the restrictionist impulse is no adequate explanation, though it may reflect something larger about the mood of the nation in the waning years of the 1990s.

As for the battle of ideas and public argument, the lengthy debate among the experts over the cost-benefit balance of modern immigration streams was essentially over. By the mid-to-late 1990s the mass immigration status quo had virtually no scholarly defenders. Cambridge, Mass., is not necessarily the epicenter of the world's intelligence, but it had for decades been one of the foremost academic centers of liberal-left thought, including the liberal dismissal of worries about immigration. It was thus a moment of sea change when in 2000 four highly respected Harvard social scientists spoke forcefully (and independently) as vocal critics of the nation's immigration regime. Sociologist Christopher Jencks, reviewing recent scholarly work on immigration, concluded that "the winners are employers who get cheaper labor" and "the losers are unskilled American-born workers," with "an adverse effect on African Americans . . . especially marked." Economist George Borjas, whose influential book *Heaven's Door* (2000) had come to the same conclusions, wrote that "our immigration policy has been spinning out of control for decades." The skills of immigrants relative to natives had long been declining, "all native workers are worse off from immigration," net economic gains are small and accrue to the American wealthy, and the numbers are too high. Nathan Glazer concluded that "immigration not only contributes to growing inequality in general, but makes life more difficult for black workers in particular." And political scientist Samuel P. Huntington minced no words: "Migration is the central issue of our time," and the "endless stream" into the United States was not assimilating as had "past waves of immigration."

And while he did not work out of Cambridge, Mass., it sent shock waves throughout the Jewish establishment when Stephen Steinlight, director of National Affairs at the American Jewish Committee, wrote a piece the summer of 2001 for the CIS in which he reported a "deeply felt conversion experience" on immigration. Steinlight now urged American Jews to set aside all taboos and discuss the remarkable demographic transformation immigration was bringing to the United States and with it "the special problem of large-scale Muslim immigration." He urged a policy of lower immigration and a rethinking of all aspects of American policy, including "the open-ended entry of Muslim fundamentalists" with no means of keeping track of them.

Taken together, these amounted to a basic statement of something quite new, a vigorous critique of current immigration from liberal turf. And something else was new. Over in the conservative intellectual encampment at the end of the century there had emerged for the first time a questioning and denunciation of the immigration status quo. William Buckley's *National Review*, flagship of conservative journals since the 1950s, gave increasing space to critics of the current immigration regime, such as Peter Brimelow, John O'Sullivan, Paul Craig Roberts, and Mark Krikorian, as the 1990s went on. Then at the end of 2000 the American Enterprise Institute, so long the home of open-border thinkers such as Ben Wattenberg, signaled an abrupt change of heart. Editor Karl Zinsmeister of the AEI's magazine, *The American Enterprise*, ran a number of articles strongly tilting toward alarm at the prospects for successful assimilation of current immigration flows. Journalist Pat Buchanan, sometime aspirant to the Republican nomination for president, launched the *American Conservative* magazine in 2002, with one of its principles stated as: "We reject the myth that open-borders immigration enriches our culture."

While intellectuals and an occasional politician in the United States at the end of the twentieth century increasingly worried out loud about immigration, the issue had become more politically acute in Europe. A central dynamic of global development in the second half of the century was the Third World moving into the First. Porous borders at the perimeter of and between European Union countries permitted sustained large-scale immigration from eastern Europe, North Africa, and the Middle East. All fifteen nations of the European Union (EU) were experiencing unprecedented immigration as the century ended. In 2001, 350,000 people sought refugee status there, and the unsuccessful ones remained to swell the ranks of illegals—500,000 to 1.5 million estimated living in Germany, one million in the UK, 300,000 in Italy, 90,000 in Belgium, 500,000 entering the entire EU each year. These population flows from "the South" to "the North" had been at first facilitated by European governments. As former colonial powers now feeling guilt about their histories, they became more hospitable to asylum-seekers and welcomed growing numbers. Additionally, in the 1970s and 1980s, several EU nations, especially Germany, initiated large guest worker programs that brought thousands of foreigners (in the case of Germany, largely Turks) who did not, as expected, return home at the end of the contractual term.

This era of high immigration generated mounting problems. A dark side of the new mass immigration included the smuggling rings delivering into

Europe women and children bound over in various forms of sexual exploitation and illicit labor—120,000 a year by an EU estimate. Fifteen million Muslims resided in the EU at century's end, ten million of them in France alone. Most were peaceful, but assimilation toward Europe's Christian and secular ways was not their intention, and the Muslim link to terrorism in the 1990s and afterward made this immigration-built subpopulation a source of multiple concerns. Crime rates escalated in large European cities, linked to the new, unassimilated immigrant populations with their youthful, male profiles. Europe, with its generous welfare state provisions and high levels of unemployment, seemed to many of its citizens to be inviting lawlessness in entry and heavy social consequences thereafter. Occasional events reminded one of the scene in Jean Raspail's novel *Camp of the Saints* when the rusty Turkish freighter *East Sea* dumped 900 Iraqi Kurds on a reef off the French Riviera, and a squeamish government allowed them to melt into the European population.

Borders out of control meant national demographic and cultural futures in play, many Europeans began to fear. Rising immigration levels, with a substantial Muslim component, came at a time when European fertility rates were below replacement levels across the entire EU. Some government officials expressed great alarm that their nations were on the verge of a shrinking population, which, if not offset by enlarged immigration numbers, might lead to elderly populations supported by a diminishing youth cohort and, eventually, no Germany or Italy. This argument did not reconcile European publics to large immigration flows, but gave them another reason to vote for parties on the right side of the political spectrum, where a tougher line on immigration could usually be heard. As the century ended European politics, especially in France, Belgium, Holland, Austria, Germany, Italy, and the United Kingdom, were being reshaped as angry voters shifted away from center-left governments that had long ignored immigration (and were vulnerable for other reasons). The political beneficiaries were usually conservative-populist parties and politicians (Jean-Marie Le Pen in France, Jorg Haider in Austria, Pia Kjaersgaard in Denmark, Filip Dewinter in Belgium) who promised, among other things (in democratic politics, there is never only one issue) to bring immigration under control. But there were some exceptions. In Holland, a political unknown named Pim Fortuyn, a gay man who was a libertarian in political leanings, gained wide European attention with his argument that large-scale Muslim immigration brought an intolerant and culturally unassimilable Islam into a survival clash with tolerant European civilization. The Dutch establishment, he charged, was paralyzed by multiculturalist dogma and politically correct reticence, and like all EU nations had largely traded in national consciousness for an enlightened, postmodern cosmopolitanism that would not permit discussion, let alone control of immigration. Islam's takeover, in Holland and elsewhere, was meeting no resistance. Fortuyn was assassinated just days before the May 15, 2002, election, but his meteoric rise to prominence was driven by a cultural and nationalistic alarm growing in other European societies. Put up signs in every port of entry announcing that Italy is "all used up" by an excessive population pressing upon resources and limited space, demanded Italian leftist Ida Magli in a mainstream newspaper, scolding Italy's "chattering classes" for a mindless "immigration enthusiasm" that overloads the country's fragile ecology. "Britain is Losing Britain" to an "unprecedented wave of immigration" driven by "sustained immigration pressure the likes of which the world had never seen," concluded a British journalist, Anthony Browne, son of an immigrant and staunch member of the leftist Labour Party. With good reason, a CNN European correspondent observed in 2001 that "Europe could scarcely be in a greater tangle about immigration. Division of several European states into "two nations" was seen by James Kurth: "the first descended from European and imperial peoples . . . secular, rich, old, and feeble. The second . . . Islamic, poor, young and virile." In this demography we see approaching "the end of the British and French national narratives themselves."

ENTERING THE TWENTY-FIRST CENTURY: BIPARTISAN IMMIGRATION EXPANSIONISM

In contrast, in the United States at the turn of the century the immigration status quo, while under attack from intellectuals on both the left and the right, seemed politically invulnerable. President Clinton had initially endorsed the Jordan commission's proposed reforms and reduction in numbers but then contented himself with vague warnings about the huge task of assimilating the millions of immigrants his own government admitted through the rest of the decade. Inaction from a Democratic president was no surprise. Liberals had been expansionists on immigration since the 1960s. Then in the 1990s came large cash contributions to the Democratic Party from Asians and Asian Americans, who made it clear that an open immigration door was expected in return, and a change of mind by the Democratic Party's only organized constituency with a historic commitment to limiting cheap labor flows, the AFL-CIO. In the 1990s organized labor veered around to a virtual open-border and mass-amnesty position, hoping to organize the ten million illegal immigrants who must now be assumed to be permanent elements of the American workforce.

At the end of the century the Republicans seemed to have moved onto a parallel track, leaving little difference between the parties on immigration. GOP leaders in California and Washington somehow concluded that Governor Pete Wilson's winning 1994 formula in resisting illegal immigration was in fact a huge political blunder that attached an anti-Hispanic label to the Republicans. It was true that the party began to weaken rapidly in California in the second half of the 1990s, losing the 1998 governor's race and, in 2000, giving up five congressional seats and falling deeper into minority status in both houses of the state legislature. That Democrats were receiving a large share of the growing Latino vote was acknowledged. Voter surveys and poll evidence pointed to the conclusion that Latinos do not have a distinctive position on immigration but instead tilt rather strongly toward Democrats because of the party's stands on health care and social-welfare spending. Republicans should not expect to win a majority among them, some analysts said, and in fact should pursue a low-immigration policy so as not to continue to import large numbers of natural Democrats.

But Republican politicians were swayed by a different explanation fostered by liberal political journalists, that "unless the California Republican Party can shed its mean-spirited, anti-immigrant, ideologically rigid, white-male image, it could wither on the electoral vine." House majority leader Newt Gingrich, well aware that the GOP problem with the Latino vote was not just a California problem, because Latinos were an explosively growing presence in many states including Gingrich's own Georgia, led a quick Republican shift to match the Democratic pandering to Latino voters. Republicans were not ready to become advocates of an expanded welfare state, but they could easily salt their speeches with *gracias* and *un gran abrazo, amigo*—and terminate their interest in controlling immigration. It was an inexpensive way to pander. While Democrats were historically committed to generous social programs, Republicans could offer open borders, a cheap, off-budget way to curry favor. The pandering did not, of course, stop with Latinos. Conservative activist Grover Norquist in a June 2001 article (that he surely now regrets) argued that Muslims are "natural conservatives" and helped George W. Bush carry Florida. Public figures who thought otherwise were few or silent. Colorado Republican congressman Tom Tancredo formed an immigration caucus in 1999 to generate reform proposals, but the caucus attracted a skimpy twenty members.

The astonishing end-of-century bipartisan consensus that immigration controls should neither be discussed nor enforced seemed therefore to rest on unshakable political if collapsing intellectual foundations. Both major parties' political leadership, with little dissent, had quietly concluded that talk of immigration reform was a political loser, in view of the dynamic growth of the Spanish-speaking population in the United States and the imagined hostility of that "voting block" toward enforcement of immigration law. A formidable if bizarre lobbying coalition in favor of open borders had somehow come together under the same tent—business groups, most visibly Silicon Valley–type high-technology industrialists; organized labor; religious groups; immigration lawyers; and organizations representing immigrants' rights. The essential backdrop was a booming economy, labor shortages everywhere, and a general euphoria that dulled the edge of public concern about much of anything, including mass immigration. Whatever America was doing should be continued.

The presidential election of 2000 reflected these dynamics. The broad dissatisfaction over mass immigration, illegal and legal, surfaced only in the platform and marginalized rhetoric of the much-weakened Reform Party and its candidate, Patrick Buchanan. The two major candidates, Vice President Al Gore and Texas governor George W. Bush, had nothing to say on immigration and were not pressed on the issue. Journalist Robert Samuelson called immigration "the great forgotten issue of the 2000 presidential campaign." Both major candidates, Bush somewhat less awkwardly, spiced an occasional speech with Spanish phrases.

After the election, President Bush moved to capitalize on the strange ebbing of immigration-reform sentiment. He responded positively to Mexican President Vicente Fox's overtures in the summer of 2001 for some sort of grand bargain between the two countries that would legalize all Mexican illegal immigrants in the United States and provide a new, permanent guest-labor program. Fox visited the United States in September to address a joint session of Congress with his proposal to change U.S. immigration policy to allow free movement of both people and goods across the U.S.-Mexican border, an unprecedented intrusion into American domestic policymaking. He demanded action by the end of the year and barnstormed in several U.S. cities. Democratic Party leaders made no objections to the Fox-Bush plan. Polls showed strong public opposition to Mexico's meddling in U.S. internal politics and to the thrust of presidential proposals, but American policymakers had never paid much attention to polls on immigration issues. As the summer ended the media generally predicted that the two presidents were on their way to an astonishing historic agreement under which Mexicans would be allowed to come northward for work and residence, without impediment.

17

SEPTEMBER 11—A TURNING POINT?

The costs of America's porous borders were stunningly piled even higher on the morning of September 11, 2001. While Mexican President Fox traveled northward to Washington on his mission to open America's southern border to his surplus population, Islamic terrorists commandeered jetliners and struck the World Trade Center in New York and the Pentagon, killing nearly three thousand persons. The Fox-Bush deal, at least for a time, slipped into limbo.

That day's terrorist attacks harshly illuminated a defect that had not formerly been high on the list of flaws in American immigration policy, that our porous borders and governmental abandonment of virtually all interior immigration controls allowed terrorists to move at will into, around, and out of the country, legally and illegally. A study of the immigration history of the forty-eight terrorists convicted of (or admitting to) acts of terrorism against the United States since 1993 found that they had readily exploited every possible means of entry into the United States. "They came as students, tourists, and business visitors," found Center for Immigration Studies research director Steven Camarota, and seventeen had worked the system to enter and stay despite their terrorist occupations, becoming lawful permanent residents and even naturalized citizens of the country they hated. Some reached this permanent status by making fraudulent marriages or applying for asylum. Twelve were illegal aliens when they attacked, and twenty-one had been in illegal status at some point in the last ten years. Several gave officials false information on entry. Joel Mowbray of *National Review* obtained access to the visa applications of fifteen of the nineteen September 11 terrorists and expert analysis found so many elementary flaws that "all the applicants among the fifteen reviewed should have been denied visas." Forty-one of the larger group of forty-eight terrorists studied by Center for Immigration Studies had gone to U.S. consulates abroad and received visas, despite their backgrounds. Judging from the experience of these forty-eight murderers who were Middle Eastern young males with terrorist pasts, there are many ways for terrorists to get into America, legally or illegally, and many ways to stay there, some lawful and some not. It is an easy country to attack, from within.

The immediate result of the events of September 11 was, of course, an angry public outcry demanding retribution, but also protection for the future. *Everything* in America was now changed, it was said—U.S. foreign and national security policy, government organization and priorities, travel, procedures for routine identification of American citizens. And immigration policy, of course. "Our vulnerability to these abominations," said Center for Immigration Studies Director Mark Krikorian, "is not merely a failure of intelligence but also of border control." Perhaps now we would hear no more of the *Wall Street Journal*'s call for open borders. Current immigration policy is an anachronism on many grounds, he went on, but after September 11 change is much more urgent. Others in the immigration reform movement were similarly optimistic about change. A Capitol Hill lobbyist for immigration limitation wrote in early 2002 that legislative changes following September 11 could include "serious immigration reforms." Congressman Tancredo's House Immigration Reform Caucus jumped to fifty members. There were signs that the media had suddenly veered over to at least an openness to a critical view of immigration policy generally. *U.S. News and World Report* conceded that after September 11, "nativist sentiment has come to be viewed not so much as an old-era paranoia as new-era prudence."

It now seemed evident from the history of the known terrorists who had already worked havoc on American soil that immigration had a vital national security dimension that only a handful of critics had foreseen. Incredibly, the Bush administration's chief spokesman for immigration policy, James Ziglar, publicly denied any connection: 'We're not talking about immigration, we're talking about evil." He was fired before the year was out, as the administration sensed what everyone else knew, that the government's immigration bureaucracy was a part of our national vulnerability to terrorism and that the government had some work to do in this area. Columnists and commentators, though not many elected politicians, declared a need for far-reaching change in both the system for handling legal entry and exit as

well as control of illegal entry or visa overstay. Presumably, with all this agitation and outrage, the government would be tightening everything up.
Some twelve hundred aliens suspected of terrorist activities were detained
by the Department of Justice for questioning in the months after September 11, taken by many as a sign that a broken system was being fixed.

But who knew? It was no one's governmental assignment to monitor and
report on an entire immigrant-control system stretched from the State Department through the INS Border Patrol and Labor Department. It was a
time for investigative journalism, and the daughter of two Asian immigrants
filled the need. The dimensions of the problem of reforming the immigration system in light of its national security vulnerabilities were stunningly
brought together in a book appearing hard on the first anniversary of September 11, *Invasion* by Michelle Malkin.

Invasion was an impassioned and unsettling indictment of our nation's incompetent immigration regime, up to and after September 11. Malkin, a
journalist and first-generation American of Filipino descent, saw herself as
"the new face of the immigration debate . . . sick and tired of watching our
government allow illegal line-jumpers, killers, and America-haters to flood
our gates and threaten our safety . . . sick and tired of watching ethnic minority leaders cry 'racism' whenever Congress attempts to shore up our borders." Her indignation was focused on the immigration bureaucracy and the
various elements of the open-border industry that, even after the terrorist
attacks of 2001, lobbied for ever-larger holes in the "Swiss cheese" that was
the American immigration system.

Malkin saw the problems as beginning with visa issuance abroad, a State
Department function shaped by external pressures from the American
tourism industry and internal pressure from high-ranking diplomats eager
to curry favor with host governments, to value only "efficient processing" of
and customer service to the high volume of foreigners headed to America.
Efficiency in visa processing, she found, is indeed a serious problem, but
one driven by a bigger problem, the rising volumes in both the immigrant
visa (IV) and non-immigrant visa (NIV) visa categories, and the increasingly
blurred distinction between the two. The latter, especially, had mush-
roomed dramatically across the 1990s. NIVs were supposed to be issued to
visitors—tourists, business people, students, and some "temporary" workers. In 1985, 9.5 million had been issued, more than tripling to 32.8 million
in 2001 (there are no limits on NIVs as there—sort of—are for IVs). There
are serious problems about this huge and growing flow (and many foreign
visitors from favored countries are permitted to enter without visas at all),
but the principal flaw made evident by the terrorist attacks is that many do

not return and some of them never intended to, becoming part of the illegal alien population (the INS estimates that 40 percent, or over 3 million, of the illegal immigrants in the United States in 2000 were NIV overstayers). To inspect the visa applications of this volume of people the State Department assigns a small pool of six hundred consular officers, who have two to three minutes to make a ruling, and fraud is rampant in the paperwork they quickly scrutinize. This clogged and easily manipulated apparatus has become a key part of the American system for deciding who comes here, and it is a user-friendly system for foreigners intending to become absconders, and among them, for terrorists who need more time to get their work done.

Malkin peeled back the layers of this system with mounting indignation. In the six months after September 11, the State Department's visa issuance process that had admitted most of the terrorists and over three million overstayers showed no signs that anyone had acknowledged the events of that day. Arab and Muslim men were going to get more strict scrutiny, the State Department promised. But in the half year following the attacks, fifty thousand new tourist, business, and student visas were issued to non-Israeli citizens of the Middle East and three times that many from southern Asia where al Qaeda had strongholds. And no one in authority proposed a contraction of the whole temporary visa (and visa waiver) program. The menu of visas, Malkin reported, seemed designed to accommodate everyone, whatever their background and intentions. H1-B visas allow (currently) nearly two hundred thousand "temporary" workers per year for stays of up to six years, from software engineers to fashion models; the Diversity Visa lottery program provides fifty-five thousand visas annually, and Malkin calculated that over seven thousand of such visas over the last five years had gone to applicants from Iraq, Iran, Syria, Libya, Sudan, and Afghanistan; the investment visas can be obtained by creating or significantly underwriting a U.S.-based business; religious worker visas admitted foreigners for up to five years to work for religious organizations in any capacity, as preacher, teacher, or even janitor.

And then there was the radically decentralized student (or F-1) visa, which several of the September 11 terrorists had used for entry as well as flight training. It came as a surprise to many to learn that the F-1 program in 1999 allowed 565,000 foreign students and their relatives to enter and stay in the country for extended periods. Yet the government had handed over the decisions as to the legitimacy of individual student study plans to 73,000 participating "schools" and made no effort to confirm either the students' arrival at these schools or their departure from the country. Econo-

mist George Borjas, in an analysis after the attacks, found that the program
had grown from 65,000 visas in 1971, had been corrupted into an open window to U.S. immigration, and currently posed two security risks: allowing
the export of high-technology knowledge that might compromise U.S. defenses or industrial secrets and opening gaping holes for terrorist entry.
Here was a large agenda for reform that had previously been stifled by research universities, who had come to cherish the cheap labor and the $14
billion in tuition from foreigners. The public did not know that taxpayers
subsidized foreign students even when (rare in graduate education) they
paid "full" tuition, because higher education in the United States costs
either taxpayers or alumni endowments between $6,000 and $9,000 per student per year. Even with the tuition paid by some of these overseas customers, Borjas estimates a $2.5 billion a year net loss.

If all other visa programs are unavailable, Malkin wrote, there is the
Transit Without a Visa Program, for people allegedly traveling through the
United States on the way somewhere else, administered, but really not enforced, by the airlines, and the Visa Waiver Program, which allowed seventeen million people (figures for 2001) to travel to the United States from
twenty-eight specified countries, where only a passport from one of those
countries is sufficient to enter for ninety days. Rarely does anyone check to
see who departs. In the 1996 immigration-reform measure, Congress at the
urging of the Jordan commission added Section 110, requiring the creation
of a comprehensive foreigner tracking system. With such a database the
government would have the ability to discover when and which visitors
failed to exit the country on schedule. A coalition of auto and trucking companies, immigration lawyers, and ethnic lobbyists (Americans for Better
Borders) successfully fought to have the law suspended, and in 2000 President Clinton signed legislation to abandon the entry-exit tracking system
and put in place a task force to study the question of a foreign visitor database to be phased in by 2005. Section 110 had no political friends and had
not survived its enemies.

Malkin's tour of the menu of visas and their lax administration was all
about getting in. As for staying in, there were many legal ways to convert
from visitor to immigrant status without going home to get in line, and
Malkin offered an astonishing account of how little the terrorist attacks of
September 2001 had altered a system of inattention, unenforcement, and
multiple legal channels leading from illegal to legal status in which, in her
words, "It ain't over until the alien wins." Asylum claims while in the country and marriage to a U.S. citizen were well-known avenues, fraught with
fraud and with a high rate of success. Malkin brought to light the many

other ways that people who ought to be outside the country remained within. Her focus was not the entire illegal population, which the Census Bureau now admitted to be nearly nine million people, and many estimated higher, one hundred thousand of them (an analysis of Census Bureau data showed) from the Middle East. This tolerated illegal population of nearly ten million was of course an old problem, now with a brand new national security dimension even though the vast majority of illegal immigrants were peaceable. Malkin was interested in how easily a terrorist, or even a run-of-the-mill criminal who was dangerous to American lives and property, could just stay in the country as long as his project required, even after he lapsed over from legal to illegal status.

Let us count the ways, starting with what should be an easy case for expeditious deportation, illegal aliens convicted of aggravated felonies. Several federal laws require that such persons be deported. Unfortunately, the INS has a long record of releasing criminal aliens after they have served their sentences, without moving to a deportation hearing, which is a lengthy process with extended appeals, "a morass" of loopholes exploited by immigration lawyers. Should a judge at such a hearing order deportation, the INS falls back on a sort of honor system, releasing aliens and then sending them letters, if their addresses are known, asking them to turn themselves in (these are called "run letters" among the aliens). Or an agreement might be struck for voluntary departure without a formal finding of deportation. The INS generally has no further contact with the alien. Malkin believes there are "untold hundreds of thousands of 'absconders' roaming the country," and even INS Commissioner James Ziglar in late 2001 admitted that he did not know the whereabouts of about 314,000 fugitive deportees, and complained that the agency only had 20,000 beds in detention facilities. Adequate resources are not the core of the problem, however. The system for resorting to deportation "is clogged by . . . incomprehensible administrative regulations, bureaucratic and judicial fiefdoms . . . and a feeding frenzy of obstructionist immigration lawyers."

Then there are the criminal aliens who are not caught or convicted, despite repeated contacts with local law and immigration law enforcement agencies, for lack of coordination, a common database, or a culture of cooperation between local and federal personnel. Angel Resendiz illegally entered the United States from Mexico at the age of fourteen, and over the next twenty-five years he had at least that many encounters with federal and local law enforcement officials. He was arrested and convicted nine times for burglary, aggravated battery, and grand theft and deported to Mexico seven times. He repeatedly returned and finally turned himself in (in 1999) after murdering twelve Americans, and possibly more. The entire American system of law enforcement had abjectly failed. Resendiz was repeatedly released by the Border Patrol in their "catch-and-release" policy designed to save money and was never entered in the INS automated fingerprint-identification system (IDENT), mandated by Congress in 1994. The databases of the FBI and the INS had never been linked, though Congress ordered this after Resendiz was convicted of murder in Texas in 2000. "Serial murder . . . serial incompetence," Malkin concluded, and governmental incompetence, before and after September 11, was her indignant theme.

WHAT NEEDED TO BE CHANGED?

What must America do? Malkin's book was about the preoccupation of the day, homegrown vulnerabilities to terrorist attack. Her last chapter listed some reforms—ban temporary visitor visas from all countries where there are al Qaeda strongholds, end the investor, H-1B, and Visa Waiver programs, replace "catch-and-release" with detention and deportation, put in place temporary militarization of the borders, and "pull up the Welcome Mat" for illegal aliens. Finally, "no more amnesty programs, period." She did not engage the rest of the immigration reform agenda—do we continue to enlarge the immigrant population by one million or more legally and half that many illegally each year, selected (or self-selected) so as to produce a foreign-born population (according to a 2002 report) in which 30 percent lack a high school diploma (3.5 times the rate for natives), with higher poverty rates and welfare use than natives?

Invasion was widely reviewed. Malkin appeared on numerous talk shows and frequently as a columnist. No one called this attractive, articulate, forceful female with unmistakable Asian features any of the "ist" words. Reviewers said the book made a strong case for changes in law and administration, which was true, but first it was a demand for a prior change in attitude, phrased with unmistakable anger at a small, obstructionist number of her fellow Americans who had built and maintained the porous system. "The safety of our citizens must come before the comfort and convenience of foreigners," she wrote, echoing the Barbara Jordan theme that immigration must serve the national interest. Whatever else they had changed, a small group of Islamic terrorists had enlarged the immigration debate beyond the questions, always in dispute, as to whether it continued to forward the national economic, social, and environmental welfare. Mohamed Atta, Marwan Al Shehhi, Hani Hanjour, and the others had made an undisputed additional point, that immigration policy could be a matter of life and death to Americans who might be, one day, in a terrorist-targeted office complex, airport, or city.

What else needed to be changed in immigration policy? It would take time to refine the answers, as it would in the areas of defense, intelligence, and identification documents both for citizens and foreigners. The Center for Immigration Studies suggested a strategy of four immigration reform thrusts. (1) Improved visa application processing overseas. The Consular Corps of the State Department has a "culture of service rather than skepticism," and now "skepticism should become the guiding principle of visa issuance." The watch list of suspected enemies of the United States should be updated and made a high priority. (2) Control the border and ports of entry. A computerized, entry-exit tracking system with biometric identifiers and photos where possible, already recommended by the Jordan commission and actually mandated by Congress in 1996 but never implemented, must be put in place for all who enter the United States. The size of the Border Patrol should be tripled. (3) Interior enforcement must be made effective through a tracking system both for the (currently) one million foreign students and one million workers, through use of a national computerized system allowing employers to submit data on new hires, followed by greatly expanded workplace inspections. (4) "Give the INS the breathing room it needs. . . . The overall level of immigration must be reduced" to give "breathing space" to hard-pressed government agencies, and especially student, exchange, and temporary worker visas. "Fewer foreign nationals living in the United States" makes it "much easier to keep track of those allowed into the country. FAIR went further than these immigrant-aimed control measures, asking for one form of secure ID for all citizens as well as either a driver's license or state identity card anchored in at least one biometric identifier." Underlying these particular recommendations was the assumption not heard since the debates over IRCA in the 1980s, that illegal entering or remaining in the United States is a crime, and that the "customers" of the INS, Border Patrol, and Consular Corps are not foreigners, for whom entry into the United States is a privilege, but the people of the United States.

"Tighter policies, and tighter enforcement of them," editorialized the conservative movement's most respected journal, the *National Review*, signaling that a deep shakeup of political outlook might be underway. The editorial went on: "Most important, lower levels of immigration overall, to shrink the haystacks in which needles must be sought. . . . We have long known that high immigration and slack enforcement were economically null and culturally disruptive. Will we be serious now that we know they are deadly?"

To some, being serious meant not only that foreign nationals must be reliably identified and tracked, but Americans themselves, so they could move without intolerable delays through the air and ground transportation system. It is time, David Simcox wrote, to acknowledge that Americans already have a "National ID card" in the form of their state driver's license, recognize its faults and vulnerabilities, and build a reliable identity system by nationalizing the driver's license and the birth certificate "breeder documents" that underlie it. "National ID Card," the sinister phrase that had spooked Ronald Reagan's cabinet, was apparently entering an era of discussion and design, rather than ritual denunciation. Harvard law professor and celebrated television liberal Alan Dershowitz said in *Why Terrorism Works* (2002) that he now fully supported national identity cards and the deportation of those illegally in the country.

CHANGE AND THE FAILURE TO CHANGE
AFTER SEPTEMBER 11

In the two years following the attacks of September 11 much was changed in the policy and outlook of the federal government. Afghanistan and Iraq were invaded and their terrorist sanctuaries shattered, at least for a time, by the military forces of a small coalition led by the United States. In the area of homeland security, the Enhanced Border Security and Visa Entry Reform Act of 2002 was signed by the president on May 14, 2002, launching some limited measures that will take much time to accomplish and assess. INS databases were to be streamlined, federal law enforcement and intelligence agencies were told to share data on noncitizens with the INS, and travel and entry documents were to be made machine readable and tamper resistant. A new Homeland Security Department was legislated in late 2002, and under its authority on March 1, 2003, President Bush formally abolished the demoralized and dysfunctional INS, transferring most of its functions to the new Department of Homeland Security (DHS).

While this long-discussed breakup and reconstitution of the INS took place, policy was tightened for foreign students. The INS installed a new tracking system and required the cooperation of schools applying for students' visas. Evaluation of these changes will take years. More contentious, and more closely focused on the terrorist problem, were DOJ-INS efforts to develop appropriate policies toward immigrants from Muslim countries, especially the young males whose look-alikes had seized the aircrafts that brought down the World Trade Centers in New York. This required crossing the line into "profiling" of some sort, treating at least some Muslim immigrants differently from other immigrants, using nationality as a proxy for religion, which was a proxy for cultural conflicts now menacing U.S. national security.

How large was this new problem that immigration was bringing into America? An August 2002 report by the Center for Immigration Studies reported that Middle Easterners (defined as people from Pakistan, Bangladesh, Afghanistan, Turkey, the Levant, the Arabian Peninsula, and Arab North Africa) were one of the fastest-growing immigrant groups in America, their total size within the United States having increased by more than sevenfold since 1970, to about 1.5 million, of whom 150,000 were illegal. Most of the Middle Eastern flow had not been Muslim in 1970, but 75 percent of the population was Muslim by 2000. Another study found the total Muslim population in the United States to have grown to three million, perhaps three-quarters of them immigrants.

It was inconceivable that young Arab males from countries known to have al Qaeda strongholds would not be the objects of some sort of special restrictions and control measures, especially because so many were known to be already in the country illegally. Public support for an absolute ban on further Islamic immigration was easy to discover. A Chicago Council on Foreign Relations poll in 2002 found 79 percent of the public agreed that the United States should simply bar all immigration from Muslim countries. "No more ragheads," I heard a newspaper reader on a Washington, D.C. street announce to no one in particular.

The government took much more limited steps. Congress had required the installation of a reliable entry-exit tracking system. And DOJ-INS took several steps in this direction. The INS decided to fingerprint, photograph, and track all visitors from Iran, Iraq, Sudan, and Libya and all males aged sixteen to forty-five from several other Muslim countries, and in late 2002 launched a special registration program for noncitizens from twenty-five Arab and Muslim countries. Of the 82,000 men who came forward to register and be interviewed, 13,000 were found to be here illegally, facing deportation. Officials claimed that these new procedures for screening incoming visitors or immigrants, as well as registering and questioning those already here, led to the arrest of more than 800 deportable criminal aliens. Another result was large-scale self-deportation as Muslims who knew themselves to be in illegal status left for Canada, Europe, or the Middle East. Was the United States "constructing a long-term, Muslim-specific immigration policy?" asked Mark Krikorian. This would be "contrary to American principles and politically unsustainable," he thought, but it did seem that Muslim terrorism against the United States, Israel, and the West had begun to create a special place for Muslim males in American immigration law.

If attempting to enter legally, Middle Easterners faced stricter scrutiny than someone entering from Japan or South Africa. If here illegally, they might find the immigration authorities serious—for the first time—about locating them, investigating their political backgrounds, and either detaining or deporting them. The Bush administration in 2003 announced its new guidelines on "profiling." It would not rely on racial or ethnic stereotypes in law enforcement, except that it would when "there was specific information that such people are preparing to mount a terrorist attack," the Associated Press summarized the new guidelines. In such cases, law enforcement authorities might single out such people for increased scrutiny at the borders, or subject them to possible surveillance and detention. Thus, the government would not use "profiling" except when national security required it, in which case it would profile. Isolated spokesmen for Muslim groups and some civil libertarians complained of these new security measures, and the inspector general of the Justice Department issued a report in mid-2003 that was critical of the government's lengthy incarceration of some terrorist suspects on flimsy evidence. Law enforcement officials promised to make appropriate "structural changes," without agreeing that they had gone too far. A federal appeals court ruled (by a 2-1 margin) in June 2003 that the government did not need to disclose the names (thus compromising the integrity of its counterterrorist strategy) of the more than 700 people it had detained on national security grounds.

Elsewhere in government, change was hard to detect. The State Department apparently had not, in the two years after the attacks, gone very far at all. Journalist Joel Mowbray exposed the outrageous results of the "courtesy culture" toward foreign visa applicants cultivated by the State Department's Bureau of Consular Affairs (CA), especially the "Visa Express" program so popular in Saudi Arabia. With strong priorities on "service first, security last," CA's goal through Visa Express was to cut the number of interviews and push much visa issuance down to Saudi travel agents. September 11 came and fifteen of the nineteen terrorists were Saudis who had initially entered the United States with visas issued through the wide open door maintained by the State Department in that country. The department's inspector general and the General Accounting Office issued separate reports in 2002 finding that "a fundamental readjustment of [State] department leadership regarding visa issuance and denial has not taken place." Under such pressures—and only after much resistance—the State Department fired CA head Mary Ryan and ended Visa Express, to which Mowbray responded, "The problems plaguing visa issuance go much deeper than just Visa Express or Mary Ryan." He was right. A General Accounting Office official told a Congressional panel in 2003 that the State Department had recently revoked the visas of 240 foreigners because of terrorist connections, but because of "major gaps" between investigation and the notification of FBI and border agents, thirty of these nonetheless entered the United States and were still at large.

Change came hard at the political level as well. Within weeks of the attacks California Senator Diane Feinstein (D-Ca.) proposed a six-month moratorium on the student visa program under which some of the September 11 terrorists had entered and trained as pilots, but she had no support from the administration and loud university complaints forced her to retreat. The immigration reform lobbyist who had "assumed . . . some serious immigration reforms" would come quickly, admitted months later that she had been "wrong." House Immigration Subcommittee Chairman George Gekas (R-Pa.) offered a bill reducing immigration by 20 percent, ending the zany "diversity visa lottery," and strengthening the tracking of foreign visitors and students. The bill attracted a puny twenty-two sponsors and, along with Congressman Tancredo's bill to reduce legal immigration to 300,000, had no pulse. The customary pressures for even more lowering of immigration barriers remained visible and aggressive. The Bush White House almost succeeded in persuading legislators to reauthorize the lapsed Section 245(i) of the 1996 law that allowed certain illegal aliens to remain legally in the country and regularize their status without returning home and facing reentry procedures—in effect, another mini-amnesty for illegal immigrants. In mid-summer 2002, the House Republican leadership sent forward a draft bill for the new Homeland Security Department that specifically prohibited "a national identification card," by which they seemed to mean a suggested nationalization of the form and content of state drivers' licenses. To prove that the Democrats could pander to ethnic minorities with the best of them, House minority leader and presidential hopeful Richard Gephart in July told a La Raza conference of cheering Latinos that he would sponsor legislation to legalize all illegal immigrants who had been in the country for five years. In California and some other states, legislators in 2002 voted to pay the tuition of illegal aliens at state colleges and universities. The growth lobby and outlook seemed to have lost little strength on Capital Hill or in parts of the country, despite what had happened in New York and Washington in early September 2001. And the Mexican government found support in some U.S. towns and cities such as Los Angeles, Chicago, and Houston for its aggressive campaign to persuade local officials and banks to accept the Mexico-issued *matriculas consulares* as official identification inside the United States

As for the flows of immigration, September 11 seemed to have made no difference either in the volume of immigration or in the public officials' thinking about any linkage between legal-illegal immigration numbers and national security. In late 2002 the Border Patrol reported that the brief slow-down of immigration pressures at the Mexican border had quickly ended and apprehensions of illegal immigrants were back where they had been before the attacks. Slightly more than 1.5 million persons immigrated (legally and il-legally) in both 2001 and 2002, and the volume was increasing. In January 2000 the INS reported that 700,000 illegal aliens entered the United States annually in the 1990s, the number rising to 817,000 in 1998 and 1 million in 1999. Some of these (a total of 1.5 million during the 1990s) were given legal status and some self-deported, so the illegal population was growing by 500,000 a year. That meant that the INS's estimate of 5.8 million illegal im-migrants in residence in the United States in 2000, an estimate revised up-ward in 2001 to 7 million illegal immigrants, implied 8 to 9 million in 2002. California attracted and held 30 percent of the total, but in the 1990s North Carolina's illegal population increased 692 percent, Colorado's 364 percent, and Georgia's 570 percent. INS official estimates had always proved to be too low, but their later upward revisions were accelerating. With so many being given green cards and "forgiven" for having come illegally, the government appeared to be encouraging border jumping as a reasonable avenue to Amer-ican jobs and amnesty. The result was expansion of the illegal flow.

Thus it is much too early to measure and assess the changes that Septem-ber 11 may yet make in immigration matters. To mention only the main un-certainty, terrorists may—we are told, very likely will—alter the future by striking again. Indeed, one has, though the media coverage did not allow the public to perceive the porous borders dimensions of the event. Seventeen-year-old John Lee Malvo, an illegal immigrant from Jamaica in the company of American passport-forger John Allen Muhammad, terrorized the Wash-ington, D.C., area with a series of sniper attacks killing fourteen people in the fall of 2002. The public perceived the older American as the responsible rifleman (the evidence now is said to point to Malvo as the main gunman). If there are more deaths next time, in an organized assault by elements of an Islamic conspiracy easily violating U.S. immigration law, then the politics of immigration will change again. We may expect an even more insistent mes-sage: Public to government—Secure the borders.

But while the public sentiment clearly moves now in this direction, the volume of immigration remains as it was, while illegal entry was actually growing. From one perspective, the September 11 attacks caused a furor about U.S. immigration policy without altering it significantly. Yet from another, the global jihad of some Islamists against the West, and especially the core country of the West, has the potential to forever alter the immigration systems of the United States and the West, and the very image of the immigrant in the United States.

18

OUR MASS IMMIGRATION ERA: HOW CAN THIS BE?

How can this be? That was the fundamental question as posed by Yale law professor Peter Schuck in 1998, even before September 11. "How can this be, when recent immigration trends have presented restrictionists with explosive political ammunition," and at a time when "the vast majority of today's legal immigrants are nonwhite and non-English speaking," when they fuel and complicate the debate over bilingual education and affirmative action, and contribute to a "wider wage gap between high and low-skill workers, especially blacks," how can this be? Schuck left out the demographic impacts, such as immigration's singular role in canceling a trend aimed at national population stabilization and replacing it with a surge of growth that expanded the suburbs, clogged the highways, and moved the goal posts of an ecologically sustainable economy farther out of reach.

How indeed could such a costly policy complex so easily shrug off its reform critics for so long? They had supplied an increasingly scathing critical assessment, as well as a set of proposals for change—though here there were naturally differences in emphasis and details. All the reformers thought the Jordan commission generally headed in the right direction. First: summon the political will to install the identification technology required to make illegal immigration difficult and unattractive and enforce the laws. Second: lower the numbers and develop a sound rationale for the annual total, which should be adjustable periodically on recommendations from the executive branch and in light of evolving economic, demographic, and social trends. Revise the selection criteria for those admitted, chiefly by cutting back on family reunification through (at least) ending the preferences for siblings and shifting emphasis toward skills leading to economic success and social integration. On the asylum and refugee muddle, repeal the Cuban adjustment act and bring the asylum and refugee components along with all legal immigration under a real ceiling, in the common understanding of that term.

This accumulation in the 1990s of a thoughtful critique of existing policy and proposals for reform led to none of the changes reformers had urged. The September 11 attacks then transformed the political climate on border and immigration issues generally, as we have seen, driving from the field the Fox-Bush ideas of further opening on the southern border. But the impressive reality even after September 11 was the survival of the mass immigration regime. Two years after September 11, reformers lacked even a legislative vehicle to move their agenda into full debate.

Here we learn again that, in modern America, it is not enough, in shaping public policy, to publicize serious flaws in existing policy and arrive at a general agreement on promising improvements. Our political system often ignores flawed and failing public policy, even after policy has lost public support. Who can defend the subsidy for U.S. sugar growers, tax breaks for corporations moving their offices offshore, the duplicitous financing of Social Security? But these are not nation-changing issues. How can this policy paralysis have been sustained for over three decades on an issue central to the nation's size, demographic composition, identity, and culture?

And how can it hang on tenaciously even after the terrorists' attacks in 2001?

The answer will have many strands, when we one day more fully understand it, and deserves book-length treatment, more than once.

Among the answers we will not, I think, find that a compelling rationale for the regime introduced in the 1960s has checkmated the critics. The architects and later expanders of the leaky system of post-1965 never defended or justified million-plus annual immigration flows, with these new Americans chosen primarily by nepotism and augmented by low-skilled illegal workers that the government allowed to enter the workforce and society. The lawmakers of 1965 had aimed their arguments and intellectual energy at the odious system of the 1920s and made no case for doubling and then tripling immigration, let alone permitting a steady illegal flow.

Once both of these results nonetheless followed from the reforms of 1965 and subsequent expansions, a defense of both has been thrown together, but it has increasingly become an intellectual embarrassment. Claims in the

1970s and 1980s that the immigration that our system permits adds up to an economic plus for the United States have collapsed under calculations of costs and benefits made in the 1990s. Strictly economic costs appear to exceed benefits, especially as the economic quality of incoming immigrants continues to decline as it has since the 1970s. The cost side would be far larger if economists' cost-benefit analyses included the full social wage. None of the leading economic studies of the 1990s, for example, attempted to add to the cost ledger the unreimbursed medical expenditures of America's hospitals and local governments. The *New York Times* reported in 2002 estimates that hospitals were writing off $2 billion a year in unpaid bills of illegal immigrants. And not even a rough estimate was offered by anyone of the costs to society of infectious diseases such as tuberculosis and leprosy that were brought to America by Third World immigrants.

But even if costs and benefits to the entire society as economists measure them were to be seen as canceling each other, the burden of the costs are not equitably distributed. They are disproportionately borne by low-income and minority Americans, while the benefits go to employers who prefer foreign to American labor, a difficult social trade-off to defend.

Beyond economics, Expansionists' assurances that assimilation of foreigners proceeds with its usual historical power are at least matched by evidence of persistent and perhaps widening social division and segmentation. The "diversity" benefit seemed to trump all concerns about "disuniting" in the 1980s and well into the 1990s, but the discussion of this complex calculation of immigration's impacts has shifted away from complacency and toward concern, a shift much reinforced by the attacks on September 11. At the end of the twentieth century, in sharp contrast to the years before and after World War I, there was little debate over immigration's connection to U.S. foreign policy. Constant replenishing of ethnic groups and growing domestic populations of new groups such as Muslims, sharpens ethnic voices. The only recent book on this subject, Alexander DeConde's *Ethnicity, Race, and American Foreign Policy: A History* (1992), takes no strong stand on whether immigration-refreshed ethnic communities harmfully complicate or usefully democratize and globalize the formation and implementation of U.S. foreign policy. The topic deserves greater attention, and will receive it, especially as growing Muslim immigrant populations in Europe and the United States bring into play their passionate anti-Israel animus.

No argument at all has been made that the United States needs to expand its population endlessly. The closest thing to a rationale for population-growth-inducing immigration has been the very recent sprinkle of claims that our low-fertility and aging population (and Europe's, even more urgently) already justify an immigrant infusion to provide the worker-base to pay for our pensions. This idea itself is a sort of reform suggestion, requiring system redesign, and even this sign of a pulse rate among proponents of large or even larger immigration has been met by counter-arguments that the immigration "solution" to the alleged "birth dearth" is a temporary fix, not without substantial costs, and unnecessary in view of other tools available to cope with the anticipated demographic changes.

As for the flagrant violation of American law represented by large and growing illegal entry and residence, the arguments against reform have been, shall we say, imaginative. We should not do anything about "undocumented persons" in the country, it is said, because nations should not make laws closing their borders to anyone in need of a better way of life, and if they do have such laws they are illegitimate and should be ignored as violating international human rights. This argument is offered to counter the foundational assumption that nations have a right to control their borders and to decide who lives within them, entry outside American law was illegal, and things illegal should be stopped. It was actually presented seriously to congressional committees during the IRCA debates, but has since ebbed away from public policy forums and retreated to fringe conferences among academic philosophers or human rights groups.

Other serious objections to illegal immigration have not been met with any substantial rebuttal. Our porous borders (Europe shares this condition) invite, indeed ensure the formation of international criminal networks designed to smuggle human capital into the affluent West, because we have made a policy decision that this will not be all that difficult or risky. Some of these criminal smugglers conveying their clients and cargo to the United States seem to be regarded as humanitarian agents, such as the Mexican "coyotes" guiding across the Southwestern and now also the Canadian borders plucky workers eager to wash American dishes and do the stoop agricultural labor. But the human smuggling our system invites inevitably has developed a very ugly side. The CIA in 2000 issued a report estimating that fifty thousand women and children from Asia, Latin America, and Eastern Europe were smuggled into the United States annually to serve as prostitutes, servants, or abused and captive laborers.

Many other components of the current U.S. legal-immigration policy system that have come under criticism are also not well defended. It has long troubled some consciences that aspects of U.S. immigration policy unconscionably foster a brain drain from poorer nations. Why should wealthy America, so (justifiably) concerned about the poorer nations in the Third World that it sends developmental aid and frets about what else it should do, allow itself to have an immigration policy that lures away from impoverished countries such as India, the Philippines, and Iran their precious few professionals in science, technology, and medicine? This issue worried liberals in the 1970s, when Senator (and Democratic presidential candidate in 1984) Walter Mondale noticed in 1967 that sixteen Nigerian doctors were practicing in the United States while Nigeria desperately needed their services, and he and others urged "forms of immigration restriction" to prevent American from draining such talent. No defense of the brain drain was offered then or later, and the term is rarely heard.

These were some of the much-criticized elements of the American immigration system that were lightly defended in the 1970s and 1980s, and by the 1990s simply remained in place without defense. The arguments for mass immigration of the sort that had fastened itself upon the United States by the hinge of the centuries were a few tottering and sentimental clichés. Western "borders were beyond control" and huge inflows were inevitable, was the best defense of the status quo offered by Columbia University economist (and immigrant from India) Jagdish Bhaqwati. "Foreigners bring pluck and grit . . . that nourish the way we live," wrote journalist Tamar Jacoby, recycling the old suspicion that America was running out of pluck and grit and required continuous transfusions. "Immigrants . . . tend to bring with them a sense of optimism, a strong family and religious tradition, and a willingness to work hard," wrote Diane Ravitch in another argument that Americans could not run their own society without overseas infusions of lots of stuff, including pluck and grit.

At the hinge of the twentieth and twenty-first centuries, then, the defenders of the immigration status quo were in firm, even unchallenged political control. But this was not because their intellectual defenses were formidable. In many cases, for example, the contribution of large-scale immigration to undesirable population growth, there was essentially no counterargument at all. Most of the Expansionist rationale has long taken the form of a cluster of sentimental slogans meant to shield any immigration pattern from criticism by associating unfettered immigration with America's very meaning and historic mission. When less or a different configuration of American immigration is suggested, protective phrases begin to be launched like the balloons over London during the Battle of Britain. Immigration is the meaning of America. America needs constant replenishment of fresh blood. Immigration diversifies America, which always means enrichment. Americans won't do their own menial labor any longer and so immigrants are essential. "If we ever closed the door to new Americans our leadership in the world would soon be lost." (Ronald Reagan uttered these vacuous words as he left office in 1989).

Possibly—no one can be sure—these slogans exert some small influence on the public. This influence must be slight, because the public, when polled, year in and year out with only minor fluctuations, does not believe that the immigration status quo is justified by these broad sentiments of the Expansionists. Writing in the economic euphoria and tight labor markets of 1998, Yale's Peter Schuck, in his "How Can This Be?" article, argued that while "most people want to admit fewer immigrants, oppose illegal immigration," and don't want immigrants going on welfare, they "will tolerate relatively high levels of immigration, and even increases in certain categories, as long as they are satisfied that newcomers pay their own way, don't get special breaks, and obey the law." The "policies enacted by the Congress in 1996 and 1997 are largely consistent with this," he thought, and the public and lawmakers are now [1998] content with "the basic American consensus on immigration," the status quo of the late 1990s. Schuck's statement of what the public does not like about the immigration system is consistent with the polls. But he wrote too soon, before it was clear that Congress had no intention in 1996–1997 of doing anything to reduce illegal immigration or immigrant use of certain social services. It was too early to declare "consensus," as what the public wanted changed remained the same—and also, presumably, the public's basic restrictionist tilt. The puny justifications of the large streams of immigration permitted by American policy are persuasive enough for the 20 to 30 percent in public opinion polls who for forty years have registered with pollsters satisfaction with what they understand the immigration status quo to be. They have made no dent in the large majorities expressing various degrees of dissatisfaction and indignation. And after September 11, the system's defenders retreated from argument altogether, falling back on other political resources.

So the search for an explanation for the leaky immigration system's ability to survive repeated reform efforts while persistently expanding the numbers, legal and illegal, must reach deeper than the power of the arguments and rhetoric of the Expansionists.

We might begin with a familiar characteristic of American political life, James Q. Wilson's concept of "client politics." When a relatively small number of people who stand to benefit organize with energy around an issue, while those who pay the costs are a diffuse, large majority who may be disgruntled but whose main concerns are elsewhere.

This fits immigration politics admirably. The coalition that came together in the 1960s to establish, and in the 1980s and 1990s to defend and enlarge the Expansionist policy, as University of Texas political scientist

Gary Freeman wrote, "was composed of organizations representing those having a direct interest in outcomes—employers [of low-wage foreign labor], immigrant-rights organizations, the churches, and immigration lawyers." It was a formidable lineup, and a vital part of it, a trio of Hispanic lobbying organizations (the well-established LULAC, and the newer, nonmembership MALDEF, and the National Council of La Raza), had been lavishly funded (approximately $50 million from 1968 to 1999) into impressive strength (especially the latter two) by the Ford Foundation beginning in the late 1960s. This coalition—really, an industry organized around human traffic into the United States—was augmented in the 1990s by an influential National Association of Manufacturers–led alliance of high-technology corporations eager to import foreign computer professionals in a tight job market. The National Immigration Forum based in Washington served as a coordinator for these efforts through the Expansionist policy successes in 1986, 1990, and 1995–1996.

On the other side is the diffuse, large majority in heavily immigrant-impacted states and communities who claim to experience harm to their interests as citizens. Their primary concerns, however, are elsewhere, and they do not know much about the issue and are virtually unorganized. In Freeman's words, the restrictionist reformers are aligned with the public's instincts and real interests, but "simply lack a serious, organized constituency." FAIR in the 1980s and 1990s mustered fifty thousand members nationwide, not enough to frighten any member of Congress (though the group had a hand in the defeat of Expansionist Michigan Senator Spencer Abraham in 2000), most of whom are in safe districts at any rate. A handful of other, smaller restrictionist groups also worked to influence national policy—Negative Population Growth, Project USA, and Numbers USA, the increasingly effective small lobbying operation established on Capital Hill by writer Roy Beck. Through the 1990s, small immigration reform groups sprouted in California, Florida, Oregon, Illinois, New York, Georgia, and North Carolina. By the end of the century one could call this a national social movement that occasionally made itself heard in the media and to some degree at the lobbying level. But in size and financial resources these restrictionist forces were vastly outmatched by the Expansionists.

The large segments of society most directly injured by massive low-skilled immigration—working-class blacks and Latinos, recent immigrants at the bottom of the economic ladder, and low-skilled whites—were politically weak and found no one to articulate their concerns. LULAC from its founding in the 1920s had opposed large-scale Mexican immigration as well as guest-worker programs, but in the late 1960s began to move away from that position toward a more nationalist, ethnic-solidarity stance advocated by the newer MALDEF and La Raza.

The leadership of organized labor had by the 1980s moved away from their historic restrictionist positions; in the maneuvers over the immigration reforms of 1996 they had actually joined the pro-immigration lobby and by 1999 were calling for the repeal of IRCA. Union leaders were responding to unionized government bureaucrats and teachers, whose constituency was expanded by the growing numbers of illegal immigrants, and the leadership had also become convinced that they could not organize the new service-sector workers, many of them illegal, if employers held the threat of disclosure of their status over them. Pro-union historian Vernon Briggs condemned this as "a betrayal of the legacy of the past," and it was unarguably a major realignment of political forces on immigration. Another such shift had come in the late 1970s when black political leadership was persuaded by Hispanics to shun the immigration issue in order to hold "the civil rights coalition" together.

The "patriotic societies" so vigorously behind restriction at the turn of the century had become strangely quiet on this and most public issues after mid-century. Their history of arid anticommunism during the decades after World War II had greatly reduced their social and political influence, and for reasons not clear, groups like the American Legion took little part in the post-1960s immigration debates. The environmental movement's leadership, as we have seen in the case of the Sierra Club, made a conscious decision that their opposition to American population growth should not be allowed to involve them in immigration policy disputes, despite the connection between the two. They feared being called the bad names associated with discussion of immigration restriction and would not rally their organizations to that prerequisite for population-stabilization.

As for the public at large, it was hard to mobilize around this issue. Taxpayers did not know immigration's cost in social services, as the economic research was too complex and the media (apart from talk radio hosts) uninterested in the topic. And while polls found Americans in general opposed to the high volumes of immigration, when asked for details they were uninformed on immigration, unable to comprehend demographic facts or trends, restrictionists without deep convictions or knowledge. On this as on many issues affecting public and national interests, the American political system responded to organized groups with deep pockets and a strong direct stake. This left immigration policymaking to distant, obscure legislative maneuvering in Washington, where special-interest lobbying invariably produced Expansionist outcomes at odds with the national interest or prevailing sentiment.

But the dynamics of "client politics," whereby small, intense, and well-financed interest groups joined in a growth lobby repeatedly outmaneuver a "diffuse majority," is an important but only partial explanation of the four-decade dominance of Expansionists over those who wanted the numbers and illegality curbed. The issue was somehow kept out of electoral politics where the public could register opinions. As we have seen, this nation-changing issue was routinely ignored in presidential primaries and general elections, by both parties, and this pattern held all the way down the electoral pyramid, from Washington to Peoria.

This is not to argue that immigration was never spoken of in public life. American politicians have been pandering to ethnic groups since the founding, and from presidents down to mayors, they overlook few opportunities to praise immigration and immigrants in general at anniversaries of the arrival of the Statue of Liberty or Columbus, at St. Patrick's Day celebrations, or at mass-naturalization occasions. What was sternly frowned on was any criticism of immigrants, which universally became also a near ban on criticism of the workings and results of the immigration policy of the United States. Large-scale and growing flaunting of immigration law by illegal entrants pushed the issue onto the national agenda in the 1980s, and a regional and more angry criticism again broke into public life in the 1990s in California and in other places heavily impacted by illegal workers.

But in retrospect we can see that the issue was generally kept under tight control, so that it could not enter, let alone realign, electoral politics. The media, politicians, academic and religious spokespersons—the national elites that shape opinion—had decided in the 1960s that there was only one legitimate position on immigration. One had to be for the mass-immigration era and see in it only wonderful benefits. Katherine Betts called these elites "the new class" in her insightful book about Australian immigration politics *Ideology and Immigration* (1988) and in a lengthy tour of the United States in 1991 found exactly the same class and ideological alignments here. Elements of this educated, cosmopolitan class in both countries (and in Europe) benefited from cheap domestic and tourist-industry labor. But Betts pointed out that the key to these elites' position on immigration was its use as a marker of social status. Immigration was "not a topic but a symbol." Hostile condemnation of any criticism of current immigration flows "was a shorthand way of demonstrating commitment to anti-racism and internationalism," and of distinguishing we cosmopolitan internationalist "better people" from average folk who were known to be narrow nationalists tainted with racist views and a "bigoted preference for cultural homogeneity."

To this new class, raising questions about immigration's costs and consequences, as currently channeled into the country by federal policy, was taboo and would be punished by being associated with the extremists of the far right in the American and European past. Any critic who wanted less legal immigration or serious efforts to curb the illegal flows was met with an arsenal of phrases lifted out of the shelf of written histories produced by historians in the second half of the century. The critics were "anti-immigrant" and "nativists" and "xenophobes" because they were at bottom "racists," motivated not by whatever they said were their objectives but by "fear" of change or the Other or the future, and beneath that motivated by "hate."

In this atmosphere, politicians would not make immigration reform an electoral issue, but treated it as the third rail of American politics. To take the lead in trying to craft legislation to curb illegal immigration was permitted in the mid-1980s, but it was probably necessary that a national commission headed by a distinguished Roman Catholic educator call for it and that Alan Simpson step forward to lead—popular in his own state, respected, well able to defend himself verbally. But for most people in public life, why raise your visibility by association with an effort to reform the whole runaway system? Why risk being identified by elite opinion as a divisive figure at best, a Nazi racist at worst? Add to this the worry that ethnic voting blocs, or at least their leaders, would inevitably be offended by talk of an immigration problem, and politicians of all parties took a pass on immigration as an electoral issue. Alan Simpson, Pete Wilson, Barbara Jordan, Richard Lamm, and Tom Tancredo of Colorado at different times took the risk of identification as immigration reformers. The list is short (and bipartisan, interestingly), which tells a story of high-perceived jeopardy.

Thus for a politician, not only were there possibly votes to be lost in being a critic of runaway immigration. There seemed none to be won. There had never developed, anywhere in the country in any election for four decades, a restrictionist voting bloc, probably because no politician had tried to build one. In all the years since Expansionist policymakers began enlarging immigration in the 1960s the only national politician to lose an election because his support for mass immigration had become a negative issue with his constituents was arguably Senator Spencer Abraham (R-Mich.), and a coalition of out-of-state immigration reform organizations rather than his opponent had exposed his leading role as an Expansionist. And there were other issues in that 2000 race. The only politician ever to win a race because of a pledge to reduce immigration was California's Republican governor Pete Wilson. He made curbing illegal immigration a winning issue in his 1994 reelection campaign, attacking not illegal immigrants themselves but Congress for allowing a porous border and did so in a state in economic recession and the destination of the most immigrants headed to America, legal and otherwise.

Had Wilson fundamentally altered American politics, by showing the way for immigration reform to become a frequent political winner, after decades in which it been universally shunned as nothing but trouble? This seemed a distinct possibility after Wilson's overwhelming reelection, and the California governor made a short run for the presidency in 1996, but withdrew when a throat ailment made him ineffective. Another ambitious Republican, political journalist Patrick Buchanan, made a speech at the 1996 Republican convention making it clear that he would add immigration restriction to his own nationalist road toward the presidency. His road was short. The exceptions ended with Wilson, proving the rule. The Expansionists counterattacked to drive the immigration issue back out of electoral politics again. Buchanan, who had never been elected to anything, was pushed out of the Republican Party by its national leadership and into the dying Reform Party ineptly incubated in 1992 by Ross Perot. Republican fortunes sagged in California after Wilson, and both party leaders and punditry declared that it was because the GOP had been tainted with the "harsh" and "divisive" themes of immigrant bashing. When Alan Simpson proposed legislation in 1996 to authorize pilot projects testing ways to verify employment eligibility, the Expansionist coalition distributed peel-off bar-code tattoos on Capitol Hill to associate Simpson's proposal with Hitler's treatment of the Jews, indeed with the Holocaust itself. Not even the popular senator from Wyoming was immune from Nazi-by-association tactics. Hannah Arendt once pointed out that the dictators of the 1930s and 1940s controlled their critics by "turning any statement of fact into a question of motive."

In Wilson's political eclipse and Buchanan's forced departure, a century-old tradition in the Republican Party seemed ended. From Henry Cabot Lodge and Theodore Roosevelt to Simpson and Wilson, the GOP had regularly produced leaders who knew how to add to their winning formula the necessity to provide the country with strong immigration controls. By the last election in the century, both parties had the same leave-the-broken-system-alone stance.

This outcome has the look and feel of inevitability, but students of history should have a keen interest in what almost happened, in turning points and roads not taken. Immigration reform has appeared to lack a political leader who could mobilize the large reservoir of public resentments against mass immigration with a positive vision of the benefits of a small immigration future and without anti-immigrant overtones. Some thought Pete Wilson had these qualifications, but he left the national stage in 1996. He almost had a replacement from the liberal side. A Democrat of national stature, a proven record of winning reelection, and a matchless ability to present immigration reform (and environmental protection and social security reform) in positive ways, however, almost joined the U.S. Senate in 1992. This was Richard Lamm, three-time governor of Colorado (1975–1987), committed environmentalist, author of books on the West, and a critic of mass immigration, who ran that year for a vacant Colorado Senate seat against Congressman Ben Nighthorse Campbell. Campbell, a self-made American Indian who rode Harley-Davidson motorcycles with his pigtail streaming behind, was sent to the Senate by Colorado voters, justifiably proud to send the first indigenous person to that body. Lamm, who had never been defeated in his Colorado political career, would have beaten anyone else. But The Lord sent Colorado voters an Indian, and they voted affirmative action. Campbell's record has not been noteworthy, and he defected to the Republicans later on. But the immigration Expansionists had used him to dodge a bullet. They did not have to contend thereafter with an articulate Senator Richard Lamm, who had the gifts to clarify the immigration connection to other issues, and give the immigration reform argument an appealing, pro-small immigration expression.

The immigration issue made no appearance in the 2000 elections, and novelist and ardent environmentalist Edward Abbey had already written a terse explanation: With mass immigration, "the conservatives get their cheap labor and the liberals get their cheap cause." When in 2001 presidents Fox and Bush began to talk of their deal to essentially remove the Mexico-U.S. border, no politician sensed in this a chance to build a voting base in opposition.

This near-total suppression of the immigration reform idea in electoral politics was not matched in the realm of general public discussion and ideas, even before September 11. There was open criticism of the stifling of discussion by invidious labeling. Barbara Jordan spoke for the Commission on Immigration Reform in 1994 when she declared that "we disagree with those who would label efforts to control immigration as being inherently anti-immigrant. Rather, it is both a right and a responsibility of a democratic society to manage immigration so that it serves the national interest." The restriction-is-nativism taboo also came under attack from a few scholars. Immigration reformers may not be numerous enough to constitute "a movement," wrote historian David Bennett, but "they certainly do not represent a return to the nativist traditions of the past," a tradition "all but finished" by the end of World War II. "The immigration debate was being conducted at a higher level than ever before," wrote Yale's Peter Schuck. He found "few traces of racism or nativism," but rather "principled restrictionism," which "contributes significantly to the overt debate." "What do you make of the nativists?" a journalist asked historian John Higham as the grassroots immigration reformers in California and elsewhere gained press coverage in the 1990s. "I don't know any nativists," Higham replied, in a subtle rebuke for such tortured and misleading, as well as argument-closing, labels. American intellectual life seemed a bit healthier at the end of the century, at least judged by the tolerance of two rather than just one point of view on this historically emotional topic. But on immigration the nation's political life was embalmed by intimidating slogans and epithets.

A key to the successful stifling of immigration reform is "elite disconnect," a phrase entering American discourse (see Thomas and Mary Edsall, *Chain Reaction* [1991], and E. J. Dionne, *Why Americans Hate Politics* [1991]), who draw attention to the remarkable gap that has opened between America's new class, in Betts's term, the liberal-cosmopolitan elites in government, media and the universities, and the Democratic Party's working and middle-class base. But the disconnect is bipartisan. One of those elite liberal Democrats, prolific author, Harvard professor, and Bill Clinton's secretary of labor (1993–1997) Robert Reich, correctly pointed out that the Republicans who ran America's corporations are also in the disconnected elite, which he designated not by political party or ideology but by education and social class. One-fifth of the American people were in the top tier of well-educated "symbolic analysts" whom globalization was making rich, as well as entirely cosmopolitan and transnational in their outlook. He feared they were withdrawing into gated communities and private clubs and schools, "seceding" from the four-fifths of "routine producers" whose incomes were under mounting pressure from a global workforce. Immigration, Reich pointed out in *The Work of Nations* (1991), brought that global labor competition home to America. This was good for the top fifth, the elites who needed nannies, gardeners, and cheap employees for the really dirty work that would have to be upgraded in pay and safety if only Americans were in the labor pool. But it was costly to the rest of America, who shouldered the labor-market competition and the taxes for expanded social services. Reich predicted that immigration "will be a point of growing contention" between the disconnecting elite who make the policies and those at the middle and bottom.

There was confirmation of this disconnect in a national poll of the public and a sample of four hundred opinion leaders taken by the Chicago Council of Foreign Relations after the September 11 attacks. "The gap between the opinions of the American people on immigration and those of their leaders is enormous," reported the Center for Immigration Studies in an analysis of the Chicago poll. Sixty percent of the public regard the present level of immigration to be "a critical threat to the vital interests of the United States," but only fourteen percent of the leadership did. On no other foreign policy-related issue was the gap wider, and it had widened since 1998, when the percentages on the "critical threat" question were fifty-five versus eighteen, respectively. In ranking large public problems in the foreign policy area, the public ranked illegal immigration sixth, opinion leaders twenty-sixth. Here the theory of elite disconnect finds grounding in data. And while opinion leaders ought perhaps to be written opinion "leaders," the fact that the latter made policy strongly against the grain of public opinion, at least in some areas for long periods of time, was one explanation for the shape of immigration policy.

Another explanation for this remarkably long run of a dysfunctional immigration system may be found in the history books. An open immigration era inherited from the birth of the republic was brought to an end early in this century after restrictionist reformers had struggled for decades to push such a large change through the American political system. As we have seen, the results were broadly favorable and the system popular. But beginning in the 1950s historians and other intellectuals who shape the national understanding and discourse mounted a severe attack on the restrictionist enterprise. Caught up in the Civil Rights Movement and rightly determined to indict racism not only in contemporary Mississippi and South Boston but down the full sweep and side eddies of the American past, some of them found ripe targets among the immigration restrictionists. Historians, then journalists and film makers and others, pulled into contemporary view some of the working assumptions and language of some of the immigration reformers, found racism and ethnic stereotyping there, and consigned that complex social movement for restriction of immigration to the bad, far-rightist tradition in America history. There are no U.S. history textbooks at the college level today that do not reflect this interpretation, not as a part of what we should know about this aspect of our past but as the deplorable essence of it.

As a result, when the new restrictionism arose in the 1970s the debate it wished to have over the real impacts of mass immigration was choked off, and policy options greatly narrowed, by labeling the reformers nativists and worse. It made no dent in this habit that prominent historians of American immigration like John Higham and David Bennett, who knew very well what nativism was and had frequently condemned it, pointed out that nativism had disappeared from America by mid-century and that questions about mass immigration should be treated as legitimate concerns for inquiry and policy redirection. But the media liked the drama conveyed by the immigration Expansionists' accusatory labels, and portrayed the new restrictionism as an eruption within America of the nativist xenophobic anti-immigrant impulse that historians had indeed found, and some of them often exaggerated, in the complex intellectual and emotional currents of a century ago. The alignment of the restrictionist project with protection of American workers' earnings and autonomy, with the ideals of civic republicanism and the rule of law, with environmental and resource conservation were all overlooked or dismissed as rationalizations disguising antiforeign prejudice. An essential national project in this era of human population surge—devising controls over the nation's demographic destiny—has been caricatured and stifled.

Finally, some share of the responsibility for the astounding persistence of bad public policy could be said to belong to the restrictionists themselves. They are against large-scale legal and any scale of illegal immigration and have communicated the manifold reasons. But they could be charged with inadequately communicating what they are for.

Here I do not have in mind the spelling out of the mechanics of policy improvement. A considerable amount of thought has gone into reforms of the machinery, as we have seen, and the core elements of a better system have emerged. A substantial curbing of illegal immigration should come through a system of identification and tracking of immigrants and visa holders; a national identification system for Americans, enhancing travel and identity security; and substantial penalties for conviction of illegal entry, including a bar against future U.S. citizenship. On the legal side, lower numbers, tailored to national population goals, achieved by real ceilings on both immigrant (including in the ceiling asylum seekers) and nonimmigrant visas; a general shift toward a skills-based system initiated by repeal of preferences for brothers and sisters; and overall selection by criteria matched to the nation's needs rather than foreigners' desires to move kinfolk to the United States.

These and other reforms have been vetted many times, and a good basket of them is the several reports of the Jordan commission. They aim us at a small-immigration future, and the terrorist threat inevitably gives the idea of such reforms a new urgency. It also gives them a defensive cast.

What is far less clear is the vision of the American (and global) future in which to anchor, emotionally as well as intellectually, the rationale for a return to a small-immigration regime in the United States and other societies. In the short run, this may not be necessary. Smaller, more manageable numbers, screened and selected from the point of view of national priorities, may possibly move through the American political system in response to national security concerns after September 11—especially if (when) hostile foreigners cross our borders again to bring more violence. But what are the intellectual and moral resources and arguments for going beyond national self-defense and connecting a small-immigration policy to a vision of a sustainable society?

Some have said that the immigration reform movement shares a shortcoming with its sibling, the environmental movement—that it has been strong on what it opposes and thin on where it would take us. The wide-minded economist Kenneth Boulding was asked as he came out of a lecture on overpopulation by the biologist Garrett Hardin what Boulding thought of the event. He replied that Hardin gave an impressive sermon on hellfire, but one came out of the church wishing more had been said about heaven.

That critical observation certainly seems apt for the immigration reform movement of a century ago. When runaway immigration was finally curbed in the aftermath of World War I, the emphasis of the reformers, in justifying this historic change in national policy, was heavily on the harms to be minimized—to American workers' wages and standards, to national cohesion, to republican political institutions, and even, to some, to national biological quality. The closest thing to a positive national goal that also pointed the country down the new restrictionist road was, perhaps, President Calvin Coolidge's terse phrase, "America must be kept American." This is sometimes quoted as a good example of the vacuous thought of the ruling class in the 1920s, but the few words in front of this phrase gave it the semblance of a positive argument, however sparse: "American institutions rest solely on good citizenship. They were created by people who had a background of self-government. New arrivals should be limited by our capacity to absorb them into the ranks of good citizenship." Coolidge himself endorsed a reformed immigration system in order to prevent many harms that unregulated immigration had permitted, but in his remarks in 1923 he also seems to have been attempting to link the new system to a larger, positive national goal. We were still making new Americans here, and this fine objective required a more moderate pace.

This sufficed as a positive policy goal for the 1920s and for several decades after. Perhaps one of the reasons that Americans have not reined in the leaky system of post-1965, in addition to those mentioned, is that while the cumulating negatives coming with mass immigration have been counted and publicized there has not emerged, or at least has not been successfully communicated to the public (and to the governing elites), a positive as well as a defensive rationale for what a reformed, small-immigration policy will lead us toward.

Nearly three decades ago, Dr. John Tanton, who would go on to organize FAIR and a cluster of other educational and lobbying immigration reform (and environmental) groups, submitted his essay, "International Migration," to the 1975 Mitchell Prize contest. It gained some brief attention when it won third place and was subsequently published in *The Ecologist*. The central argument was that, given global population growth, mass migrations "will have to be stringently controlled, or no region will be able to stabilize ahead of another. . . . A more hopeful scenario calls for some regions stabilizing at an early date and then helping others to do so." Then, "in the world of a stationary state" for all societies, "international migration could become free and unfettered, because there would be little incentive to move. Contentment with conditions at home . . . would serve to keep most people in place." This was a long-range vision indeed, if short on details of this future America "in balance with . . . [the] environment," except that Americans in the post-migration epoch would do their own menial labor and be the better for it. Kenneth Boulding might say that the immigration reform movement, necessarily engaged in a critique of the status quo and its implications, would have been wise to pay more attention to constructing plausible scenarios of an American society, and the larger world, after the growth binge was over.

19

DOGMAS OF THE PAST

The dogmas of the quiet past, are inadequate to the stormy present. . . .
We must disenthrall ourselves, and then we shall save our country.

—Abraham Lincoln, Annual Message to Congress, December 1, 1862

The twenty-first century arrived for Americans with a terrorist shock that altered some aspects of national outlook and policy. As we have seen, however, the impact of these events on immigration policy was initially modest, and a disappointment to those who hoped that the starkly obvious connection between porous borders and national security vulnerability would bring a broad reconsideration and reform.

History aids in our understanding of this tenacious resistance to reform of a four-decade regime of large-scale immigration, roughly half of it illegal. The regime itself—and now its current persistence despite internal attacks by foreigners gaining entrance and residence by gaming the system—are products of history.

This book has offered an account of the immigration issue beginning with American nation-builders, and it is time to reprise it. The founding Americans saw themselves as colonists, not immigrants, and the founders of the American nation were mostly residents. They expected immigration, and the official stance was one of welcome. But they were also ambivalent about immigration, in recognition of the teaching of experience that it always brings costs and risks with the benefits. Colonists and nation-builders accepted for two centuries a modest inflow from Europe and Africa, and said many positive things about this refreshing infusion, as well as uttering some cautionary thoughts and grumblings. The American population expanded mostly through domestic increase; immigration made a smaller but important contribution.

Then the young nation, after several decades without a national immigration policy, experienced the arrival of the Great Wave (when the Second Great Wave arrived in the 1960s, it was possible to rename this the first one) after the Civil War. These incoming numbers from new places forced a debate over a new idea—immigration restriction. The beginnings of that system were legislated in the 1880s, but it was not completed until the 1920s. The principles on which it was grounded were a mixture of those of which we contemporaries still tend to approve (firm national control over a primal nation-changing force, immigration, and protection of the wage levels and work conditions of the American worker) and those that now to some seem odious and unenlightened where not racist (a bias in favor of some nationalities and against others, as well as a conception of America as fundamentally and permanently white European in derivation). For four decades this system, aided by a worldwide economic depression and World War II, brought the mass immigration of the First Great Wave to an end, and provided a period of negligible immigration. The economic and social benefits of this era of restriction were considerable, giving the U.S. a half-century modern tradition of small immigration that was popular and well-aligned with national needs as the public perceived them.

The principle of selection built into the system, however, came under intense criticism as the civil rights era arrived after World War II, with its invaluable suspicion of racial categorization. Immigration policy was fundamentally altered in 1965, as part of the liberal reforms of the Great Society. Here there was more than a historic policy change, but also evidence of a change in the national memory, itself an independent and potent new force. The historic policy change was the ending, after 1965, of the favorable quotas for Europe, replaced by a radical shift in source countries toward Latin America and Asia, and a fourfold increase in the numbers. The memory change came through the brilliant efforts of writers, publicists, and historians, who, in order to undermine and destroy the national origins quota system of the 1920s, created powerful myths—America is "a nation of immigrants"; the Statue of Liberty's torch expresses the core meaning of America as a land of permanent asylum; and immigration restriction in the American past is a shameful expression of a form of bigotry called nativism. In and after the 1960s, this mythistory tilted America's educated elites against the very idea of restricting immigration, even as it became an indispensable policy tool.

Combine this with interest group power mobilized to sustain flows of cheap labor and ethnic kin, and the United States deployed an expansionist immigration policy against all criticism, as the Second Great Wave of migratory peoples began to arrive in the West, set in motion by the culminating century of the world population spike and against a dismal background of uneven global development and the spoliation of ecological systems. For decades behind and ahead, and with accelerating momentum, the world's increasingly mobile poor along with some of the cosmopolitan elites from developing countries press toward the richest places they can see on television. To manage this transforming influx of peoples, the United States minds the gates with an inept policy system that is a combination of the anachronistic and the unintended.

There are many signs that the Second Great Wave, which can in retrospect be discerned in the American Southwest in the 1920s and began in earnest in the 1960s, will not be controlled as was the first. Immigration momentum has been allowed to build up over decades, and mainstream politicians seem both intellectually and politically paralyzed. Sociologist Douglas Massey seemed to summarize the situation in 1999, when he declared that the United States was now "a country of perpetual immigration," because "a significant reduction in the immigration rates no longer can be legislated." There will be no pause, he thought; the stream will only grow. Any "migration flow," noted Myron Weiner, "once begun, induces its own flow" through networks of information and contacts. Western democracies, David North told an Organisation for Economic Co-operation and Development (OECD) group in 1991, "cannot cope with illegal immigration." The unique porosity of America's borders made it the leading though not the only Western society struggling in the 1980s and 1990s with mass immigration. Having themselves launched the First Great Wave, Germany, the Scandinavian countries, the United Kingdom, France, Italy, and the rest of Europe were—with the neo-Europes, now the United States, Canada, and Australia—the favored destinations of the second wave, its annual size estimated by Harvard's Samuel P. Huntington as 130 million people (100 million legal immigrants, 19 million refugees, 10 million illegals) in 1990. A UN tally in 2002 raised that number to 175 million, a doubling since 1975. More were on the way across borders, and generally from south to north. We are "destined to be overwhelmed by people from the failed societies of the South," commented France's Pierre Lellouche. You are indeed, said Malaysian Prime Minister Mahathir Bin Mohamad in 1997: "We do have the ultimate weapon. People are more mobile now. They can go anywhere. . . . If we are not allowed a good life in our countries . . . we should migrate north in our millions, legally or illegally. Masses of Asians and

Africans should inundate Europe and America." From his Malaysia back across the Middle East to Algeria, these "Asian and African masses" were Muslim masses, the prime minister might well have said, his phrase "the ultimate weapon" encouraging questions of whether they would come as migrants or settlers and warriors.

When the UN Population Division reported in 2002 that 175 million people currently live in a country other than where they were born, this was 3 percent of global population. The UN did not speculate on how many more might be driven or tempted into border crossing by the mounting disruptions of climate change, civil unrest, drought, or war. Failed states in Africa and the Middle East—and on the edge of Europe, where high-fertility Albania had sent migrants north to further destabilize an unstable Yugoslavia—set refugee masses in motion. As the century ended there seemed an increase in stories of dislodging crises from teeming, 1.2 billion-peopled China—reports of water shortages and blowing soils, massive rural displacement of labor, unrest, discontent, all generating a restless flow of perhaps 100 million, or one-tenth of the population, toward the cities, as China slipped from a controlled communist society toward the chaos of transition. Harbingers of a potentially immense overseas migration of Chinese began arriving in the 1990s in rusty steamers carrying smuggled immigrants again to the Golden Mountain—the rusty Indonesian tanker *Golden Venture* running aground outside New York harbor in 1993 with 286 Chinese would-be immigrants (most were given asylum) and other landings in Vancouver, Los Angeles, even Savannah, Georgia. Another potential source of even larger immigration pressures on the United States was nearby Mexico. That nation's population ended the century at 100 million and, despite downward trends in fertility rates, a doubling time of thirty-two years, massive unemployment, political unrest, and millions of channels to family and kinship anchors north of the border in what was often called Greater Mexico. "We are really just at the start," observed writer David Simcox, "of a worldwide phenomenon that is going to intensify and irrevocably change many countries." "Can either Europe or the U.S. stem the migrant tide?" Huntington asked, with considerable doubt revealed in his tone.

Unlike the First Great Wave that sent the full component of the excess populations of Europe spilling into the population-thin neo-Europes, the twentieth–twenty-first-century Second Great Wave out of Asia, Latin America, the Middle East, and Africa will not solve the problems of the people-exporting societies. Contemporary migratory flows amount to only 1 to 2 percent of the world's annual *increase* of population. There is no relief from population pressures here. Whether remittances from First World wages are a beneficial form of foreign aid to people-exporting countries is a contested issue, and even if helpful, they were matched or overmatched by the drain from the developing world of scarce professional and technical talent that decides to abandon the struggling homeland. The first of these modern mass migrations moved the surplus populations of Europe to regions with space. The second cannot similarly ease the epochal human crowding that is ahead for humanity but can only insure that all spaces fully share it.

Thus as we move deeper into this testing time when the human population finishes the surge through six billion to ten, and recalling Rostow's language about "a global crisis of Malthusian consequences," it is clear that migration pressures will be an increasingly central issue in the West.

In answer to Huntington's question, most Western elites continue to urge the wealthy West not to "stem the migrant tide" but to absorb our global brothers and sisters until the horrid ordeal has been endured and shared by all, ten billion humans packed onto an ecologically devastated planet. In this vision of human solidarity, immigration will have equally overpopulated and culturally altered every society. One result may well be the end of mass migration to the United States, because in that crowded place it will be risky to drink the water. Or perhaps it will be the former United States, its power for global mischief fragmented into successor regions in a post-nationalist, post-American future.

Or perhaps not. What are we to make of the signs that, whether or not this open-border instinct is wise advice, events may not quite stay on the track that Christian-sharing ethics or left-wing internationalism or corporate cheap-labor appetites prefer? Mass immigration seems in these times to meet with the approval of American and European elites, but it tends to have disruptive political effects among ordinary citizens in receiving societies. Already in Europe and in Australia at the hinge of centuries, the inability of established governments to limit immigration has produced fast-growing restrictionist factions or new parties. The swirl of Western politics is complex and much more is involved than immigration. But uncontrolled immigration has in the past been a reliable formula for generating a populist-nationalist politics.

Many have wondered how long the United States, the nation receiving more immigrants than all of Europe together, can avoid this pattern of populist churning and new leaders and parties combining mass migration backlash with other complaints against ossified and unresponsive governments. While there is little sign of this as yet in American or Canadian political life, events in Europe and Australia suggest that mass immigration in the face of passive or ineffective governments poses a hazard for those grouped around the cautious center. They can ignore complaints and suppress discussion and thereby cede the issue to nationalist parties of order, which may mean invigorating populist, possibly rightist politics and parties within the West, with all of the dangerous consequences that history suggests.

Or moderate political leadership in the West can respond to public resentment of expansive immigration regimes and summon the political will to bring immigration down to modest numbers selected by the nation to forward its own interests. Nothing prevents a small-immigration policy from including commitment of larger amounts of aid for developmental and refugee assistance overseas. Indeed, nothing prevents it from taking left-populist directions, stressing the protection of American jobs and labor standards. A politics that includes a small-immigration component will be a nationalist politics, and people with short memories may assume that the entire American left is on another track, irremediably two decades into a cosmopolitan antinationalistic internationalism. Yet there are at least intellectual stirrings of a new liberal-centrist nationalism, with a growing appreciation of the linkage between strong feelings of solidarity as Americans and the reform movements of the progressive era and the New Deal. A small but growing number of American conservatives have already broken with Reagan-Bush open-borderism.

In the American past, low levels of immigration, whether brought by global events or public policy, have reliably led to economic and social benefits, and also cleared the way for our politics to focus on homegrown economic and environmental problems from which ethnic politics steals attention. Given our place and time in global history, it is possible to see here a chance in the United States and across the West for visionary leadership, providing to the world models of appropriately sized populations with lifestyles so altered that at long last the developed nations are no longer making a disproportionately large negative contribution to global warming and planetary ecosystem abuse. Nations' responsibilities to pass on a sustainable ecology and economy to their posterity trump their obligations to foreigners, and will finally have been put first. When global flight, with attendant brain drain, is increasingly infeasible and even condemned, all nations will be obliged to face and fix the problems of overpopulation, poverty, and environmental decay where they are.

Significantly restricting immigration flows as part of new national paths in the West toward sustainability is not all that should be done in the West and would be morally and politically difficult to defend without a complement. Providing models for what nations should aim for instead of the end-less growth that was the West's once-appropriate but in the long run disas-trous trajectory is the highest challenge for the developed world at this tran-sitional era. These models will repudiate large-scale immigration as a solution of the problems of any society, sending or receiving. The model is not Send Me Your Poor, but Liberty and Sustainability Enlightening the World. This was our original, now again timely, model, as an example, point-ing the world where the high road ran. With that example should go in-creasingly generous birth control, technical and economic aid in helping poorer nations solve problems where they are, on their own paths to popu-lation stabilization and ecological sustainability. This promises to be a far better way to spend a dollar, pound, mark, or yen on impoverished peoples than relocating a small fraction but population-expanding number of them to the North, including much of their top talent.

Of all the reforms of the long Progressive Era, immigration reform was the most difficult, and took longer even though it began early. We have explored some of the reasons why the Expansionist regime launched in 1965 persists, despite a gathering corps of critics. We have also weighed the possibilities that change may come, spurred perhaps by a series of terrorist attacks on and in the U.S. by foreigners, and/or by a border-crossing disease epidemic.

Yet policy change triggered by disaster ought to have intellectual prepa-ration. At a deeper level, reform in the United States requires and awaits a rethinking of the role of immigration itself, in our past and future.

A growing immigration reform literature has made a beginning, arguing that, whatever the benefit-cost ratio of essentially unmanaged mass immigra-tion during our earlier national experience with it in a population-thinner time, it must now be seen as solving no international or national problems while intensifying or creating many. Small-scale, managed immigration can enrich a nation's life (always at the expense of other societies), and some re-turn migration may in the future play a small role in compensating for inter-nal demographic change. Large-scale plus illegal immigration drains reser-voirs of trained and talented people from struggling societies and strains the social fabric of receiving developed countries whose best service to them-selves and the earth is early population stabilization, which large-scale immi-gration prevents. Whatever the scale of immigration America (and the West) chooses, unsupervised borders and flows of foreigners are incompatible with national security in this new century. A nation's immune system is enfeebled if it allows sentimental myths and half-truths about its historic experience with immigration to insulate outmoded policy from criticism and revision.

This has been our circumstance for half a century now, but when we place this in historical perspective it appears as an aberration Americans themselves may well correct. William Leach argues, in an important recent book about internal rather than foreign immigration, *The Destruction of Place in American Life* (1999), that Americans have always been both restlessly migratory and place-centered, their society at times in a centrifugal and at others a centripetal pattern. In the late twentieth century "the centripetal pull that always seemed to check the centrifugal side of the American experience . . . no longer has the strength it once had," and we live amid "the weakening of place as a centering presence in the lives of ordinary people." Americans increasingly are drifters and movers, changing jobs and homes, affiliations, relationships. Larger migration flows, both internally and from abroad, are at the center of this pattern, though beneath it are the real culprits: globalization of economies and mass communication. Leach regrets the costs of this habit of disaffiliation from place and community. Economist Albert O. Hirschman points out in *Exit, Voice and Loyalty* (1970) that "exit"—cutting and running, bailing out, leaving the problems behind and moving west— "has been accorded an extraordinarily privileged position in the American tradition." He argued for an appreciation of and rebalancing with more of the other, nonmigratory options, "voice"—staying where you are and joining the effort to resolve problems—and "loyalty," which perhaps needs no elaboration. This is what Wallace Stegner meant when he deplored that there were so many "splitters" or "boomers" in America, and so few "stickers." Faced with difficulties, we Americans migrate away from them, choosing a solution (of sorts) for individuals or families while we leave social problems rooted in the place abandoned by the young and the dreamers of greener fields. But our heritage also contains the stickers, for whom the act of migration would be a sort of defeat, if not betrayal. Both impulses are woven into the American grain, but Stegner found them badly out of balance in this century's second half. More honor for stickers, less for splitters.

They are out of balance internationally, as well. These voices beckon us to add to our rethinking of the function of national gates in the twenty-first century a fundamental reassessment of the act of immigration itself, globally, and especially in the United States, where it decimated an indigenous civilization, played a part in building an unprecedentedly free and successful society, and now in a second mass wave augments the centrifugal forces and environmental harms that are emerging as the American nation's chief challenges.

NOTES

INTRODUCTION

xiii *These polls are one form*   Public opinion polls on immigration issues from the 1960s to the present have not been adequately analyzed together. A useful summary is found in Rita J. Simon, *Public Opinion and the Immigrant: Print and Media Coverage, 1880–1980* (D. C. Heath, 1985). See also Edwin Harwood, "American Public Opinion and U.S. Immigration Policy," *Annals of the American Academy of Political and Social Science* (Sept. 1986).

xiv *Illegal entry should be firmly*   The commission issued preliminary reports in 1994 and 1995 and then the final report, U.S. Commission on Immigration Reform, *Report of the U.S. Commission on Immigration Reform* (Washington, D.C., 1996).

xiv *top five failures*   Paul C. Light, *Government's Greatest Endeavors of the Second Half of the Twentieth Century* (Brookings, 2000). The failures were devolving responsibilities to the states, immigration control, simplifying taxes, expanding urban mass transit, and renewing poor communities.

xiv *"vast social experiment"*   Christopher Jencks, "Who Should Get In?" parts 1 and 2, *New York Review of Books*, Nov. 29 and Dec. 20, 2001, p. 101.

xiv *Apologists for the mass*   See, for example, Sanford Ungar, *Fresh Blood: The New American Immigrants* (Simon and Schuster, 1993), and Michael Barone, *The New Americans: How the Melting Pot Can Work Again* (Regnery, 2001).

CHAPTER I

3 *"the immigration stamp"* Victor Greene, "Immigration Policy," in *Encyclopedia of American Political History*, ed. Jack P. Greene (1984), 2:579.

3 *a virtual genocide* Carl Waldman's estimate of the population north of the Rio Grande is ten to twelve million, in *Atlas of the North American Indian* (Facts on File, 1986), p. 29, while Shepard Krech, *The Ecological Indian: Myth and History* (New York: Norton, 2000), p. 93, puts the consensus at four to seven million, and Russell Thornton settles on two to seven million or more (in Thornton, "Population History of Native North Americans," in *A Population History of North America*, ed. M. E. Haines and R. H. Steckel (Cambridge University Press, 2000). For a discussion of the animated disputes over indigenous populations and thus deaths attributable to European contacts, see Charles C. Mann, "1491," *The Atlantic Monthly* (March 2002), James Wilson, *The Earth Shall Weep* (Atlantic Monthly Press, 1998), and David Henige, *Numbers From Nowhere* (University of Oklahoma Press, 1998).

4 *"Slums and alleys"* Marion T. Bennett, *American Immigration Policies* (Public Affairs Press, 1963), p. 5.

4 *"The bosom of America"* Matthew Spaulding, "Immigration and the Founding Fathers," *Policy Review* (Winter 1994): pp. 35–41; John P. Sanderson, *Republican Landmarks: The Views and Opinions of American Statesmen on Foreign Immigration* (J. P. Lippincott, 1956).

4 *"the importation of foreigners"* On the Founders' views on immigration, see Thomas Jefferson, "Notes on the State of Virginia," in *Thomas Jefferson: Notes on the State of Virginia*, ed. William Peden (University of North Carolina Press, 1955), pp. 82–87; Maldwyn Jones, *American Immigration* (1960), pp. 40–48; Martin Marty, *The One and the Many* (1997); Michael Lind, *The Next American Nation* (Free Press, 1995), p. 42.

5 *"swarmed and swarmed again"* Alfred Crosby, *Ecologic Imperialism: The Biological Expansion of Europe, 900–1900* (Cambridge University Press, 1986), pp. 2–3.

7 *Economic historian Richard* Richard Easterlin, "Immigration: Economic and Social Characteristics," in *Harvard Encyclopedia of American Ethnic Groups*, ed. Stephan Thernstrom (Belknap Press, 1980), p. 476.

7 *"lived much closer to serfdom"* John Higham, *Send These to Me: Immigrants in Urban America*, 2nd ed. (Johns Hopkins University Press, 1984), p. 39.

CHAPTER 2

10 *"sober, industious, and inoffensive"*; *"Transported and largely controlled"* Higham, *Send These*, p. 35.

10   *They fled, or were sent into virtual slavery*   See John K. Fairbank and Edwin
     O. Reischauer, *China: Tradition and Transformation* (Houghton-Mifflin,
     1989), pp. 262–377; Immanuel C. Y. Hsu, *The Rise of Modern China* (Oxford
     University Press, 1975), chap. 10; and H. M. Lai, "Chinese," in *Harvard
     Encyclopedia*, pp. 217–25.

11   *"disease-breeding, miserly"*   Arnold Shankman, *Ambivalent Friends: Afro-
     Americans View the Immigrant* (Greenwood, 1982), p. 13.

11   *It was the first sharp*   See Ronald Takaki, *Strangers from a Different
     Shore: A History of Asian Americans* (Penguin, 1989), pp. 110–12. The dis-
     tinction between the Immigration Law of 1882 and the Chinese Exclusion
     Act is clearly drawn in John Higham, *Strangers in the Land: Patterns of
     American Nativism 1860–1925* (Rutgers University Press, 1963), pp.
     42–45.

11   *"no race that will be willing"; "we do not object"; "If they are brought rap-
     idly"; "The public peace is disturbed"*   Quotations in these two paragraphs
     are from Andrew Gyory, *Closing the Gate: Race, Politics and the Chinese
     Exclusion Act* (University of North Carolina Press, 1998), pp. 232–34, 240,
     248, 252.

CHAPTER 3

15   *The appeal for immigration control*   Keith Fitzgerald, *The Face of the Nation:
     Immigration, the State, and the National Identity* (Stanford University Press,
     1996), p. 117.

16   *Had black Americans been*   See Shankman, *Ambivalent Friends*, pp.
     152–65, and Louis R. Harlan, *Booker T. Washington: The Making of a Black
     Leader* (Oxford University Press, 1972), esp. pp. 204–28.

16   *"heartily approve all legitimate efforts"*   Kirk Porter and D. B. Johnson,
     eds., *National Party Platforms 1840–1964* (University of Illinois Press,
     1966), p. 166. See also Rita Simon, *Public Opinion and the Immigrant*, chap.
     2, for a survey of party platforms on immigration from 1876 to 1980.

16   *"is a grave responsibility"*   Samuel Gompers, *Seventy Years of Life and Labor*,
     ed. Nicholas Salvatore (1925; reprint, Ithaca: Cornell University Press, 1984),
     p. 162.

16   *"immigrants crowded into any"*   Gompers, *Seventy Years*, p. 161.

17   *long-term upward trend"*   A. T. Lane, *Solidarity or Survival? American
     Labor and European Immigrants, 1830–1924* (Greenwood Press, 1987),
     p. 121.

17   *"crowded tenement districts"*   Martin Melosi, *Garbage in the Cities*
     (Dorsey, 1981), p. 16.

18   *Chicago social worker* Edith Abbott, *Historical Aspects of the Immigration Problem*   (University of Chicago Press, 1926).

18   *An outbreak of the disease*   On immigration and disease in the late nineteenth century, see Alan M. Kraut, *Silent Travellers: Germs, Genes, and the "Immigrant Menace"* (Johns Hopkins University Press, 1994), and Howard Markel, *Quarantine! East European Jewish Immigrants and the New York City Epidemics of 1892* (Johns Hopkins University Press, 1997).

18   *"the 'cholera scare'"*   H. Sidney Everett, "Immigration and Naturalization," *The Atlantic Monthly* (March, 1895), pp. 345–53.

18   *"to close the floodgates"*   Lane, *Solidarity*, p. 84.

19   *"more rackrent for slum landlords"*   Lane, *Solidarity*, p. 148.

19   *"more than whites [they] suffered"*   David J. Hellwig, "Black Leaders and U.S. Immigration Policy, 1917–1929," *Journal of Negro History* 66 (1981): 111.

19   *"Blacks in Steelton"*   John Bodnar, "Impact of the 'New Immigrants' on the Black Worker: Steelton, Pa., 1880–1920," *Labor History* (Spring 1976).

19   *"Every hour sees the black man"*   Frederick Douglass, *My Bondage and My Freedom* (Dover, 1969), pp. 454–55.

19   *"To those of the white race"*   Booker T. Washington, Atlanta Exposition Address, in Louis R. Harlan, *The Booker T. Washington Papers* (University of Illinois Press, 1972), 1:73–76. See also Jeff Diamond, "African-American Attitudes Towards United States Immigration Policy," *International Migration Review* 32 (Summer 1998), pp. 451–70, and Lawrence Fuchs, "The Reactions of Black Americans to Immigration," in *Immigration Reconsidered*, Virginia Yans-McLaughlin, ed. (Oxford University Press, 1990).

20   *"substantial and rising negative"*   Claudia Golden and Gary D. Libecap, eds., *The Regulated Economy* (University of Chicago Press, 1994), p. 8. See also Claudia Golden, "The Political Economy of Immigration Restriction in the U.S., 1890 to 1921," National Bureau of Economic Research Working Paper 4345 (April 1993), pp. 21–22.

21   *"They do not (unlike Americans)"*   George M. Stephenson, *A History of American Immigration, 1820–1924* (Russell and Russell, 1964), p. 88.

21   *"to be American was to be free"*   Fitzgerald, *Face of the Nation*, p. 123.

24   *"there is now being injected"*   Thomas Gossett, *Race: The History of an Idea in America*, rev. ed. (Oxford University Press, 1997), p. 294.

24   *"peasantry, degraded below"*   Gossett, *Race*, p. 303

24   *"Throughout the century men"*   Quoted in Hans Vought, "Division and Reunion: Woodrow Wilson, Immigration and the Myth of American Unity," *Journal of American Ethnic History* (Spring 1994), pp. 28–29.

24   *"The long-suppressed, conquered"* Madison Grant, *The Passing of the Great Race*, (Charles Scribner's Sons, 1916), p. xxxi.

25   *Theodore Roosevelt, for example* Gary Gerstle, "Theodore Roosevelt and the Divided Character of American Nationalism," *Journal of American History* (Dec. 1999), pp. 1280–1307.

25   *"Foreigners do not bathe often"* Peter Roberts, *The New Immigration* (Macmillan, 1912), pp. vii–xiv, 307.

CHAPTER 4

28   *The organization collapsed* On the APA, see Carl Wittke, *We Who Built America* (Prentice-Hall, 1939).

28   *Most of the IRL's members* John A. Garraty, *Henry Cabot Lodge* (Alfred Knopf, 1953), p. 141. On the IRL, see Barbara Miller Solomon, *Ancestor and Immigrants* (John Wiley, 1956). Teddy Roosevelt agreed with Lodge, approving of the work of the IRL and disdaining the APA.

28   *This does not take us* The *Oxford English Dictionary*, 2nd ed. (1989), for nativism, after the definition "prejudice in favor of natives against strangers," offers also a definition from anthropology ("the movement of societies back toward a reaffirmation of their native tribal cultures"), philosophy ("the doctrine of innate ideas"), and psychology ("the doctrine that certain capacities . . . are innate rather than acquired").

29   *"suffered one of the most severe"* Robert W. Fogel, *Without Consent or Contract: The Rise and Fall of American Slavery* (Norton, 1989), p. 69; Elliott J. Gorn, "'Good-Bye Boys, I Die a True American:' Homicide, Nativism, and Working-Class Culture in Antebellum New York City," *Journal of American History* (Sept. 1987).

29   *fear "eventually proved mistaken"* Stephan Thernstrom, "Ethnic Groups in American History," in *Ethnic Relations in America*, ed. Lance Lieberman (Prentice Hall, 1982), p. 8.

29   *"Reasonable Protestants"* Charles R. Morris, *American Catholic: The Saints and Sinners Who Built America's Most Powerful Church* (Times Books, 1997), pp. 50–72. See also David O'Brien, *Public Catholicism* (Macmillan, 1989).

30   *"Powerful and overbearing in Europe"* Ray Allen Billington, *The Protestant Crusade, 1800–1860: A Study of the Origins of American Nativism* (1938; reprint, Quadrangle Books, 1964), pp. 289–321.

30   *"genuine fears rooted in"* Thomas Archdeacon, *Becoming American: An Ethnic History* (Free Press, 1983), pp. 74–101, and Billington, *Protestant Crusade*, pp. 322–38.

31 *"How could bedrock republican virtues"* Gorn, "Good-Bye Boys," pp. 392, 398.

31 *"Our movement is plain Americanism"* The best source on the Know-Nothings is Tyler Anbinder, *Nativism and Slavery: The Know-Nothings and the Politics of the 1950s* (Oxford University Press, 1997). See also Michael F. Holt, "The Politics of Impatience: The Origins of Know-Nothingism," *Journal of American History* 60 (Sept. 1973), and Bruce Levine, "Conservatism, Nativism, and Slavery: Thomas R. Whitney and the Origins of the Know-Nothing Party," *Journal of American History* 88 (Sept. 2001).

33 *That is quite a spectrum* The causal linkage between large-scale immigration and such nativism as well as other social tensions is asserted in John Higham, "Cultural Responses to Immigration," in *Diversity and Its Discontents*, Neil Smelser and Jeffrey Alexander (Princeton University Press, 1999).

34 *"nativism now looks less"* John Higham, "Another Look at Nativism," *Catholic Historical Review* (July 1958), pp. 148–58; Higham, *Strangers*, p. xiv.

34 *Higham's continuing second thoughts* See especially his "Instead of a Sequel, Or How I Lost My Subject," *Reviews in American History* 28 (2000): 327–39.

35 *"was all but finished"* David H. Bennett, *The Party of Fear: From Nativist Movements to the New Right in American History* (University of North Carolina Press, 1988), p. 285.

35 *"Xenophobia did not matter"* Timothy Hatton and Jeffrey G. Williamson, *The Age of Mass Migration: Causes and Economic Impacts* (Oxford University Press, 1998), pp. 245–247.

CHAPTER 5

38 *As the new century arrived* John R. Commons, *History of Labor in the United States* (Macmillan, 1935), 3:26.

38 *"our present immigration laws"* Marion Bennett, *American Immigration Policies* (Public Affairs Press, 1963), pp. 22–23, and Leonard Dinnerstein and David Reimers, *Ethnic Americans: A History of Immigration*, 3rd ed. (Harper and Row, 1988), p. 72.

39 *"a competent race"* Bennett, *American Immigration*, p. 37.

39 *Japanese immigration continued:* George Mowry, *The Era of Theodore Roosevelt* (Harper and Row, 1958), pp. 185–89.

39 *If you're pestered by critics"* See Geoffrey Parsons, "Royal Commission," *Punch* (Aug. 24, 1955). Copyright Punch, London.

39   *"separate the ignorant"*   Mowry, *The Era of Theodore Roosevelt*, p. 169.

40   *"a definite solution"*   Quoted in Lawrence Fuchs, "Immigration Reform in 1911 and 1981: The Role of Select Commissions," *Journal of American Ethnic History* (Fall 1983): 59, 63–65.

40   *"enormous influence on the future"*   Fuchs, "Immigration Reform," p. 65.

40   *mountains of data*   On the lower "human quality" of the new immigration relative to the old, see Hatton and Williamson, *Age of Mass Migration*, chap. 8.

40   *The commission affirmed*   U.S. Immigration Commission, *Reports of the Immigration Commission 1907–1911* (Arno Press and *New York Times*, 1970), 5:145–47.

CHAPTER 6

41   *"an abiding faith"*   Dinnerstein and Reimers, *Ethnic Americans*, pp. 72–73.

41   *Congress overrode a second veto*   Higham, *Strangers*, pp. 189–91. Roy Garis, *Immigration Restriction* (Macmillan, 1927), p. 123. An extensive discussion of the literacy test may be found in Golden, "Political Economy of Immigration Restriction."

42   *They established programs*   Otis L. Graham, Jr., and Elizabeth Koed, "Americanizing the Immigrant, Past and Future: History and Implications of a Social Movement," *The Public Historian* 15 (Fall 1993): 37.

42   *found two faces*   Edward G. Hartmann, *The Movement to Americanize the Immigrant* (Columbia University Press, 1948); Higham, *Strangers*, chap. 9.

43   *"The conformist tendency"*   Otis L. Graham Jr. *The Great Campaigns* (Robert Krieger, 1987), p. 110.

44   *Don't Preach! Don't Patronize!*   Aileen Kraditor, *Ideas of the Woman Suffrage Movement, 1890–1920* (Columbia University Press, 1965), p. 142.

43   *"Americanization is an ugly"*   M. E. Ravage, "The Immigrant's Burden," *New Republic* (1919), p. 211.

44   *The attractive achievements*   See for example David Hollinger, *Postethnic America* (Basic, 1995), Gary Gerstle, "Liberty, Coercion, and the Making of Americans," in *International Migration: The American Experience*, Charles Hirschman et al., eds. (Sage, 1999), and Gary Gerstle, *American Crucible: Race and Nation in the Twentieth Century* (Princeton University Press, 2001).

44   *The Dillingham Commission estimated*   Golden, "Political Economy of Immigration Restriction," pp. 236–38.

46   *More than ten million*   Bennett, *American Immigration*, p. 41.

46   *if there were in existence*   U.S. Senate Report 1515, *The Immigration and Naturalization Systems of the United States*, 81st Cong., 2nd sess., 1950, p. 55.

46   *a deluge of immigration*   Henry Pratt Fairchild, *Immigration* (Macmillan, 1925), p. 453.

46   *Annual immigration would*   Senate Report 1515, p. 55. Senate Committee on Immigration, *Emergency Immigration Legislation* (13 vols.), 66th Cong., 3rd sess., January 3–30, 1921.

46   *"There is a limit"*   U.S. Congress House Report 1351, *Temporary Suspension of Immigration: Conference Report*, 66th Cong., 3rd sess., Feb. 22, 1921. Senate Report 1515, p. 57.

47   *"We favor reducing it to nothing"*   A. Philip Randolph, editorial, "Immigration and Japan," *The Messenger*, Aug. 1924, p. 247. See also Daryl Scott, "Immigrant Indigestion: A. Philip Randolph, Radical and Restrictionist," *CIS Backgrounder* (June 1999): 3.

48   *"abnormally twisted"*   Higham, *Strangers*, p. 309; *Congressional Record* (April 8, 1924), p. 5868.

48   *"the worst kind of discrimination"*   Gerstle, *American Crucible*, p. 117.

48   *"The committee has not dwelt"*   U.S. Congress, House Report 350 (April 1924), pp. 12–16; *Congressional Record* (April 8, 1924), p. 5911. For a detailed analysis of the congressional debates of 1924, see Kevin MacDonald, "Jewish Involvement in Shaping American Immigration Policy, 1881–1965: A Historical Review," *Population and Environment* 19 (March 1998).

49   *"that the restrictionists of Congress do not"*   *Congressional Record* (April 8, 1924), p. 5922.

50   *"Nations come of slow growth"*   Edward Lewis, *America: Nation or Confusion?* (Harper and Brothers, 1928), pp. 14–15.

50   *One of the more influential*   Gino Speranza's articles of 1923–1924 were published as *Race or Nation* (Bobbs Merrill, 1925).

50   *Thirty-four biologists*   *Congressional Record* (Jan. 18, 1927), p. 1904.

51   *Rita Simon's survey*   Simon, *Public Opinion*, pp. 69–71.

51   *Joining Congressman Johnson*   Fairchild, *Immigration*, p. 452.

51   *"If . . . the principle of individual liberty"*   "Restriction of Immigration," *House Report* No. 350, 68th Congress, 1st session (Washington, D.C., 1924), p. 13.

51   *"It has always seemed to me"*   U.S. Congress Senate Hearings, 68th Congress, 1st session *Selective Immigration Legislation* (Feb. 14, 1924), p. 30.

52   *"If one were to"*   Stephen T. Wagner, "The Lingering Death of the National Origins Quota System: A Political History of U.S. Immigration Policy, 1952–1965" (Ph.D. diss., Harvard University, 1986), University of Michigan Microfilms, 1994, pp. 8–19.

52   *"If we will only check the tide"*   Wagner, "The Lingering Death," p. 19.

52   *"reproducing in miniature the American composite"*   U.S. Congress House
      Report 716, *Immigration of Aliens into the United States: Conference Report*,
      68th Cong., 1st sess., May 12, 1924; Marion Bennett, *American Immigration*,
      p. 52; George Wheeler Hinman, "National Origins: Our New Immigration
      Formula," *The American Review of Reviews* 70 (Sept. 1924): 309.

53   *"Most of the support"*   John Higham, *Send These To Me: Immigrants in
      Urban America*, rev. ed. (Johns Hopkins University Press, 1984), p. 49;
      Higham, *Strangers*, p. 301. The role of "Patrician race thinkers" promot-
      ing the findings of eugenics and of intelligence testing is in dispute. Con-
      gressman Albert Johnson had cordial relations with Eastern intellectuals
      such as Harry Loughlin and others who pressed their ideas on intelli-
      gence testing on Congress. But their role in the legislation was "insignif-
      icant" in the view of Carl N. Degler, *In Search of Human Nature* (Oxford
      University Press, 1991), pp. 52–53), a view corroborated by Mark Sny-
      derman and R. H. Herrnstein, "Intelligence Tests and the Immigration
      Act of 1924," *American Psychologist* 38 (Sept. 1983): 994.

53   *"America must be kept American"*   Fred Israel, ed., *The State of the Union
      Messages of the Presidents*, 1790–1966 (Chelsea House, 1966) 3:2651.

54   *"For a decade or more"*   John Higham, "Cultural Responses to Immigra-
      tion," in *Diversity and Its Discontents*, eds. Neil Smelser and Jeffrey C.
      Alexander (Princeton University Press, 1999), pp. 51–52.

CHAPTER 7

57   *"Anglo-Saxon and Latin-dominated alike"*   Senate Report 1515, pp. 27–41;
      Bennett, *American Immigration*, chap. 7.

58   *William S. Bernard estimated*   Bernard, *American Immigration*, p. 34.

58   *Demographer Leon Bouvier*   Leon Bouvier, *What if . . .? Immigration
      Decisions: What Could Have Been, What Could Be* (FAIR, Oct. 1994), p. 6.

58   *In 1933, with immigration almost*   President's Research Committee on
      Social Trends, *Recent Social Trends* (McGraw-Hill, 1934), pp. 48–49.

59   *Sacco and Vanzetti*   On the lengthy and torturous debates over the guilt or
      innocence of Sacco and Vanzetti, see a recent review by Nunzio Pernicone,
      "Carlo Tresca and the Sacco-Vanzetti Case," *Journal of American History*
      (Dec. 1979).

59   *Many employers in both*   On productivity increases after immigration
      restriction, see Vernon Briggs, *Mass Immigration and the National Inter-
      est* (M. E. Sharpe, 1992), p. 70. And see also Jeffrey Williamson and Pe-
      ter Lindert, *American Inequality: A Macroeconomic History* (Academic
      Press, 1980), pp. 206–212.

59   *Economic historians include* Claudia Golden, "The Political Economy of Immigration Restriction to the U.S., 1890–1921," National Bureau of Economic Research Working Paper 4345 (April 1993), pp. 21–22. "In the absence of mass migrations [of the nineteenth century] the real wage would have risen faster and unequal trends would have been more pronounced," concludes Jeffrey Williamson, "Immigration-Inequality Trade-Offs in the Promised Land," in *The Gateway*, ed. Barry Chiswick (1981), p. 254. See also Stanley Lebergott, *Manpower in Economic Growth* (McGraw-Hill, 1964), and Hatton and Williamson, *Age of Mass Migration*, chap. 8.

60   *"The [immigration] laws are on the books"* E. E. Cummins and F. T. De Vyner, *The Labor Problem in the United States*, 3rd ed. (Van Nostrand, 1947), p. 269.

60   *"The decline of European immigration"* John Bodnar, Roger Simon, and Michael Weber, *Lives of Their Own: Blacks, Italians, and Poles in Pittsburgh 1900–1960* (University of Illinois Press, 1982), p. 238.

60   *"this process was aided by the curtailment"* Foster Rhea Dulles, *Labor in America* (T. Y. Crowell, 1960), p. 243.

60   *Writing of Italian Americans* Victor Alba, *Italian Americans: Into the Twilight of Ethnicity* (Prentice Hall, 1985), p. 168.

62   *"caused America to sacrifice"* Thomas A. Bailey et al., *The American Pageant* (Houghton-Mifflin, 1998), pp. 748–49.

65   *Secretary of State Charles* On the politics of Japanese immigration and citizenship, see Yuji Ichioka, *The Issei: The World of the First Generation Japanese Immigrants, 1885–1924* (Free Press, 1988). For the legislative struggle over the handling of Japan, see Don McCoy, *Calvin Coolidge* (University Press of Kansas, 1988), pp. 231–32.

CHAPTER 8

68   *"The Goddess of Liberty"* U.S. Congress House Report 3472, *Report of the Select Commission on Immigration and Naturalization*, 51st Cong., 2nd sess., Jan. 15, 1991, p. 5.

69   *no longer Liberty enlightening the world* Betty Koed, "A Symbol Transformed," *The Social Contract* (Spring 1992).

69   *"we might say that for all practical purpose"* Collis Stocking, "Adjusting Immigration Requirements to Manpower Requirements," *Annals of the American Academy of Political and Social Science* (March 1949): 113.

69   *"I concluded"* Herbert C. Hoover, *The Memoirs of Herbert Hoover: The Great Depression, 1929–1941* (Macmillan, 1952), pp. 47–48.

70 *"America needs to give herself"* Louis Adamic, *My America* (Harper Brothers, 1938), pp. 208–9.

CHAPTER 9

71 *"A steady stream of men and women"* Samuel I. Rosenman, ed., *The Public Papers and Addresses of Franklin D. Roosevelt*, vol. 5, *The People Approve: 1936* (Russell and Russell, 1938), p. 542.

73 *They included physicists Albert Einstein* See Richard Breitman and Alan Kraut, eds., *American Refugee Policy and European Jewry 1933–1945* (Indiana University Press, 1987), and Henry Feingold, *Bearing Witness: How America and Its Jews Responded to the Holocaust* (Syracuse University Press, 1995).

73 *Close to 75 percent* See William D. Rubenstein, *The Myth of Rescue: Why the Democracies Could Not Have Saved More Jews from the Nazis* (Routledge, 1997), and Yehuda Bauer, *American Jewry and the Holocaust: American Jewish Joint Distribution Committee, 1939–1945* (Wayne State University Press, 1981).

73 *"few Jews of any persuasion"* David M. Kennedy, *Freedom From Fear: The American People in Depression and War, 1929–1945* (Oxford University Press, 1999), pp. 412–15.

75 *Human traffic around the national origins system"* Marion T. Bennett, "Immigration and Naturalization Act of 1952, as amended," *Annals of the American Academy of Political and Social Science* 367 (Sept. 1966).

76 *"any theory of Nordic superiority"* Senate Report 1515, pp. 12–14, 65, 285–89, 371–73, and appendix II for committee recommendations. Congressman Francis Walter, obviously impressed by Senate Report 1515, frequently set immigration issues in the context of global demographics. See for example U.S. Congress, 84th Cong., 2nd sess., *Congressional Record—House*, pp. 9162–63.

76 *"rising tide of immigration"* Senate Report 1515, p. 285.

77 *a passionate enemy of communism* The only biography of McCarran pays almost no attention to his immigration policymaking; see Jerome E. Edwards, *Pat McCarran: Political Boss of Nevada* (University of Nevada Press, 1982).

77 "a rational method" U.S. Statutes at Large, Public Law 414, p. 66 (June 17, 1952) (GPO, 1953), p. 69.

77 *"we can correct an historic mistake"* Congressional Record (Oct. 11, 1943), p. 8176.

78   *"Stripped of its intellectual respectability"*   Bennett, *Party of Fear*, p. 185.

78   *"racist, fascist, reactionary"*   Bennett, "Immigration and Naturalization Act," p. 132. For a passionate criticism of the National Origins system, see Oscar Handlin, "The Immigration Fight Has Only Begun," *Commentary* (July 1952).

78   *"a barely disguised restatement"*   Israel Goldstein, "An American Immigration Policy," *Congress Weekly: A Review of Jewish Interests* (Nov. 3, 1952), p. 2.

79   *"immigration policy is"*   "Veto of Bill to Revise the Laws Relating to Immigration, Naturalization, and Nationality," June 25, 1952, *Public Papers of the Presidents of the United States: Harry S. Truman, 1952–1953* (Washington, D.C., 1966), pp. 441–47.

80   *"professional immigrant-handlers"*   Congressional Record—House, 84th Congress, 2nd session (GPO), p. 9162.

80   *"the greatest vice"*   *Public Papers: Truman*, p. 442.

80   *Immediately after his veto*   President's Commission on Immigration and Naturalization, *Whom We Shall Welcome* (Washington, D.C., 1953)

81   *Francis Walter, in a 1956 Memorial Day*   "Immigration or Invasion," Extension of Remarks by Francis E. Walter, House of Representatives (84th Cong., 2nd sess,), *Congressional Record*, pp. 9462–65.

81   *"When they glibly advocate"*   Robert C. Alexander, "Our National Origins Quota System—Mirror of America," *The American Legion Magazine* (Sept. 1956), pp. 52, 55. Alexander and Liskovsky are quoted in Wagner, "Lingering Death," p. 299; Nathan Glazer, in *Law and Contemporary Problems* 21 (Spring 1956): 269, 300.

82   *a 1958 bouquet of praise*   John F. Kennedy, *A Nation of Immigrants* (Harper and Row, 1964). And see Ira Melhman, "John F. Kennedy and Immigration Reform," *The Social Contract* (Summer 1991): 201–6.

83   *a golden alliance*   Earl Raab, *Jewish Bulletin* (July 23, 1993), p. 17; Nathan C. Belth, *A Promise to Keep: A Narrative of the American Encounter with Anti-Semitism* (Times Books, 1979); S. M. Neuringer, *American Jewry and United States Immigration Policy 1881–1953* (Arno Press, 1980); Kevin MacDonald, "Jewish Involvement in Shaping American Immigration Policy, 1881–1965: A Historical Review," *Population and Environment* 19 (March 1998): 295–356; Betty Koed, "The Politics of Immigration Reform" (Ph.D. diss., University of California, Santa Barbara, 1995), p. 43. See also Abba P. Schwarz, *The Open Society* (Morrow, 1968).

CHAPTER 10

87   *These hearings should have served*   U.S. Congress, House, Committee on the Judiciary, Subcommittee 1, *Study of Population and Immigration Problems*, Special Series, 17 vols., 1–14 (Washington, D.C., 1962–1963).

88   *Kennedy sent a special message*   John F. Kennedy, "Letter to the President of the Senate and to the Speaker of the House on Revision of the Immigration Laws," July 23, 1963, *Public Papers of the Presidents of the United States* (Washington, D.C., 1964), pp. 594–97.

88   *"We ought to never ask"*   Wagner, "The Lingering Death," p. 388.

88   *"in smaller cities and towns"*   Koed, "Politics of Immigration," pp. 130, 144.

89   *"It would be impossible to draw up a law"*   "Controversy over U.S. Immigration Policy," *Congressional Digest* (May 1965): 150–51.

89   *We need "an immigration policy reflecting"*   Koed, "Politics of Immigration," pp. 133, 136. A summary statement of the liberal critique of the national origins system was by Senator Edward M. Kennedy, "The Immigration Act of 1965," *Annals of the American Academy of Political and Social Science* 367 (Sept. 1966).

89   *A Harris poll released*   Wagner, "Lingering Death," p. 421.

90   *"The McCarran-Walter Act is":*   *Congressional Record—Senate* (Mar. 4, 1965), p. 4143.

90   *"Every other country that is attractive":*   *Congressional Record—Senate* (Sept. 14, l965), p. 23793.

90   *The patriotic societies, the American Legion:*   "In view of the vehemence of past opposition, it was surprising in a sense how little the present opposition counted," wrote Jerome Lieberman (*Are Americans Extinct?* (Walker and Co., 1968), p. 156.

91   *African American leaders*   See Lawrence Fuchs, "The Reactions of Black Americans," pp. 298–99.

91   *"expressed little overt defense"*   Edward M. Kennedy, "The Immigration Act of 1965" *Annals of the American Academy of Political and Social Science* 367 (Sept. 1966): 142.

91   *"the reformers consistently denied":*   Wagner, "Lingering Death," pp. 478–79.

91   *"insured that the new immigration pattern":*   *Wall Street Journal* (Oct. 4, 1965).

92   *"Congressmen don't want*:   Koed, "Politics of Immigration," p. 69.

92   *"There is not much pressure:"*   U. C. Congress, Senate, Subcommittee on Immigration and Naturalization, Committee on the Judiciary, "Hearings on S. 500 98th Congress, 1st Session, Mar. 4, 1965 (GPO, 1965), p. 17.

92   *Was it not "discrimination":*   Ibid., pp. 16–17. See the discussion of this exchange in Lieberman, *Are Americans Extinct?*, pp. 154–55.

93   *"the [proposed new] distribution":*   Statement by Senator Robert F. Kennedy before the Subcommittee on Immigration, "Hearings on S. 500," pp. 218–24.

93   *"Our cities will not be flooded":*   *Congressional Digest* (May, 1965): 152.

95   *"No wonder the 1965 Act":*   A good account of the surprising pattern of immigrant countries of origin and of chain migration after 1965 may be found in David Reimers, *Still the Golden Door*, 2nd ed. (Columbia University Press, 1992), pp. 92–96, and Hugh Davis Graham, *Collision Course: The Strange Convergence of Affirmative Action and Immigration Policy in America* (Oxford University Press, 2002), chap. 5.

95   *"the transfer of policy control"*   Eugene McCarthy, *A Colony of the World* (Hippocrene Books, 1992), pp. 57, 59.

95   *"The bill that we will sign today"*   *Weekly Compilation of Presidential Documents* (Oct. 11, 1965), pp. 364–65.

96   *"the most thoughtless of the many acts"*   Theodore White, *America in Search of Itself* (HarperCollins, 1984), p. 363. See also David M. Reimers, "An Unintended Reform: The 1965 Immigration Act and Third World Immigration to the United States," *Journal of American Ethnic History* (Fall 1983), and "Three Decades of Mass Immigration: The Legacy of the 1965 Immigration Act," *CIS Backgrounder* (Sept. 1995).

97   *"a period of maximum strain on resources"*   W. Walt Rostow, *The Great Population Spike and After* (Oxford University Press, 1998), pp. 187–88; Hamish Macrae, *The World in 2020* (HarperCollins, 1995). E. O. Wilson refers to the era of cresting global population growth as "the Bottleneck" in Edward O. Wilson, "The Bottleneck," *Scientific American* (Feb. 2002), an excerpt from his *The Future of Life* (Knopf, 2002).

CHAPTER 11

100   *Disapproval might have been stronger*   See Graham, *Collision Course*, p. 108; Reimers, *Still the Golden Door*, chap. 6.

100   *President Ronald Reagan*   Roger Daniels, *Coming to America* (Harper and Row, 1990), pp. 380, 382.

100   *Monthly flows reached*   Elliott R. Barkan, *And Still They Come: Immigrants and American Society 1920 to the 1990s* (Harlan Davidson, 1996), pp. 135–38.

101   *Resettlement costs were disguised*   Daniels, *Coming*, p. 376. See also Reimers, *Still the Golden Door*, p. 178.

CHAPTER 12

103   *Annual totals of legal immigration*   Vernon Briggs, *Mass Immigration and the National Interest*, data from table on p. 120.

103   *"immigrants are an unsettling force"*   Higham, "In Place of a Sequel," p. 19.

104   *"welcome and plan for a stabilized population"*   U.S. Commission on Population and the American Future, *Population Growth and the American Future* (Washington, D.C., 1972). See also David E. Simcox, "Twenty Years Later: A Lost Opportunity," *The Social Contract* (Summer 1992).

104   *"the pressures of a steadily rising population"*   "NPCA Urges Strong Controls to Stem the Tide of Illegal Aliens," *National Parks and Conservation Magazine* 52 (July 1978).

104   *Washington-based staff*   For the story of the rise and decline of the population issue, see Roy Beck and Leon Kolankiewicz, "The Environmental Movement's Retreat from Advocating U.S. Population Stabilization (1970–1998): A First Draft of History," in Otis L. Graham, Jr., ed., *Environmental Politics and Policy, 1960s–1990s* (Penn State University Press, 2000).

104   *the nation's foremost organization working for*   John Tanton, letter to author, March 15, 2000, and Judith Kunofsky, letter to author, Feb. 9, 1998; Melanie Wirken, conversation with author, March 1978.

105   *FAIR provided the organizational*   Otis L. Graham, Jr., "Illegal Immigration and the New Reform Movement," *The Center Magazine* (1977). See also the papers of FAIR, Gellman Library, George Washington University, including the oral history of John H. Tanton, "A Skirmish in a Wider War." On Tanton's perspective on global immigration, see his essay "End of the Migration Epoch? Time for a New Paradigm," in *Immigration and the Social Contract*, ed. John Tanton et al. (Avebury, 1996). See also John Rohe, *Mary Lou and John Tanton: A Journey into American Conservation* (Fair Horizon Press, 2002). The author was a founding board member of FAIR.

105   *"a hot second-tier issue"*   Roberto Suro, *Watching America's Door: The Immigration Backlash and the New Policy Debate* (Twentieth Century Fund, 1996), p. 32.

220NOTES

105   *"there is more product"*   Ray Marshall, "Immigration in the Golden State," in *U.S. Immigration in the 1990s*, ed. Simcox (Westview Press, 1988), p. 181.

106   *"tried in vain to stem the tide"*   Richard W. Etulain, ed., *Cesar Chavez: A Brief Biography with Documents* (Palgrave Press, 2002), p. 18.

106   *"This immigrant labor subsidy"*   Phillip Martin, "Good Intentions Gone Awry," *Annals of the American Academy of Political and Social Science* (July 1994): 55.

106   *tomato prices would rise*   Wallace Huffman and Alan McCunn, "How Much is that Tomato in the Window? Retail Produce Prices Without Illegal Farmworkers," *CIS Backgrounder* (Feb. 1996). UC economist Phillip Martin estimates that if the influx of immigrant labor were curbed and farm wages allowed to rise, the retail price of "a pound of apples or a head of lettuce . . . would rise by 2 to 3 cents." Martin, "Mexico-U.S. Migration in the Twenty-First Century," *Handout #9* (Oct. 20, 2002).

106   *"Latinos will always be handicapped"*   Suro, *Strangers among Us* (Alfred A. Knopf, 1998) p. 264.

106   *a natural and unstoppable part*   An early voice for this open-border fatalism was Mexican economist Jorge Bustamente. A recent version of the argument that illegal immigration was a vital part of a "complicated piece of [economic] machinery" in the Southwestern region that required the seasonal cross-border flows of illegal labor is Douglas S. Massey, Jorge Durand, and Nolan J. Malone, *Beyond Smoke and Mirrors: Mexican Immigration in an Age of Economic Integration* (Russell Sage, 2002), p. 1.

106   *"particularly troubled by"*   Suro, *Watching*, p. 33.

107   *"The American people are so very fed up"*   Suro, *Watching*, p. 10. For the administration's relations with Simpson and role in IRCA, see Otis L. Graham, Jr., "Failing the Test: Immigration Reform," in *The Reagan Presidency*, ed. W. Elliot Brownlee and Hugh Davis Graham (University Press of Kansas, 2003).

108   *A Gallup poll in the fall*   For Gallup polls, see *The Gallup Poll: Public Opinion*, an annual publication of Scholarly Resources.

108   *"The change in the farm labor market"*   Phillip Martin, "Good Intentions," p. 44.

109   *Demographer David Simcox*   Simcox, "Measuring the Fallout: The Cost of IRCA Amnesty after Ten Years," *CIS Backgrounder* (Jan. 1997). Vernon Briggs counts four amnesties within IRCA: the general one, the SAW, a special amnesty for Cubans and Haitians entering during Mariel, and moving the Registry date from 1948 to 1972. See Briggs, *Mass Immigration*, p. 160.

109   *"the most generous immigration law"*   Reed Ueda, *Postwar Immigrant America: A Social History* (St. Martins Press, 1994), p. 48.

CHAPTER 13

112   *"Post-1965 immigrants"*   Vernon Briggs, "U.S. Immigration Policy and the Plight of its Unskilled Workers," *People and Place* 7 (1999), p. 3.

113   *a RAND Corporation researcher*   Georges Vernez, "Community Costs of Low-Skilled Immigrants," *The Social Contract* (Fall 1999), a version of his testimony before the House Committee on the Judiciary, Subcommittee on Immigration, March 11, 1999.

113   *accusing the study's director of falsely*   Borjas, Freeman, and Katz are cited in John Cassidy, "The Melting-Pot Myth," *The New Yorker*, July 14, 1997, p. 41.

113   *"the magnitude of the current flows"*   National Research Council, *The New Americans: Economic, Demographic, and Fiscal Effects of Immigration* (National Academy Press, 1997); Steven Camarota and Leon Bouvier, "The Impact of New Americans: A Review and Analysis of the National Research Council's *The New Americans*," (Center for Immigration Studies, Nov. 1999).

114   *"supporting an astonishing transfer of wealth"*   George Borjas, *Heaven's Door: Immigration Policy and the American Economy* (1999), p. 13. See also Borjas and Freeman, "Findings We Never Found," *New York Times*, Dec. 10, 1997, A29, and Borjas, "The New Economy of Immigration," *The Atlantic Monthly* (Nov. 1996).

114   *"Immigration is an income redistribution program"*   George Borjas, "The Top Ten Symptoms of Immigration," *CIS Backgrounder* (Nov. 1999): 5. See also Georges Vernez, "Community Costs of Low-Skilled Immigrants," *The Social Contract* (Fall 1999): 24–27.

114   *"indentured servants"*   Dan Stein, interview on CNN, Oct. 6, 2000 at www.nexis.com (accessed July 14, 2003).

115   *the rate among immigrants now roughly double*   See Camarota and Bouvier, "Impact of New Americans," and Camarota, "Does Immigration Harm the Poor?" *The Public Interest* (Fall 1998), and Camarota, *Importing Poverty*, Center for Immigration Studies Paper 15, 1999.

115   *"balance is shifting to the cost side"*   Kevin McCarthy and Georges Vernez, *Immigration in a Changing Economy: California's Experience* (RAND Corporation, 1997), and see Patrick J. McDonnell, "Immigration Study Urges New Curbs and Criteria," *Los Angeles Times*, Sept. 15, 1997, a front-page report on the study.

115   *"The fact that immigration hurts the poor"*   Cassidy, "Melting-Pot Myth," pp. 42, 43.

115   *"They brought in all these Guatemalan and Mexican workers"*   Marcus Stern, "Jobs Magnet," Copley News Service, reprinted in Eugene Katz Award brochure (CIS, 1998).

115   *"America's older black poor"*   Jack Miles, "Blacks vs. Browns: Immigra-
       tion and the New American Dilemma," *The Atlantic Monthly* (Oct. 1992),
       pp. 52–66. For a similar view of black loss of political power and economic
       opportunity to immigrants, see Peter H. Schuck, "The Evolving Civil
       Rights Movement: Old Civil Rights and New Immigration," *Current* (Jan.
       1994).

115   *"lazy, defeated, and corrupt"*   Roberto Suro, *Strangers among Us* (Knopf,
       1998), pp. 247, 252–53, 260.

116   *"People do not blow into our country"*   Miles, "Immigration and the New
       American Dilemma," p. 60. See also William Julius Wilson, *When Work
       Disappears* (Random House, 1996), p. 246.

116   *too many immigrants are entering America*   Roger L. Connor, Oral His-
       tory, January 27, 1989, Gellman Library, George Washington University,
       pp. 136–37. Rodolfo de la Garza et al., *Latino Voices* (Westview Press,
       1992), p. 101. An excellent analysis of polls of Hispanics on immigration is-
       sues is found in Peter Skerry, *Mexican Americans: The Ambivalent Minor-
       ity* (Free Press, 1993), pp. 300–304. While Hispanics, however defined by
       the pollsters, have complex views that do not exactly match up with overall
       national opinion, their opposition to illegal immigration levels is captured
       in every poll.

116   *"if anyone had cause for complaint"*   Higham, *Strangers*, 45.

CHAPTER 14

117   *"a federation of distinct nationalities"*   Horace M. Kallen, "Democracy
       versus The Melting Pot," *Nation* (Feb. 18–25, 1915).

118   *"the spirit of ethnicity"*   Quoted in Arthur Mann, *Immigrants in American
       Life* (Houghton-Mifflin, 1974), pp. 242–43. On the rise of cultural plural-
       ism, see Philip Gleason, *Speaking of Diversity: Language and Ethnicity in
       Twentieth Century America* (Johns Hopkins University Press, 1992).

118   *took on the name Multiculturalism*   Richard Bernstein, *Dictatorship of
       Virtue* (Knopf, 1994), p. 4.

118   *"Struggling to be born"*   Michael Novak, "The New Ethnicity," *The Center
       Magazine* (July–Aug. 1974), p. 25.

119   *"We seem incapable yet"*   Quoted in Virginia Abernathy, *Population Politics*
       (Insight Books, 1993), p. 11.

119   *"Something good—movement towards a more inclusive"*   Robert Pickus,
       "Current Work Strategy: Rescuing and Improving A Common Civic Culture,"
       The James Madison Foundation (1997).

120   *"The balance is shifting from unum to pluribus"*   Arthur M. Schlesinger, Jr., *The Disuniting of America* (W. W. Norton, 1992), pp. 2, 70–71, 78–80.

120   *this third republic had the outward trappings*   Michael Lind, *The Next American Nation* (Free Press, 1995). On the replacement of the founding American story by a cacophony of stories, see Nathan Glazer, "American Epic: Then and Now," *The Public Interest* (Winter 1998).

120   *"ethno-racial tensions are acute"*   John Higham, "In Place of a Sequel or, How I Lost My Subject," unpublished MS, author's possession, pp. 16–17. See the cover and story, "Who Are We?" *Time* (July 8, 1991).

120   *"Some of them in North America?"*   Daniel Patrick Moynihan, *Pandaemonium: Ethnicity in International Relations* (Oxford University Press, 1993), p. 168.

121   *"If the American people truly want"*   Lawrence Auster, *The Path to National Suicide* (American Immigration Control Foundation, 1990), pp. 8–9.

121   *Brimelow agreed that small numbers*   Peter Brimelow, *Alien Nation: Common Sense About America's Immigration Disaster* (Random House, 1995), pp. 20, 57, 123. See also Brimelow's influential article, "Time to Rethink Immigration," *National Review* 44 (June 1992), and "Alien Nation: Round 2," at www.vdare.com (accessed September 15, 2002).

122   *America had always been a society*   Mark Krikorian, "A Flawed Jewel," *Immigration Review* 22 (Summer 1995): 14–16. See also Otis L. Graham, Jr., "A Second Opinion," *Immigration Review* (Fall 1995): 14–16.

122   *"glue of a sense of community"*   Bouvier and Grant, *How Many Americans?* pp. 147, 115.

122   *"a new wave of immigration larger"*   William Jefferson Clinton, commencement address at Portland State University, *Weekly Compilation of Presidential Documents*, 34 (June 13, 1998), pp. 1121–25.

123   *"that word earned a bad reputation"*   Barbara Jordan, "The Americanization Ideal," *New York Times*, Sept. 11, 1995.

123   *"The U.S. has experienced these effects"*   Weintraub quoted in Leon Bouvier, *Peaceful Invasions*, p. 126.

123   *Our national culture had not been splintered*   A typical argument of this kind is found in Michael Barone, "Our Immigrants Always Melted Before," *The American Enterprise* (Dec. 2000)

125   *"flowing into a defined region"*   David Kennedy, "Can We Still Afford To Be a Nation of Immigrants?" *The Atlantic Monthly* (Nov. 1996).

126   *"docile, obedient, inherently honest"*   Clare Sheridan, "Contested Citizenship: National Identity and the Mexican Immigration Debates of the 1920s," *Journal of American Ethnic History* (Spring 2002): 23.

126   *Public opinion polling*   Polls on immigration are analyzed in Gimpel and
        Edwards, *Congressional Politics*, chap. 2.

128   *Several scholars there had been slowly breaking*   The American equiva-
        lent of Weber, in a sense, was Edward Banfield, whose *The Moral Basis of
        a Backward Society* (Free Press, 1958) was a brilliant cultural explanation
        of Italian regional disparities, appearing just as the Weberian point of view
        was about to disappear beneath a new orthodoxy for half a century. A pio-
        neer in reviving discussion of the role of culture was Lawrence Harrison,
        whose *Underdevelopment Is A State of Mind* (University Press of America,
        1985) and *Who Prospers? How Cultural Values Shape Economic and
        Political Success* (Basic Books, 1992) led to an alliance with Harvard's
        Samuel Huntington, leading to the publication of the multiauthor study,
        Harrison and Huntington, eds., *Culture Matters: How Values Shape
        Human Progress* (Basic Books, 2000). See also the influential economic
        history of the world, David Landes, *The Wealth and Poverty of Nations*
        (Norton, 1998). Harrison acknowledge his considerable debt to Latin
        American writers such as the Venezuelan Carlos Rangel, the Peruvian
        Mario Vargas Llosa, and the Argentinian Mariano Grondon.

128   *"chronic malaise of political instability"*   Eugene Robinson, "Why Doesn't
        Latin America Work?" *Washington Post National Weekly Edition* (Jan.
        6–12, 1992), p. 11.

129   *"failure to build solid democratic"*   Harrison, *Who Prospers?* p. 175.

129   *"Mexican immigration poses challenges"*   Samuel P. Huntington, "The
        Special Case of Mexican Immigration: Why Mexico Is a Problem," *The
        American Enterprise* (Dec. 2000): 20–22, and Chavez, "Are Mexicans
        Melting Into America or Not?" Ibid., p. 25.

130   *"Mexican immigration reduces wages"*   Steven A. Camarota, "Immigra-
        tion From Mexico: Assessing the Impact on the United States," Center for
        Immigration Studies Paper 19 (July 2001): 5–10. See also Hugh Graham,
        Collision Course, pp. 180–85.

130   *Just months later, the Mexican*   The Mexican report, Consejo Nacional de
        Poblacion (CONAPO), *La Migration Mexico-Estados Unidos 2001* (Nov.
        2001), was reviewed in David Simcox, "Another 50 Years of
        Mass Mexican Immigration," *C IS Backgrounder* (Mar. 2002) at www.
        conapo.gob.mx/m_en_cifras/principal.html (accessed March 15, 2003).

131   *"must accept the fact that"*   Suro, *Strangers*, pp. 247–77.

131   *"I have proudly proclaimed that"*   Roger McGrath, "Letter From Califor-
        nia," *Chronicles* (Oct. 2000), p. 34, and "Mexico Admits Plan of 'La Re-
        conquista' in California," *Voice of Citizens Together* (Mar.–April 1998), p.
        1. Angel Osuna commented on news reports of his remarks that he was
        "partly serious, partly joking, about Reconquista."

132   *"will result in the browning of America"*   Brimelow, *Alien Nation*, p. 25.
      McGrath, "Letter From California," p. 36.

132   *red, white and green flag of Mexico*   For a picture of the event and dis-
      cussion, see David G. Gutierrez, "Migration, Emergent Ethnicity, and the
      'Third Space': The Shifting Politics of Nationalism in Greater Mexico,"
      Journal of American History (Sept. 1999): 481–517.

132   *"Somos Mexicanos!"*   From *Immigration: Threatening the Bonds of Our
      Union*, video produced by Voices of Citizens Together (Los Angeles); and
      see review by J. P. Lubinskas, *The Social Contract* (Summer 1999): 269.

132   *"The question is not whether"*   Fred Siegel, *The Future Once Happened
      Here* (Free Press, 1997), p. 145.

132   *"This constant influx"*   Linda Chavez, "Our Hispanic Predicament,"
      Commentary (June 1998): 49.

132   *a Texas town passed an ordinance*   "Texas Town Holds Meetings in Spanish
      Only," *New York Times*, Aug. 22, 1999.

132   *"the possibility looms that"*   Kennedy, "Can We Still Afford."

132   *Peter Skerry has cautioned*   Skerry's point is found in *Mexican Americans*,
      esp. chap. 10. For survey data confirming Mexican assimilation, see
      Rudolfo de la Garza et al., "Will the Real Americans Please Stand Up,"
      American Journal of Political Science 40 (May 1996).

132   *Others, like Californian*   Victor Davis Hanson, *Mexifornia: A State of Be-
      coming* (Encounter Books, 2003), pp. 147–48.

133   *"transnationalization"*   David Gutierrez, *Walls and Mirrors: Mexican
      Americans, Mexican Immigrants, and the Politics of Ethnicity* (University
      of California Press, 1995), esp. chap. 6. See also Peter Andreas, "The Mak-
      ing of Amerexico: Mishandling Illegal Immigration," *World Policy Journal*
      (Summer 1994).

CHAPTER 15

135   *"There is simply nothing"*   Daniel Patrick Moynihan, "Defenders and
      Invaders," *Washington Post*, June 13, 1977.

136   *"the increase in human population"*   Bill McKibben, "A Special Moment
      in History," *The Atlantic Monthly* (May 1998), p. 56.

136   *some experts estimated*   All global population estimates are from the
      United Nations Population Division (UNPD) publications, most notably
      World Population Prospects: The 1998 Revision (1999) and *World Popula-
      tion Prospects: The 2000 Revision: Key Findings* (2001); see also
      www.un.org/esa/population/unpop.htm.

136   *demographers recalculated their projections*   David R. Francis, "New
       Global Forecast," *Christian Science Monitor*, Mar. 11, 2002, p. 7.

136   *The second was more an opportunity*   The title of the UNPD report, *Re-
       placement Migration: Is It a Solution to Declining and Ageing Populations*
       (UN, 2001), implied that there were nations declining in population, but
       this was not so. Low fertility rates and aging of populations was real and
       eventual decline in overall numbers was inevitable somewhere ahead if
       these fertility rates persisted. Such societies will then have to accept
       shrinking populations for the multiple benefits that would bring. At some
       point, however, stabilization at desired levels could come from only some
       combination of rising fertility and immigration. Compared with the popu-
       lation spike we are living through, these are nice problems to have.

137   *When shrinkage begins*   For a positive view of the shift to stable, older
       populations, see Lincoln Day, *The Future of Low-Birthrate Populations*
       (Routledge, 1992).

137   *"Human beings and the natural world"*   This document is reprinted in
       Paul and Anne Ehrlich, *Betrayal of Science and Reason* (Island Press,
       1996), pp. 242–50. The 1993 Scientific Summit on World Population, a
       meeting of fifty-six of the world's scientific academies, urged global zero
       population growth, and declared that "the earth is finite, and . . . natural
       systems are being pushed ever closer to their limits." National Academy of
       Sciences, *Population Summit of the World's Scientific Academies* (Wash-
       ington, D.C.: National Academy Press, 1993).

137   *"it is impossible to know whether"*   J. R. McNeill, *Something New under
       the Sun: An Environmental History of the Twentieth-Century World* (W.
       W. Norton, 2000), pp. 358–59.

138   *Not all who shared these concerns*   Paul R. and Anne H. Ehrlich, *The
       Population Explosion* (Simon and Schuster, 1990), pp. 132–33.

138   *"It will be very brief"*   Walter Youngquist, *GeoDestinies: The Inevitable
       Control of Earth Resources over Nations and Individuals* (National Book
       Company, 1997), chap. 12.

138   *There were Deep Greens*   Hal Rothman to author, July 10, 2003.

139   *"There is no meaningful physical limit"*   Julian Simon, *The Ultimate
       Resource* (Princeton University Press, 1981). Simon confessed that he had
       been able to recover from deep personal depression only when he wrote pos-
       itive things about bringing new babies into the world. So that is what he did.

140   *"This is my long-run forecast"*   Quoted in Ed Regis, "The Environment is
       Going to Hell . . ." *Wired* (1997), p. 198.

140   *his clones such as journalist*   Conservative, free-market, and business-
       oriented foundations supported a small stable of writers who argued, in the

Simonite mold, that natural resources were becoming more plentiful, the environment cleaner, and population growth bringing rising living standards, but none had Simon's inflammatory boldness or achieved his notoriety. A representative selection of Brownlash argument is found in Ronald Bailey, ed., *The True State of the Planet* (Free Press, 1995). On the Brownlash movement, see the Ehrlichs's *Betrayal* and Andrew Rowell, *Green Backlash: Global Subversion of the Environmental Movement* (Routledge, 1996).

140   *Two years after Simon's death*   See Bjorn Lomborg, *The Skeptical Environmentalist: Measuring the Real State of the World* (Cambridge University Press, 2001).

140   *This time the scientific community*   Reviews of Lomborg's work include critical reviews in *Scientific American* (Jan. 2002), Lomborg's reply in the same journal (May 2002), Lomborg's web site (www.lomborg.org), an exchange in *Grist Magazine*, Dec. 12, 2001 (www.gristmagazine.com), an article in *The Economist* (Aug. 23, 2001) and in *Environment* (July/Aug., 2002). On the face of it, Simon and Lomborg were superficially informed across the range of the environmental sciences. More important, they were essentially uninterested in and profoundly wrong about the massive and undeniable deterioration of the ecological foundations of human life and the contribution of population growth in intensifying the damage. "The ecologist has a different world view" from "the cornucopian economist," wrote Harvard biologist Edward O. Wilson in "The Bottleneck," *Scientific American* (Feb. 2002), an article that offers an extended comparison of these two world views, and a critique of "the cornucopian economist" view. The article is excerpted from Wilson, *The Future of Life* (Alfred Knopf, 2002).

141   *There was some attention to population*   In a remarkable book of 1950 in which the immigration policy choices were placed in a demographic context, William Bernard asserted with no real supporting data that the U.S. could absorb a population of three hundred million. He worried that our slowing birth rates would not get us there and urged immigration expansion to reach his three hundred million goal. (William Bernard, *American Immigration Policy: A Reappraisal* [Harper, 1950], pp. 185–95).

141   *Then in the 1962–1963 House hearings*   See the seventeen-volume special series of the hearings of the Committee on the Judiciary, Subcommittee No. 1, U.S. Congress, House of Representatives, *Study of Population and Immigration Problems* (GPO, 1962–1963).

142   *"What is the cause?"*   Stefan Collini, introduction to *The Two Cultures*, rev. ed., by C. P. Snow (Cambridge University Press, 1993), p. lxxi.

142   *attempted "carrying capacity analysis"*   For a discussion of such estimates over time, see Joel E. Cohen, *How Many People Can the Earth Support?* (W. W. Norton, 1995), and Leon Bouvier, "The Demography of America's Future," University of Denver Center for Public Policy and Contemporary

Issues (1993). Paul and Anne Ehrlich, "The Most Overpopulated Nation," in *Elephants in the Volkswagen*, ed. Lindsey Grant (W. H. Freeman, 1992), chap. 10, and David and Marcia Pimentel, "Land, Energy and Water: The Constraints Governing Ideal U.S. Population Size," unpublished manuscript, author's possession, Jan. 1990.

142   *If ending national population growth*   Commission on Population Growth, *Population Growth*, chap. 13.

143   *"In my opinion"*   Quoted in Bernard, *American Immigration Policy*, p. 197.

143   *Over the remaining years*   Congressman Scheuer, who had served on the Rockefeller commission on Population Growth and the American Future, established a Select Committee on Population in the House of Representatives, providing a small rallying point for the population-based critique of mass immigration. See, for example, "Legal and Illegal Immigration to the United States," Report of the Select Committee on Population, U.S. House, 95th Cong., 2nd sess. (Dec. 1978), which states: "Decisions must be made about the future size of the U.S. population, and population policy cannot be made without a corresponding immigration policy" (p. 32).

143   *Demographer Leon Bouvier*   Leon Bouvier, "How to Get There from Here," in Grant, *Elephants*, chap. 13.

143   *But it did not*   Beck, *The Case Against*, chap. 4; and see www.numbersusa.org. See also Camarota and Bouvier, "Impact of New Americans."

144   *With immigration pushing*   "2100 Census Forecast: 2000 x 2, Minorities Expected to Account for 60 Percent of U.S. Population," *The Washington Post*, Jan. 13, 2000, A5.

144   *Even these projections*   Steven Camarota, "The Impact of Immigration on U.S. Population Growth," testimony prepared for the House Judiciary Committee, July 19, 2001), Center for Immigration Studies, www.cis.org.

144   *"Do we really want an America"*   Richard D. Lamm, "Immigration: The Ultimate Growth Issue," typescript (March 1995); Lamm, "Bigger Isn't Better for U.S. Immigration Policy," *Seattle Post-Intelligencer*, Sept. 4, 2001.

146   *"California . . . will be twice as crowded"*   Ed Lytwak, "A Tale of Two Futures," *NPG Forum* (Mar. 1999); Bouvier and Grant, *How Many Americans?*; Bouvier quoted in Roy Beck, "Immigration #1 in U.S. Growth," *The Social Contract* (Winter 1991–92); Bouvier, "The Impact of Immigration on U.S. Population Size, 1950–2050," *NPG Forum* (1998); "State Population of 47 Million Forecast by 2050," *Los Angeles Times*, April 21, 1994, A27; review of National Research Council, *The New Americans*, in *Immigration Review* (Spring 1998); "Prediction: 50 Million Californians," *Los Angeles Daily News*, Nov. 29, 1998, A5; Vir-

ginia Ellis, "Study Says State's Population Will Double by 2040," *Los Angeles Times*, Dec. 18, 1998.

146   *"we believe that reducing"* President's Council on Sustainable Development, *Sustainable Development: A New Consensus for Prosperity, Opportunity, and a Healthy Environment for the Future* (Washington, D.C., 1996).

146   *But the Green organizations* See Roy Beck and Leon Kolankiewicz, "The Environmental Movement's Retreat from Advocating U.S. Population Stabilization: 1970–1998," *Journal of Policy History* 12 (2000). On the Wilderness Society's almost unique courage on the population-immigration connection, see "The Wilderness Society: TWS Population Policy," at www.wilderness.org.

147   *"the single most important environmental issue"* For a review of the controversy, see 30-year Sierra Club member Ben Zuckerman's account, "Immigration and the Sierra Club," *Immigration Review* (Fall 1998), James Ricci, "The Sierra Club and the Immigration Freight Train," *Los Angeles Times Magazine* (June 9, 2002), and John H. Cushman, "An Uncomfortable Debate Fuels a Sierra Club Election," *New York Times*, April 5, 1998.

148   *"the quality of the American environment today"* Schuck, *Citizens*, p. 355; Cushman, "Uncomfortable Debate"; Ricci, "Immigration Freight Train."

148   *"there is no doubt some truth"* David Kennedy, letter to the editor, *The Atlantic Monthly* (Feb. 1997), pp. 13–14.

148   *Hal Kane, author* 86th American Assembly Conference on "World Migration and U.S. Policy," Arden House, Harriman, N.Y., Nov. 10–13, 1994.

149   *"Apart from some business executives"* Christopher Jencks, "Who Should Get In?" *The New York Review* (Dec. 20, 2001), p. 97.

149   *"per capita national emissions allocations"* Peter Singer, *One World: The Ethics of Globalization* (Yale University Press, 2002), pp. 35–47.

CHAPTER 16

153   *Historian David Reimers* David Reimers, *Unwelcome Strangers: American Identity and the Turn Against Immigration* (Columbia University Press, 1998), pp. 70–71.

154   *"Congress was clearly more liberal"* Barkan, *And Still They Come*, p. 82.

154   *It was in California* For an account of the battle over Proposition 187, see Peter Schrag, *Paradise Lost: California's Experience, America's Future* (Berkeley: University of California Press, 1998), pp. 229–34; Otis L. Graham, Jr., "California's Proposition 187," *Conservative Review* (Mar./Apr.

1995), pp. 25–26; Ron Unz, "California and the End of White America," *Commentary* (Nov. 1999): 17–29.

154   *"This meant that approximately"*   Graham, *Collision Course*, p. 129–30. Before Graham's superb account of how this came to be there had been scant attention paid to the intersection of these two programs. An exception is James S. Robb, "Affirmative Action for Immigrants: The Entitlement Nobody Wanted," *The Social Contract* (Winter 1995–1996).

155   *Geographer William Clark*:   William A. V. Clark, *The California Cauldron: Immigrations and the Fortune of Local Communities* (Guildford Press, 1998), pp. 167–72.

156   *"Legal immigration, however, has costs"*   Jordan, "Americanization Ideal," p. 15; Jordan testimony before House Judiciary Subcommittee on Immigration, June 28, 1995, Federal Document Clearing House; Testimony of Barbara Jordan, House Committee on the Judiciary, Subcommittee on Immigration and Claims, Mar. 30, 1995 (www.utexas.edu/lbj/uscir); Testimony of Barbara Jordan, House Subcommittee on Immigration and Claims, Feb. 24, 1995; (www.utexas.edu/lbj/uscir). See also Mary Beth Rogers, *Barbara Jordan: American Hero* (Bantam, 1998).

156   *"consistent with my own views"*   John F. Harris, "Clinton Backs Call to Reduce Immigration," *Washington Post* (June 8, 1995), A1.

156   *"We are not against immigration"*   FAIR packet, "Immigration Reform Awareness Week," Washington, D.C., Apr. 23–25, 1998.

157   *Congress seemed to move*   *Congressional Record Daily Digest* (Mar. 19, 1996), H-2373–74.

157   *"the American people are so very fed up"*   Quoted in Roberto Suro, *Watching America's Door: The Immigration Backlash and the New Policy Debate* (New York: Twentieth Century Fund, 1996), p. 10.

158   *"The pro-immigration coalition desired"*   Reimers, *Unwelcome Strangers*, pp. 142–43, For the politics of immigration reform in the mid-90s, see Reimers, chap. 7.

158   *"We kept them from getting almost anything"*   John Heilemann, "Do You Know the Way to Ban Jose?" *Wired* (Aug. 1996), p. 7.

158   *"remarkably muted and civil"*   Nathan Glazer, "America's Open Door," Jan.–Feb. 2000, at http://www.harvard-magazine.com.

158   *When the new century arrived*   Camarota, "The Impact of Immigration on U.S. Population Growth"; Camarota, "Immigrants in the U.S.—2002: A Snapshot of America's Foreign-born Population," *CIS Backgrounder* (Nov. 2002); "Now, a Nation of More Immigrants Than Ever," *Christian Science Monitor*, Feb. 7, 2002; Cindy Rodriguez, "Census: Undocumenteds Affect Economy," *Boston Globe*, Feb. 6, 2001.

158   *The INS quietly gave up*   See the comments of INS associate commissioner for policy and planning Robert Bach, in Louis Uchitelle, "I.N.S. Looks the Other Way on Illegal Immigrant Labor," *New York Times*, Mar. 9, 2000, A1.

159   *"The winners are employers who get"*   Jencks, "Who Should Get In?" parts 1 and 2; George Borjas, "Let's Be Clear about Whom We Want to Let in," *Washington Post*, Dec. 23, 2001, B2; Borjas, "Top Ten"; Glazer, "America's Open Door," p. 2.

159   *"Migration is the central issue"*   Samuel P. Huntington, *New Perspectives Quarterly* (Spring 2001): 22–24.

159   *"deeply felt conversion experience"*   Stephen Steinlight, "The Jewish Stake in America's Changing Demography: Reconsidering a Misguided Immigration Policy," *CIS Backgrounder* (Oct. 2001): 1, 2, 12, 14.

160   *William Buckley's* National Review   The first *National Review* opening to the restrictionist outlook was probably Peter Brimelow's influential article, "Time to Rethink Immigration," *National Review* (June 1992). See also the five articles from the symposium "Does America Have An Assimilation Problem?" *The American Enterprise* (Dec. 2000).

160   *the issue had become more politically acute*   "Huddled Masses, Please Stay Away," *The Economist* (June 25, 2002); Robin Oakley, "Europe's Tangle Over Immigration," June 4, 2001, at http://europe.cnn.com; Molly Moore, "900 Fleeing Kurds Stranded off France," Feb. 17, 2001, at www.washingtonpost.com; Marc Champion, "Immigration Moves to Front Burner in Europe," *The Wall Street Journal*, April 24, 2002; Omer Taspinar, "Europe's Muslim Street," *Foreign Policy* (Mar.–April 2003); Rod Dreher, "On Tiptoe through the Tulips," *National Review* (July 15, 2002); Alan Cowell, "Migrants Feel Chill in a Testy Europe," *New York Times International* (April 28, 2002); Paul Gottfried, "All Used Up,"www.vdare.com (November 1, 2001); Anthony Browne, "Britain Is Losing Britain," *London Times* (August 7, 2002); Marion Donhoff et al. *Weil Das Land Sich Andern Muss* (Why the Country Must Change), edited and translated by Jack Miles, in *The Social Contract* (Fall 1995).

162   *Division of several European states*   James Kurth, "Migration and the Dynamics of Empire," *The National Interest* (Spring 2003).

162   *In the 1990s organized labor*   See Vernon Briggs, *Immigration and American Unionism* (Cornell University Press, 2001), and David Bacon, "Labor Fights for Immigrants," *The Nation* (May 21, 2001).

163   *Voter surveys and poll evidence*   James G. Gimpel and Karen Kaufmann, "Impossible Dream or Distant Reality?" *CIS Backgrounder* (Aug., 2001). Another argument that the GOP was headed in exactly the wrong political direction by sponsoring amnesties and porous borders was made by Peter

Brimelow and Ed Rubenstein, "Electing a New People," *National Review* (June 16, 1997).

163   *"unless the California Republican Party"*   Sherry Jeffe, "California Conservatism's Worst Nightmare Revealed," *Los Angeles Times*, Aug. 18, 1997; Chris Parkes, "Republicans Fade in California," *London Financial Times*, Jan. 23, 2001.

163   *House majority leader Newt Gingrich*   Jodi Wilgoren, "Chastised GOP Softens Stance on Immigration," *Los Angeles Times*, Nov. 23, 1997, Al.

163   *Muslims are "natural conservatives"*   Grover Norquist, "Conservatives Grow Up," *The American Spectator* (June 2001).

164   *A formidable if bizarre lobbying coalition*   Peter Grier and Dante Chinni, "On Immigrants, a Great Softening," *The Christian Science Monitor*, July 31, 2001; Thomas Edsall and Cheryl Thompson, "Alliance Forms on Immigrant Policies: Business, Church, Labor Groups Unite on Liberalization," *The Washington Post*, Aug. 7, 2001.

164   *The broad dissatisfaction*   Buchanan's critique of immigration policy, and much else, is found in Patrick J. Buchanan, *The Death of the West: How Dying Populations and Immigrant Invasions Imperil Our Country and Civilization* (New York: 2002). For the platform positions of the three parties, see *FAIR Immigration Report* (Oct. 2000).

164   *"the great forgotten issue"*   Robert Samuelson, "Ignoring Immigration," *Washington Post*, May 3, 2000.

164   *President Bush moved to capitalize*   Eric Schmitt, "Bush Panel Backs Legalizing Status of Some Immigrants," *New York Times*, July 24, 2001; Editorial,"Rethinking Mexican Immigration," *New York Times*, July 23, 2001; Donna Smith, "Top House Democrat Backs Broad Immigration Plan," Reuters News Service, July 20, 2001, at dailynews.yahoo.com.

CHAPTER 17

165   *The Fox-Bush deal*   Ronald Brownstein, "Green Light, Red Light," *The American Prospect* (Nov. 19, 2001).

165   *"They came as students, tourists"*   Steven A. Camarota, "The Open Door: How Militant Islamic Terrorists Entered and Remained in the United States, 1993–2001," Center for Immigration Studies Paper 21 (May 2002). See also Michelle Malkin, *Invasion: How America Still Welcomes Terrorists, Criminals, and Other Foreign Menaces to Our Shore* (Regnery, 2002), chap. 2. *The National Review* obtained copies of fifteen of the visa applications of the nineteen hijackers of September 11, and experts with foreign-service experience concurred that all of them would have been denied if the law and

administrative regulations had been followed. See Joel Mowbray, "Visas That Should Have Been Denied," *National Review* (Oct. 28, 2002).

166   *"Our vulnerability to these abominations"*   Mark Krikorian, "Get Tight: Now More Than Ever, Immigration Should Be Curtailed," *National Review* (Mar. 25, 2002).

166   *"serious immigration reforms"*   Rosemary Jenks, "The Changing Dynamics in Congress," *The Social Contract* (Winter 2002).

166   *"nativist sentiment has come to be viewed"*   Chitra Ragavan, "Coming to America," *U.S. News and World Report* (Feb. 18, 2002).

166   *"We're not talking about immigration"*   Quoted in Mark Krikorian, "Asymmetrical Warfare and Immigration," Dec. 6, 2002, at www.inthenationalinterest.com. Ziglar was not alone. "There's no relation between immigration and terrorism," said Cecelia Munoz of the National Council of La Raza. Mark Krikorian, "Safety in (Lower) Numbers," *CIS Backgrounder* (Oct., 2002), p. 1.

167   *"the new face of the immigration debate"*   Malkin, *Invasion*, pp. xiii–xiv, 14–21.

167   *but one driven by a bigger problem*   Jessica Vaughan, "Shortcuts to Immigration: The 'Temporary' Visa Program Is Broken," *CIS Backgrounder* (Jan. 2003).

168   *Economist George Borjas*   George Borjas, "Rethinking Foreign Students," *National Review* (June 17, 2002).

171   *the rest of the immigration reform agenda*   See Camarota, "Immigrants in the United States—2002."

171   *"The safety of our citizens must come before"*   Malkin, *Invasion*, chap. 10; pp. xvi, 75–77. See also Malkin, "The Deportation Abyss," *CIS Backgrounder* (Sept. 2002).

172   *The Center for Immigration Studies suggested*   Testimony of Stephen A. Camarota, director of research of the CIS, before the Senate Judiciary Committee, Subcommittee on Technology, Terrorism, and Government Information, Oct. 12, 2001, at www.cis.org. See also Camarota, "The Open Door," Krikorian, "Safety," "How a Document Security System Would Work," *FAIR Issue Brief* (September 27, 2002), and John O'Sullivan, "May We Get Serious Now?" *National Review* (April 22, 2002).

172   *"Tighter policies, and tighter enforcement"*   NR Editors, "Time for Realism," *National Review* (May 31, 2002).

173   *Americans already have a "National ID Card"*   David Simcox, "Making Our De Facto National ID Card Work," *The Social Contract* (Winter 2002).

173   *Harvard law professor*   Alan Dershowitz, *Why Terrorism Works* (Yale University Press, 2002), and Stephen Brill, "The Biggest Hole in the Net," *Newsweek* (Dec. 30, 2002).

173   *the Enhanced Border Security and Visa Entry*   Rosemary Jenks, "The Enhanced Border Security and Visa Entry Reform Act of 2002," *CIS Backgrounder* (June 2002).

174   *An August 2002 report*   Steven A. Camarota, "Immigrants from the Middle East," *CIS Backgrounder* (August 2002); Daniel Pipes and Khalid Duran, "Muslim Immigrants in the United States," *CIS Backgrounder* (August 2002).

174   *"long-term, Muslim-specific immigration policy"*   Krikorian argued that cutting immigration across the board would facilitate all the antiterrorist reforms being discussed and achieve other desirable objectives, besides. Krikorian, "Safety," p. 6.

175   *new guidelines for "profiling"*   Curt Anderson, "Federal Agencies Announce Ban on Practice of Racial Profiling," and Mark J. Prendergast, "Court Sides with 9-11 Secrecy" in the *New York Times* (June 18, 2003).

175   *"a fundamental readjustment of [State] Department"*   James Dao, "U.S. Embassies Remain Lax in Issuing Visas, Report Says," *New York Times*, Dec, 21, 2002.

176   *A General Accounting Office Official told a Congressional panel*   Joel Mowbray, "Visa Express Axed,"   *National Review Online* (July 10, 2002); "Possible Terrorists May Be in U.S.," *Hearst News Service* (June 19, 2003).

176   *She had been "wrong"*   Rosemary Jenks, "The Enhanced Border Security and Visa Entry Reform Act of 2002,"   *CIS Backgrounder* (June 2002).

176   *prohibited a "national identification card"*   David Firestone and Elizabeth Baker, "House Leadership Bows to President on Security Department," *New York Times*, July 19, 2002.

177   *September 11 seemed to have made no difference*   Jim Yardley, "Human Cargo Again Treads from Mexico North to U.S.," *New York Times*, Nov. 24, 2002; Camarota, "Immigrants in the U.S.—2002," and Camarota, "800,000+ Illegals Entering Annually in Late 1990s," Center for Immigration Studies, "CIS This Week," Feb. 4, 2003, at www.cis.org.

CHAPTER 18

179   *"How can this be, when recent"*   Peter H. Schuck, "The Open Society," *The New Republic* (Apr. 13, 1998): 16.

179   *all the reformers thought*   The range of reform proposals for more restricted immigration, along with two arguments in favor or reform toward open borders, may be found in Richard Lamm and Alan Simpson, eds.,

"Blueprints for an Ideal Legal Immigration Policy," Center for Immigration Studies Paper 17 (Mar. 2001).

181 *hospitals were writing off $2 billion*   Dana Canedy, "Hospitals Feel Strain of Illegal Immigrants," *New York Times*, Aug. 25, 2002; Julia Malone, "Hospitals: Illegal Immigrants Costly," July 30, 2002, at www.palmbeachpost.com; Center for Disease Control, "Increase in African Immigrants and Refugees with Tuberculosis—Seattle-King County, Washington, 1998–2000," Oct. 11, 2002, at www.cdc.gov/mmwr/preview; "Doctors Say Leprosy Cases on Rise in Northeast U.S.," *New York Times*, Feb. 23, 2003.

182 *the human smuggling our system invites*   Joel Brinkley, "CIA Depicts a Vast Trade in Forced Labor," *New York Times*, April 2, 2000. See also John Hagan and Alberto Palloni, "Immigration and Crime in the United States," in *The Immigration Debate*, ed. James P. Smith and Barry Edmonston (National Academy Press, 1998).

183 *Walter Mondale noticed in 1967*   Walter Mondale quoted in Reimers, *Still the Golden Door*, p. 258. For a critique of the brain-drain aspects of U.S. policy, see Graham, *Collision Course*, chap. 5.

183 *Western "borders were beyond control"*   Jagdish Bhagwati, "Borders Beyond Control," *Foreign Affairs* (January–February 2003); Tamar Jacoby, "Don't Slam the Door," *Reader's Digest* (March 2002); Diane Ravitch, "Diversity, Tragedy, and the Schools," *Brookings Review* (Winter 2002).

184 *"most people want to admit fewer immigrants"*   Schuck, "The Open Society," p. 17.

185 *"was composed of organizations representing those"*   Gary P. Freeman, "Reform and Retreat in U.S. Immigration Policy," *People and Place* 6 (1998): 9. See also Carolyn Wong, "The Politics of Immigration: An Analysis of Policy Reform in Congress, 1965–1996" (Ph.D. Diss., University of California, Los Angeles, 1997). An important account of the formation of the open-borders lobby and the Ford Foundation's role is William R. Hawkins, *Importing Revolution: Open Borders and the Radical Agenda* (American Immigration Control Foundation, 1994); see also Joseph Fallon, "Buying Open Borders," *The Social Contract* (Summer 2000): 256.

185 *LULAC from its founding in the 1920s*   See Gutierrez, *Walls and Mirrors*, and Katsuyuki Murata, "The (Re)Shaping of Chicano Ethnicity through the Inclusion/Exclusion of Undocumented Immigrants," *American Studies International* (June 2001).

186 *"a betrayal of the legacy of the past"*   Briggs, *Immigration and American Unionism*, pp. 164–69; Georgie Anne Geyer, "Union Cards for Illegals," *The Social Contract* (Summer 2000).

188   *Immigration was "not a topic but a symbol"*   Katherine Betts, *Ideology and Immigration* (Melbourne University Press, 1988), p. 5, revised and extended as *The Great Divide* (Duffy and Snellgrove, 1999), pp. 5–6.

189   *distributed peel-off bar-code tattoos*   Stern, "Jobs Magnet."

189   *Hannah Arendt once pointed out*   As noted by Senator Moynihan in an interview with Jeffrey Toobin, "Pat 'N' Bill," *The New Yorker* (Feb. 8, 1999), p. 30.

190   *"the conservatives get their cheap labor"*   Edward Abbey, "Immigration and Liberal Taboos," in *One Life at a Time Please* (Henry Holt, 1988).

190   *"we disagree with those who would label"*   U.S. Commission on Immigration Reform, *U.S. Immigration: Restoring Credibility: Executive Summary* (Washington, D.C., 1994).

191   *"they certainly do not represent a return"*   David H. Bennett, *The Party of Fear: From Nativist Movements to the New Right in American History* (University of North Carolina Press, 1988), pp. 372–73.

191   *"The immigration debate was being conducted"*   Peter Schuck, *Citizens, Strangers, and In-Betweens: Essays on Immigration and Citizenship* (Westview, 1998), p. 6.

191   *"What do you make of the nativists?"*   Conversation with the author, June 1995.

191   *well-educated "symbolic analysts"*   Robert B. Reich, *The Work of Nations* (A. A. Knopf, 1991), pp. 288–89.

192   *"The gap between the opinions"*   The CCFR poll results, with little comentary, are found at www.worldviews.org/detail reports/usreport/html/ch5s5.html. For analysis, see Roy Beck and Steven Camarota, "Elite vs. Public Opinion: An Examination of Divergent Views on Immigration," *CIS Backgrounder* (Dec. 2002).

194   *Hardin gave an impressive sermon*   Boulding, quoted in Garrett Hardin, *Living within Limits* (Oxford University Press, 1993), p. 58.

195   *"will have to be stringently controlled"*   Tanton's essay is reprinted in Rohe, *Mary Lou and John Tanton*, appendix A.

CHAPTER 19

197   *"The dogmas of the quiet past"*   Abraham Lincoln, Annual Message to Congress, December 1, 1862.

199   *"a country of perpetual immigration"*   Quoted in August Gribbin, "Hispanics Growing in Numbers, Political Clout," *The Washington Times*, Oct. 4, 1999.

199   Any *"migration flow"*   Quoted in Samuel P. Huntington, *The Clash of Civilizations and the Remaking of World Order* (Simon and Schuster, 1996), p. 199.

199   *"cannot cope with illegal immigration"*   David North, "Why Democratic Governments Cannot Cope with Illegal Immigration," (Paris: OECD, 1991). See also Christian Joppke, "Why Liberal States Accept Unwanted Immigration," *World Politics* (Jan. 1998).

199   *"destined to be overwhelmed"*   Huntington, *Clash*, pp. 203–4.

199   *"We do have the ultimate weapon"*   "Could There Be A Flood?" *The Social Contract* (Winter 1997–98): 99

200   *When the UN Population Division*   United Nations Population Division, *International Migration 2002* (UN, 2002); see www.unpopulation.org.

200   *teeming, 1.2 billion-peopled China*   Lena H. Sun, "The Dragon Within," *Washington Post*, Oct. 9, 1994, C1. Elisabeth Rosenthal, "100 Million Restless Chinese Go Far from Home for Jobs," *New York Times*, Feb. 24, 1999, p. 1.

200   *"We are really just at the start"*   Ramon McLeod, "Human Migration Enters New Era," *San Francisco Chronicle*, Aug. 1994.

200   *"Can either Europe or the U.S. stem"*   Huntington, *Clash*, 203.

202   *intellectual stirrings of a new liberal-centrist nationalism*   See David Hollinger, "Nationalism, Cosmopolitanism, and the U.S.," in *Immigration and Citizenship in the Twenty-First Century*, ed. Noah Pickus (Lanham, Md.: Rowman & Littlefield, 1998); Hollinger, *Postethnic America* (Basic Books, 1995), and Lind, *The Next American*.

204   *"the centripetal pull"*   William Leach, *Country of Exiles: The Destruction of Place in American Life*, (Pantheon Books, 1999), pp. 20–21.

204   *"an extraordinarily privileged position"*   Albert O. Hirschman, *Exit, Voice, and Loyalty* (Harvard University Press, 1970), pp. 106, 126.

204   Wallace Stegner, conversation with the author, Palo Alto, California, December 10, 1985. Jackson J. Benson quotes Stegner using the term "boomer" for his father and "sticker" for his mother in his story "Big Rock Candy Mountain." See Benson, *Down by the Lemonade Springs* (University of Nevada Press, 2001), p. 52.

INDEX

Abbey, Edward, 190
Abbott, Edith, 18
Abraham, Spencer, 188
Adamic, Louis, 70
African Americans and immigration, 19, 60, 115
Aldrich, Thomas Bailey, xv
Alexander, Robert, 81
Alien Nation (Brimelow), 122
American environment, and the "immigration connection," 58
The American Enterprise, 160
American Federation of Labor (AFL), 16
American Jewish Committee, 88
American Party, 31–32. *See also* Know-Nothings
Americanization, 42–44
Asylum seekers: Central American, 100; Cuban, 99–101; Haitian, 100
Auster, Laurence, 121

Beck, Roy, 143, 185
Beecher, Henry Ward, 11
Bennett, David, 78, 191, 193

Bennett, Marion, 4
Betts, Katherine, 187
Beyond the Melting Pot (Glazer and Moynihan), 61
Billington, Ray Allen, 30
Borjas, George, 112–13, 159
Boulding, Kenneth, 194
Bouvier, Leon, 58, 122, 143
Bracero Program, 71–72, 105
brain drain, 182–83
Briggs, Vernon, 112, 186
Brimelow, Peter, 121
Brookings Institution, xiv; 205n
Buchanan, Pat, 160, 164, 189
Bush, George W., 164, 190

California, 146, 154–56; population growth in, 228n
Camarota, Steven, 115, 130
Carter, Jimmy, 107
Center for Immigration Studies, 122–29, 172, 174, 192
Chavez, Cesar, 105–6, 131
Chavez, Linda, 132